MANAGING SHIFTWORK

THE AUTHOR

©

*Robert Sergean is now occupational psychologist
with the TUC Centenary Institute of Occupational
Health at the London School of Hygiene and
Tropical Medicine. He was for fifteen years a
member of the scientific staff of the Medical
Research Council*

Managing

Shiftwork

Robert Sergean

Gower Press · Industrial Society

First published in Britain by Gower Press Limited
140 Great Portland Street, London W1N 5TA
1971

ISBN 0 0033 9

Set in 10 on 12 point Times and
Printed in Britain by Tonbridge Printers Ltd
Peach Hall Works, Shipbourne Road, Tonbridge, Kent

Contents

Illustrations

Preface

It is not the purpose of this book to exhort employers on economic grounds to introduce and extend shiftwork, or to present to them moral arguments why they should not do so. Nor is it intended as a how-to-do-it set of instructions in six easy lessons. What it tries to do is simply to take shiftwork as it finds it, to describe the practices which are common in industry and the kind of problems—for both manager and shiftworker—to which these can give rise.

In writing this book I have made use of two sets of information. The first of these is derived from my own experience as an industrial psychologist in a wide range of firms throughout the country, from small and transitory backstreet concerns to long established industrial giants with household names. I have drawn particularly on two fact-finding surveys which I made in the late 1960s, and which featured in unpublished reports—"Problems of shiftworking: a review of management opinion" and "Shiftworking in London and the South-East"—which I wrote for the Medical Research Council. The first of these surveys was largely carried out by lengthy correspondence with managers in 76 of the companies which participated in the 1966 PERA symposium, *Benefits and Problems of Shiftworking*. The second was based on factory visits, lasting from a matter of a few hours to several weeks, in 50 companies in London and South-East England—a supposedly non-traditional shiftworking region which turned out to conceal some highly traditional enclaves.

In the second place, I have made use extensively of the experience of others: I have, in fact, tried to survey the "literature," which comprises a very mixed bag indeed. I am frequently asked to recommend "a book on shiftwork" or "a few good references." There is, however, no such animal—or, at least, none which will satisfy the varied needs of those who inquire. This book in turn will certainly not provide all the answers. But as a result of bringing together different aspects of the subject I hope that the reader will be better able to assess the state of play in this complex field and, by the provision at the end of a sizeable list of titles to which reference has been made in the text, that he will be better able to follow up his own lines of interest.

I invite readers who are exasperated by particular omissions in the following pages to work off their frustration by writing to point them out to me. For any additional information, from no matter what source, on terminology, rotas, special problems, successful techniques and the like, I shall be most grateful.

Acknowledgements

My thanks are due, first, to the Medical Research Council and to the London School of Hygiene and Tropical Medicine, in whose time this book was largely written. I am also grateful to Dr C B Frisby, formerly Honorary Director of the MRC's Industrial Psychology Research Unit, who first prodded me into an interest in hours of work and into writing this book, and to Dr P J Taylor, of the TUC Centenary Institute of Occupational Health, who subsequently kept me at it.

I am very much indebted to my former colleagues, Gwen de la Mare and Dr James Walker, from whose work I have borrowed extensively. Dr Walker's own interest and research in shiftwork date at least from 1960, long before the subject became the bandwaggon which it now is. I should also like to thank Jean Martin and Pat Werr, Paul Branton and Larry Currie, for their help in factory visits.

There are very many people in industry to whom I am also indebted. To all of them may I say how very grateful I am that in the middle of their own working problems they took the time and trouble to help me with mine.

A special word of thanks to Dr Alex Wedderburn, of Heriot-Watt University, Edinburgh, who should have written this book—and who would have made a much better job of it if he had.

Finally, my thanks to Gower Press, for their patience and for their forbearance every time I broke my delivery promise.

Robert Sergean

Part One
Characteristics of Shiftwork

ONE

Historical Background to Shiftworking

HOURS OF WORK AND THEIR ARRANGEMENT

Although the use of multiple shifts is largely a product of modern industrial society, occupational activity at night is by no means a new phenomenon. Soldiers and sailors, shepherds and herdsmen, innkeepers and servants, tollgate keepers, customs men, sewer-workers and police—from medieval watchman to Bow Street Runner and Peeler—all these are workers whose jobs throughout the centuries kept them up and about at times "when all good men should be abed." Not that such work always continued uninterruptedly throughout the night. The tollgate keeper might doze off and the shepherd get his head down with his sheep. But all were as much "on call" in case of emergency as the works manager of a modern plant with a telephone beside his bed.

Night hours in early Biblical times were divided into three or four watches, but customary working hours were marked by sunrise and sunset. And it was doubtless to make use of the element of the un-expected that Gideon attacked the Midianites in the middle watch and Saul fell upon the Ammonites in the morning watch. It was in the morning watch, too, that the Egyptians, in pursuit of the fleeing Israelites, were engulfed, much to their surprise, in the waters of the Red Sea. The Old Testament, indeed, is full of examples of tactical opportunism at times in the 24 hours when the opposition least expected it.

The question "Are there not 12 hours in the day?" defines the daytime pattern of New Testament times. To these the Romans added four military night watches: evening, midnight, cockcrowing and morning. The injunction that "the night cometh when no man can work" may well reflect contemporary attitudes to daylight and darkness. But some civilian activities did take place during the latter. Peter, James and John, it is related, as fishermen, had caught nothing in spite of having "toiled all night." And in the parable of the master who departed into another country, he left his servants their instructions and "commanded also the porter to watch," so as to be prepared for his return even if this should be in the middle of the night.

In medieval society most work was again scheduled for the hours between dawn and dusk, as is natural in a predominantly rural society. On the manors the Rolls refer to a day's work as cutting two acres of wheat between 4 a.m. and 10 p.m. In the towns work was controlled by the guilds, and night work was frowned on, partly because quality was easier to supervise in daylight hours, and partly because of the additional fire hazard in the timbered houses of the time. [It is interesting to note several centuries later that in *Fire*, December 1967, J W Leavis discusses the increased fire risks in a large paper mill following the introduction of four-shift working.] Exceptionally, work did extend into the hours of darkness, for example, in the lengthy process of smelting metal, and certain work in shipbuilding depended more upon the tides than the sun. Bakers were permitted to make an early start, but they do not appear at this time to have begun much before dawn.

With the development of cottage industry in the later Middle Ages, as in textiles, there was no doubt some flexibility in the arrangement of working hours within the family. There was a division of labour here between women spinning and men weaving, with the man "second jobbing" in husbandry for the upkeep of his family. But although the pattern of the working day might vary within the family, its duration would still be limited by the extent of daylight —artificial light being beyond the average cottager's means.

Dorothy George (1966) has given an absorbing account of the length and irregularity of working hours in London of the eighteenth century. She reports that working days of 14–15 hours were common in many trades, and these represented the normal day during which the apprentice was required to work and in which the journeyman on piecework could reach a standard wage. The hours of shop assistants were as long and, in the busy season, could be even longer.

4

Two interesting examples of nightwork are also quoted by George. One concerns rope-makers who could not make ropes when the sun shone and, therefore, in the words of one of them, "we begin at 8 o'clock at night and work till 8 in the morning, and sometimes we work all day if we can hold it." The other relates to washerwomen who were employed as outworkers by the day, and whose practice it was to arrive at their employer's house overnight in order to work all that night and the following day.

It is with the industrial development of the late eighteenth and early nineteenth centuries, and with the transition from an agrarian to an industrial society, that the length of the "normal working day" grew to have less and less relation to the hours of daylight. Under a factory system of manufacture, making use of new machine developments, it was profitable for an employer to extend the working day of his employees as much as he could. That it was possible for him to do so resulted from the movement from countryside to town and the concentration there of large pools of labour of both sexes dependent upon wages alone.

Men, women and children in factories regularly worked long hours. The movement for the reform and control of the working day was a painfully slow development covering the whole of the nineteenth century and continuing into the twentieth. It also took place piecemeal, affecting some sections of industry long before it touched others. The Factory Act of 1833, for example, applied only to textiles. And 10 years later we can still read, in the second Report of the Commissioners on the Employment of Children, of cases where employment is continued "for 15, 16, and even 18 hours consecutively" and where "the children work as long as the adults" (Pike, 1966).

Writing as late as the 1860s, Marx (1867) (citing official sources of the day) gives numerous examples of the long hours worked during both day and night by men, women and children, particularly in sections of industry not covered by factory legislation. Inevitably such long stints involved work outside daytime hours. In the Nottingham lace trade children of 9 and 10, wakened at 2, 3, and 4, in the morning, are reported as working until 10, 11 and 12 at night. And, if necessary, the "ordinary" working day would continue throughout the night. The evidence to an official committee of a 12-year old boy employed in the Staffordshire potteries ran as follows:

I come at six. Sometimes I come at four. I worked all last night till six o'clock this morning. I have not been in bed since the night before last. There were eight or nine other boys working last night. All but one have come this morning. . . . I do not get any more for working at night.

How close we are to working conditions of this kind is brought home by the realisation that the boys referred to here could well have become the grandparents of men now working in industry.

What we would understand as multiple shifts, making use of different teams of workers, were also in use by this period under the name of the "relay system." Marx describes, for example, an "alternation between two sets of workers" where "part of the workers are engaged on daywork one week and on nightwork the next": a system, he says, dating back to the early days ("the full blooded youth") of the cotton industry. In addition, according to an employer witness from the steel industry before the Children's Employment Commission in 1865, "some of the hands always work in the night, without any alternation of day and night work."

Among other restrictions which the Factory Act of 1833 placed upon the employment of children and young persons was one which forbade the employment of those between the ages of 9 and 18 on nightwork (defined as from 20 30 to 05 30). Out of this grew up the practice of "working double sets of children," from 05 30 to 13 30 and from 13 30 to 20 30—in fact a double-day system. But this, too, appears to have been abused by certain employers who found that it was difficult for factory inspectors to check that the law was being observed if the work and rest periods of the same employees were continuously shifted and shuffled within the allowed range (05 30 – 20 30) of daytime hours. An account of this "shifting system" is to be found in the Reports of Inspectors of Factories for 31 October 1848. And in the same year a petition to the Queen was presented by the clergy of Ashton and neighbourhood against the abuses of what Marx calls "this spurious system of relays."

Examples, about the 1860s, of continuous manufacture using a multiple-shift system within a 24-hour period include blast furnaces, forges, plate-rolling mills and other metallurgical establishments, paper mills and glass works. A common length of shift hours in such "relay work" was 2 × 12, over seven days, but there appears to have been overworking beyond even these limits. Absence might mean double-shifts, or even several shifts in a row, for those who remained.

Development of systems of multiple shiftworking beyond these nineteenth century examples depended upon further control of working hours, and in particular upon the eventual acceptance of the 8-hour day and 48-hour week. Just how recently this has come about is emphasised by the fact that "Even in the years just before 1914 only a few isolated groups had achieved it" (Evans, 1969).

The adoption of an 8-hour day and a 48-hour week was largely a post First World War development. These standards were in fact incorporated in the first Convention of the International Labour Conference in 1919, the Hours of Work (Industry) Convention, although allowance was made for a 56-hour week in certain types of manufacture under three-shift working. Three-shift operation, although not unknown before this date, is almost exclusively a product of the last 50 years.

RESEARCH INTEREST

Some men, then, have always worked unusual hours, whether this was dictated by military expediency, by the technical demands of the job or by sheer economic pressure. And there has been continuing government and legislative interest in the subject of the length and arrangement of working hours at least since 1802 when the Health and Morals of Apprentices Act aimed at limiting the time which young persons spent at work, particularly at night.

Research interest is inevitably of more recent origin, but this again is far from being a development of the immediate present. For example, the effect upon performance and health of the duration and arrangement of working hours has been a recurrent interest of Medical Research Council workers in this country for over 50 years.

An early publication of the Council (Industrial Fatigue Research Board, 1924) suggests 1893 as the date when the human factor in industry was first recognised as deserving of scientific study. This was the year in which the firm of Mather and Platt, of Manchester, abolished the pre-breakfast spell of work, so reducing the working week from 54 hours to 48. This experiment [*see* William Mather's article in *The Times*, 29 March 1894] resulted in both an increase in production and a reduction in lost time, and on the basis of its success the 48-hour week was adopted in government arsenals and dockyards. In general, however, this lead was not followed by the private sector of industry.

The First World War provided both a stimulus and an opportunity for research into the effects of working hours. To meet increased production demands in the munitions industry, hours of work were increased as an emergency measure at this time; "seventy to ninety hours a week being common and over ninety not infrequent" (Industrial Health Research Board, 1940). For example, one shell-making factory in the early months of the war worked 7×12 hour shifts each week under an alternating day and night system. Many women were also putting in working weeks of 70 hours. The assumption in this situation was that if x units of work could be performed in 1 hour, $2x$ units could be done in 2 hours, $10x$ units in 10 and so on. Actual production, however, failed to obey this apparently simple logic, and accidents and absence from work increased alarmingly.

In order to investigate these problems the government in 1915 set up a Health of Munition Workers Committee, "to consider and advise on questions of industrial fatigue, hours of labour, and other matters affecting the personal health and physical efficiency of workers in munition factories and workshops." The findings of this body are summarised in its Final Report, (1918) (presented to the then Minister of Munitions, Winston Churchill) and cover maximum hours of work for men and women; single, double and three-shift working; rest pauses and length of individual stint; and nightwork. The efforts of this Committee not only had an effect on wartime conditions of work, but also influenced events post-war.

The Committee was succeeded in 1918 by the Industrial Fatigue (later Health) Research Board, which in the two decades between the wars carried out a pioneering series of investigations concerning conditions and methods of work and their relation to the health and effectiveness of the worker. This research covered a variety of topics, but only those relating to hours of work need concern us here.

Interest centred first on the *duration* of hours of work and its effects. Studies of both men and women operatives in a range of industries compared the effects of shifts of different lengths. One study, for example, looked at the performance of men in tinplate manufacture on 4-, 6- and 8-hour shifts (Vernon, 1919), and another that of women munition workers under a 12- or a 7- and 8-hour shift arrangement (Osborne, 1919). These and other studies clearly demonstrated the superiority in terms of improved hourly output of the shorter shift.

These early exercises, aimed at determining the optimum length of shift in any given work situation, were supplemented by others which sought the most effective way of breaking down a single spell of work by the use of rest pauses. In general it was found that when suitable rest intervals were introduced in industrial work the result was an improvement in quantity and quality of output (Wyatt, 1927). Other investigations included the speed of adaptation of output to altered hours of work (Vernon, 1920) and the effects of variety and uniformity in the task performed (Wyatt and Fraser, 1928).

Interest was not directed at this time specifically towards multiple-shift situations or the effects of multiple shifts upon performance. But it was inevitable that in their wide ranging inquiries into hours of work the Board's investigators should find themselves in factory situations where two or three shifts in the 24 hours were worked, and so should be led to examine the comparative advantages of day-work and shiftwork, and of the various shifts within a multiple-shift situation.

A 1924 study in the Yorkshire glass bottle industry, for example, although setting out as a best-length-of-shift inquiry, comparing the merits of a 10- and an 8-hour working stint—"a definite problem of practical importance to the trade"—later examines the comparative efficiency of morning, afternoon and night turns within a 3×8 hours system (Farmer, 1924).

Four years later we find the report of an investigation which set out directly to consider the effects of a double-day system for women in a number of factories, it being "of interest to the employer to know how the output will be affected by a change from ordinary daywork to shiftwork" (Smith and Vernon, 1928). As well as comparing the two systems on the basis of output, loss of working time, sickness absence and labour turnover, this study also makes some comparisons between performance on early and late turn under the two-shift arrangement.

The findings of the early studies about the dangers, in terms of greater absence and injury and reduced output, of excessive hours and uninterrupted spells of work, acquired a fresh relevance through the production demands made upon industry by the Second World

War. A need for further research under prevailing industrial conditions became apparent, and in the wartime investigations of Wyatt and his associates the possible effects on performance and health in multiple-shift arrangements received more attention than before. A number of these investigations will be referred to in later chapters.

DEVELOPMENT OF INTEREST AFTER 1945

Although multiple shifts had been worked prior to 1939, these had been largely confined in peacetime to such continuous process industries as steel, paper, glass and chemicals, where they were technically necessary. The material and economic conditions of the postwar years saw a growth of propaganda in favour of an extension of shiftworking into sections of industry where it had previously hardly been known. The argument here was based on the need for shiftwork as part of a policy of sound economics and good management. This kind of propaganda has continued in one shape or form ever since.

In March 1945 the government appointed a committee, under the chairmanship of Professor J L Brierly, to inquire into the economic need for, and social consequences of, the double-day system in manufacturing industry. The Brierly Committee was as much concerned with the introduction of double-day work as a normal and permanent feature of industrial organisation as with its use to cope with temporary difficulties in the immediate postwar period. In its report two years later the Committee concluded that "the wider use of the double-day shift system is undoubtedly capable of making an important contribution to the economic well-being of the country," (Ministry of Labour, 1947) but stressed that the likelihood of its extension was dependent upon the attitudes of both employers and workpeople.

Prominent advocates of the need for more shiftwork at this time were the industrial groups whose postwar visits to the United States were organised by the Anglo-American Council on Productivity. In his book, *We Too Can Prosper*, published in 1953, Graham Hutton analysed the reports of 66 of these productivity teams and saw the more intensive use of capital equipment through an extension of multiple shiftworking in Britain as an important means of increasing productivity. He also emphasised the far wider practice of shiftworking in the USA as compared with this country, and the more favourable climate of opinion there which helped to make the use of shifts possible. What he wrote still has relevance. He observed:

> ... in industries in which no naturally continuous process is involved, there is almost a traditional or constitutional British ... dislike of a multiple shift system, even where shifts work to rota. It is probable that the big increase in productivity rendered possible by shiftwork would enable ... industries to pay wages high enough to over-come social and other resistances, provided enough of the extra pay remains with the worker and is not taken by taxes (Hutton, 1953).

At this time, too, the National Joint Advisory Council representing the (then) British Employers' Confederation, the TUC and the nationalised industries, considered the desirability of extending double-day and other forms of shiftworking in industry as a practical means of contributing to production and productivity and of making better use of existing plant and equipment. Although the Memo-randum (Ministry of Labour, 1953) which this body produced on the subject lacks the enthusiastic presentation of Hutton's case, it does come down, albeit somewhat cautiously, in favour of more shiftwork. It makes clear that there is no suggestion of an immediate and wholesale change to two-shift working because "in general, British industry is equipped for single-shift working." But it does see shiftwork as having value where a firm has expensive plant and equipment in only partial use and where markets can be developed and labour recruited to expand production.

Encouragement of shiftworking practices from government and other official sources continued through the 'fifties and 'sixties. The results of the two surveys carried out by the Ministry of Labour in 1954 and 1964, showing the distribution of men and women on some form of shiftwork and the marked increase in their numbers over the decade, did much to stimulate interest. In 1966 the National Joint Advisory Council again considered the subject and concluded that not enough was known concerning problems associated with the introduction of shift systems. Accordingly, at the Council's request, officers of the Ministry of Labour carried out a short investigation of a number of companies which had recently introduced, or attempted to introduce, some form of shift rota (Ministry of Labour,

1967b). In the same year the subject featured on the agenda of the Prime Minister's National Productivity Conference. Finally, in 1969, the National Board for Prices and Incomes was given the task of examining the relationship between the length and pattern of the working week, including hours of overtime and shiftwork, and earnings, costs and productivity. The Board's findings were published in December 1970.

The growth of shiftworking in this country since the Second World War, and particularly during the 1950s and 1960s, has resulted from a variety of factors: economic, technological and social. The sophisticated nature of much modern plant and equipment has meant that continuous operation, and continuous manning, have been increasingly necessary on technical grounds. But even where considerations of technical necessity have not applied, the high cost of such plant has usually been economically justifiable only if intensive use has been intended. The speed of technological development, and the consequent need for early replacement, has also placed a premium upon intensive use. These factors have been accompanied by more competitive market conditions which have acted as a stimulus towards modernisation and efficiency.

Quite apart from these considerations in areas of continuous three-shift operation, however, such factors as shortage of labour and reduction in the length of the standard working week have obliged many employers to consider new ways of arranging working hours in order to cope with staffing problems. Many employers in the retail distributive trades, for example, who previously ran their businesses with a single group of employees all working the same hours, now employ part-timers and overlapping groups of workers. Those engaged on this basis may not regard themselves as shiftworkers, but the fact remains that the employer has the administrative headache of dovetailing the activities of Box and Cox so as to maintain the service that is expected of him.

There has also been a growing tendency in manufacturing industry to use a second shift, even if only temporarily or seasonally, to deal with fluctuations in demand. Shiftwork in this sense has been used more and more as a form of overtime working to give the supplier greater flexibility in production. Shiftwork has even been used in this sense in the building and construction industries and in agriculture in order to meet delivery deadlines and to make use of favourable weather conditions.

All these developments have seen the introduction of various forms of shiftwork into industries and occupations in which day-work was previously the rule. One of the most striking features of recent years has been the extension of shiftwork into white collar activities, mainly through mechanisation and the use of computers. Enterprises employing staff on shifts on electronic data processing equipment include insurance offices, banks and local authorities.

These developments have also affected new categories of workers: management, clerical, administrative, scientific and technical. Geographically, shiftwork has been introduced and accepted in parts of the country traditionally considered to be solely dayworking.

The level of interest in multiple shiftwork at the present time is reflected in the number of conferences and discussion groups on the subject which are organised by such bodies as the British Institute of Management, the British Productivity Council, the Industrial Society and the Production Engineering Research Association, as well as in the increasing amount that is being written on the subject, both "pop" and serious, in management and scientific journals.

Questions affecting the length and arrangement of working hours will inevitably continue to be of concern to both employer and employed during the 1970s.

TWO

The Pattern of Contemporary Shiftwork

DEFINITION AND CLASSIFICATION OF SHIFTWORK

The *Oxford English Dictionary* includes among the meanings it attributes to the word "shift," "a relay or change of workmen or of horses."

The Handbook of the International Confederation of Free Trade Unions defines shiftwork as "the regular change of one group of workers for another on the same type of job and in the same workplace" (International Confederation of Free Trade Unions, 1964).

The Industrial Relations Service of the Ministry of Labour refers to "...a system of working in which production is continuous or continuous over a very long day, but each worker works only normal or even a relatively short number of hours each day" (Ministry of Labour, 1967*a*).

This type of organisational definition simply specifies the manning of an establishment by more than one set of employees in a particular period of time. This is multiple shiftworking, the use of more than one shift team.

There is no reference in this type of definition to the alternation or rotation of the same group of workers between the different shift periods, to the swapping of the periods of time during which each shift team attends for duty. In practice, however, shiftwork is often thought of in this way. "Shift working *by definition*," one Yorkshire work study engineer insisted, "means that a man rotates through three shifts round the clock." He had been born and brought up in an iron and steel town in the north of England, and his whole working experience had been that of continuous working in which men changed weekly from one shift to the next.

At an engineering factory in Kent the writer was interested in looking at the output records of permanent day and permanent night crews and, for this purpose, was passed on to the work study department. This section's only brief about their visitor was that he was "interested in shiftwork." "We thought you wanted to talk about women on double-days," they told him after some minutes at cross-purposes, "because we don't think of permanent day and night men as shiftworking." On double-days the women changed shifts weekly.

In line with this way of thinking a distinction is often drawn between "shiftwork" (meaning an arrangement with a rota of some kind in which each man takes a turn on different periods of duty) and "nightwork" (meaning a stabilised, permanent arrangement in which the same men always work nights). "No, my dad wasn't a shiftworker," a London dockworker reported, "he worked nights most of his life." This distinction is commonly made in collective agreements. Stability is found, of course, though less frequently, in systems other than permanent nights. Stabilised as well as changing arrangements will be regarded as shiftwork for the purposes of this book.

The descriptions quoted at the beginning of this chapter are also organisational definitions, looking at shiftwork from the company standpoint rather than that of its employees. This, too, can give rise to some confusion. Take two examples.

At an oil refinery with a continuous three-shift system a "permanent morning support shift" was introduced when the working week was reduced from 42 to 40 hours so as to allow the three-shift men to take an additional free day each month. Each "support" man regularly works the 07 00 – 15 00 shift, standing in as a relief for a different shiftworker each day.

Are such "support" men to be classified as shiftworkers? From the company's point of view they are an integral part of the shift system, although paid at day rates, since without them a new three-shift rota would have to be devised and more operators incorporated into it. But the members of the support shift do not regard themselves as shiftworkers: recruitment for this shift come from men on the three-shift cycle who want to revert to daywork, and from new recruits who use it as a stepping stone to a three-shift vacancy.

A second example is provided by a firm which managed to change, after difficult negotiations, from permanent days and nights to a discontinuous three-shift arrangement over five days. An unusual feature of this three-shift system is that it is non-rotating, the previous permanent night men taking the new night shift, the old permanent day men taking the new morning shift, while the afternoon shift is manned by new recruits.

Administratively the firm now has a three-shift system and thinks of itself in these terms. But the new morning shiftworkers, even though their hours have been altered, regard themselves as day men as much as they did under the old system.

Many examples of this kind can be cited where organisationally a man's role may be defined in a way which he himself would not recognise. Organisational definitions may be satisfactory in economic terms, but less so psychologically and socially.

Sometimes, of course, although shifts are being worked, neither side thinks in these terms. The medical department in one factory is "manned" for 14 hours a day by four nursing sisters as follows: two fulltimers working 08 00 – 16 00 and 09 00 – 17 00 respectively; two parttimers working 14 30 – 22 00 on alternate days. These girls get on well together and largely arrange their own hours of work. But might the company regard this as a shiftwork situation if the girls did not see eye to eye, and if problems of link-up and takeover occurred daily?

There would, indeed, be an advantage in ceasing to draw a distinction between shiftwork and non-shiftwork, and in simply thinking of "different arrangements of working hours." In this sense daywork could be regarded as another kind of shift. Day shifts, after all, can themselves vary, in the attitudes they attract and in their behavioural effects, according to their length, starting and stopping times, the way they are broken up by rest periods, their relation to total weekly working hours, whether they operate in conjunction with other shifts and so on.

Many arrangements of working hours, not now regarded as shiftworking, may be subjectively "worse" than certain shift schedules, and may certainly present problems of social and physical adaptation for the people concerned. One has only to think, for example, of the routines of doctors in general practice, midwives, parish priests, country vets, on call at odd hours in addition to a regular daily schedule; of farmworkers and members of parliament, with long and erratic hours; of actors and entertainers, with nighttime public performances and daytime rehearsals; or of the "voluntary overtime" of members of the Royal Family, senior civil servants, barristers, journalists, teachers, research workers, probation officers, sales representatives, housewives, company directors, retail shop-keepers, trade union officials, the self-employed and so on. Problems arising from working hours are not exclusive to shiftworkers in receipt of "inconvenience allowances."

If we are committed to the concept of shiftwork, in broad distinction to the idea of single-shift daytime working, then at least we can try to be specific when we refer to it. Generalisations about shiftwork abound. We read about its effects and its growth, about the attitudes of workers and of management towards it, about the problems to which it gives rise. As a matter of convenience this kind of abbreviation is often inevitable, but we ought to qualify such generalisation wherever we can by putting it in context. Shiftwork is not one kind of activity, but many. Nor, of course, do shiftworkers make up one uniform population. Shiftworking is a field of operations where we should continually remember to ask "what?" and "who?" and "where?"

Different kinds of shiftwork may bear little resemblance to each other in the extent to which they are accepted or resisted, in the administrative problems they present, and in the demands they make upon the worker. What relation is there, for example, between a part-time "granny" shift and one involving two alternating 12-hour day and night turns of duty?; between the intricacies of a "continental" rota and the uniformity of a permanent "graveyard" shift?

Also to be remembered are the qualifications "when?" and "for how long?" A lifelong shiftworker in a traditional shift area differs very much from the man temporarily working shifts to pay off the instalments on a colour TV set, or one intermittently doing so during a firm's busy season.

Nor do the same labels always refer to the same commodities. Take "day" and "night," for example. What constitute day and night hours in collective agreements of different industries vary considerably. In two branches of the catering industry "night" is of six hours' duration, midnight to 06 00 and 23 00 to 05 00. At the other end of the scale, in keg and drum manufacture, nighttime has a $14\frac{1}{2}$ hours' coverage, from 17 00 to 07 30, while in one section of the brick industry nightwork consists of "any complete shift commencing on or after 15 00." In between we have examples of eight hours' coverage (22 00 – 06 00, laundry and cutlery; 21 00 – 06 00, cast stone) and 12 hours (18 00 – 06 00, bakery and brewing;

1900–0700, fur trade (Department of Employment and Productivity, 1969*b*; T & GWU, 1966).

Such differences in definition not only indicate different ways of perceiving "nightwork," but also themselves help condition such perception. Observations about nightwork may need to be identified by industry in order to have meaning.

The terms "morning," "afternoon" and "night" in a three-shift system are again examples of labels which lack a constant meaning. In some cases the night shift is longer than the two earlier turns, and in others all three-shifts are of unequal length. Not only duration, but also starting/stopping times need to be stated before we can generalise about particular effects. A 06 00 – 14 00 and an 08 00 – 16 00 morning shift, for example, may have different effects in terms of, say, single-day absence, timekeeping or accidents.

These questions of definition and classification are not just academic quibbles. They are of concern to the manager who has to introduce, recruit for and administer shifts, as well as to the worker who has to adapt to new shift arrangements. They are relevant in the interpretation of research results and the understanding of official statistics.

In this book we shall be concerned with shifts of all kinds which are used in addition to, or as an alternative to, a main single-shift operating in the hours of daylight. These will include:

1 Part-time shifts
2 Double-day shiftworking
3 Shift arrangements involving nightwork, including permanent night duty as well as alternating day and night shifts
4 Three-shift arrangements, including discontinuous systems covering part of the working week as well as continuous systems which give full seven days' cover.

In addition, various other arrangements will be mentioned which do not seem properly to belong in any of these categories. Figure 1 illustrates diagrammatically the principal arrangements of working hours.

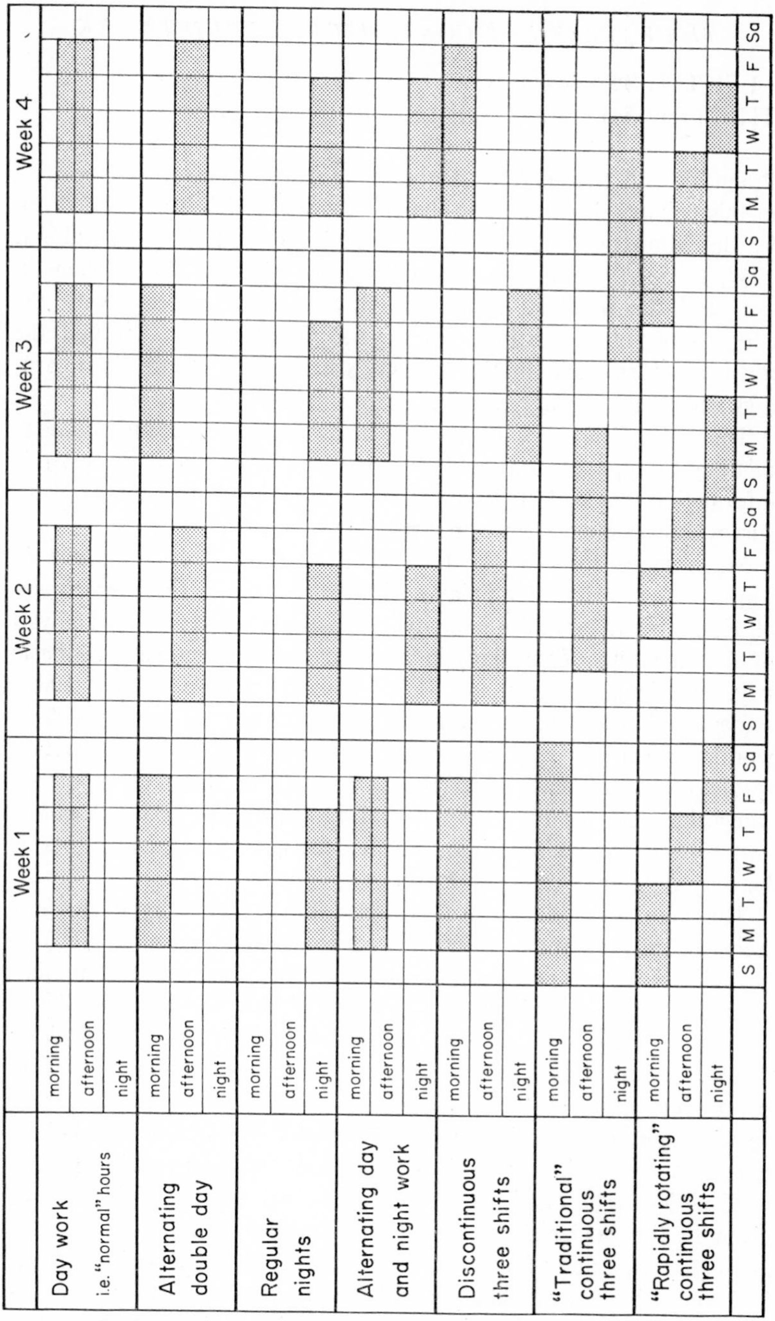

FIGURE 1   PRINCIPAL ARRANGEMENTS OF WORKING HOURS

c

OFFICIAL STATISTICS:
THE TWO MINISTRY OF LABOUR SURVEYS

Practically all that is known about the distribution of shiftworking in this country depends upon the two surveys which were carried out by the Ministry of Labour in 1954 and 1964 (Ministry of Labour, 1954, 1965a, 1965b). Information about the different shift systems in use, and the numbers employed on each, was collected with the cooperation of the British Employers' Confederation through the form of return used for the Ministry's half-yearly inquiry into earnings and hours of wage earners in April in each of these years.

The 1951 Census of Production also contained certain questions relating to type of shift and numbers employed thereon. But this information was collected on a different basis to that of the Ministry surveys and comparison was not possible.

Much more recently (in 1968–9), as part of its new survey of wages and salaries of employees in Great Britain, the Department of Employment and Productivity (1969a) has presented an analysis of the make-up of earnings in terms of such components as basic pay, overtime, bonuses and shift payments. These results enable some rough estimate to be made of the extent of full-time shiftworking (men and women separately) in broad occupational groups (professional, clerical, supervisory, manual) in different industrial categories, and for different national agreements in both the public and private sector. This information does not distinguish, however, between different types of shiftworker.

The industries and services sampled by the Ministry of Labour were the manufacturing industries generally, mining and quarrying, gas, electricity and water supply, government services and a number of miscellaneous services such as laundry and dry cleaning. Since certain activities such as coal mining were excluded, the Ministry figures tend to under- rather than over-estimate the numbers working on a shift basis in the country as a whole. Also excluded were certain night shift workers such as cleaners and watchmen, and all part-time shiftworkers with the exception of those on evening shifts.

The 1964 returns provide some additional detail which was not given in the earlier figures. In 1964 numbers for men and women are stated separately for all types of system, whereas this breakdown had only been available for double-day and part-time evening shifts in 1954. What had been one general category for three-shift workers in 1954 was now split into continuous and non-continuous working, and the former further divided into four-crew systems and those manned in other ways. Finally, the 1964 figures were usefully broken down regionally.

No information was given by the Ministry as to the basis on which establishments were included or not included in their samples, but it was estimated that some 70 per cent in 1964, and nearly 75 per cent in 1954, of the total number of manual workers employed in the industries sampled were covered by the returns received.

The numbers of manual workers employed in firms for which returns were received by the Ministry in 1964 totalled roughly five and half million, and 18 per cent of these [the proportion rises to 20 per cent if manufacturing industries alone are considered]—something over one million—were reported to be working on some kind of shift system. These figures should be borne in mind in the paragraphs which follow which will describe the 1964 distribution of shiftworkers mainly in percentage terms. Reference to "all shiftworkers," for example, will indicate all shiftworkers in the Ministry sample.

Proportions on different types of shift system
The proportions of all shiftworkers in the Ministry's 1964 sample on different types of system were, approximately:

Continuous three-shift	22%
Discontinuous three-shift	19%
Alternating day and night	23%
Permanent night	12%
Double-days	17%
Part-time evening	7%

About a quarter of all shiftworkers, that is to say, are found in systems occupying the hours of day and evening. Another third are engaged in two-shift systems involving nightwork. The remainder is involved in some form of three-shift system.

Men and women
Shiftworking is predominantly a male activity, only 12 per cent of the total numbers on shifts being made up of women. This is to be

expected since the type of shift system on which women (and young persons) can work is controlled by the provisions of the Factories Act 1961, the Employment of Women, Young Persons and Children's Act 1920, and the Hours of Employment (Conventions) Act 1936. Although exemptions can be granted, women are at present largely excluded from shift systems involving night turns of duty. (But see the section on women in Chapter 12.)

Over half (55 per cent) of the women on shifts work a part-time evening shift, while another 39 per cent are employed on a double-day basis. Part-time evening work is the only turn which they dominate as a "women's shift." Women make up 98 per cent of the total employed in twilight hours, although they contribute substantially (30 per cent) to the total double-day labour force.

Industries in which most shiftworkers are to be found
Well over half of Britain's male shiftworkers are located in the four industrial groups of metal manufacture (20 per cent), vehicles (17 per cent), engineering and electrical goods (12 per cent) and textiles (9 per cent).

Women on shifts have an even greater industrial concentration. Over 70 per cent are to be found in the three industrial groups of textiles (32 per cent), food, drink and tobacco (21 per cent) and engineering and electrical goods (18 per cent).

But the greatest numbers on different *types* of shiftwork vary with industry (Appendix 1). Metal manufacture, for example, has most men on both continuous and non-continuous three-shift work, while vehicles and engineering/electrical goods use most men on two-shift systems involving nightwork. Vehicles, along with textiles, also has most men on double-days.

The relative importance of shiftwork in different industries
Apart from the absolute numbers of shiftworkers, and of the different types of shiftworker, there is also a difference by industry in the ratio of shiftworkers to dayworkers.

The industrial groups employing the highest proportions of shift-workers in their total labour force are metal manufacture (44 per cent), vehicles (33 per cent) and the chemical and allied industries (29 per cent). At the other end of the scale, leather goods, timber and furniture, and clothing and footwear have only 3, 2 and 1 per cent respectively of their workers on shifts.

There are also differences in the relative importance of different *types* of shiftwork in the various industrial groups (Appendix 2). For example, "gas, electricity and water" and "chemical and allied industries" have over 80 per cent of their shiftworkers on three-shift systems, whereas in "shipbuilding and marine engineering" alternating day and night and permanent night arrangements account for more than 90 per cent of the shift force.

Regional differences

Appendix 3 shows the distribution of the shiftworking population through the country, as well as the relative importance of shiftwork in the different regions. It is in the Midlands and the North-West that the highest proportions of the country's shiftworkers are to be found, but it is in Wales and the North, with smaller working populations, that the ratio of shiftworkers to dayworkers is highest.

Regional differences are also to be found in the incidence and importance of different types of shiftwork.

Comparison of 1954 and 1964 figures

The returns made to the Ministry for 1954 and 1964 each covered some five and half million manual workers. Twelve per cent of this total were reported as working shifts at the earlier date, but this figure rose to 18 per cent in 1964. No comparable data for the two periods are available with regard to region, or in the proportions of men and women separately. It is clear, however, that the proportional increase is much higher in the case of women. The Ministry did publish information about relative amounts of growth in different industrial groups.

There was in fact no single industrial group which failed to show an increase between 1954 and 1964, although in some cases the amount was quite small. Greatest increases were recorded in vehicles where the proportion of shiftworkers to all workers in that industrial group rose from 13 to 33 per cent; in textiles, 11 to 22 per cent; and in paper, printing and publishing, 14 to 24 per cent.

There was also an increase in all types of shiftwork, but some variation in the extent of this. The figure of 52.8 per cent—the overall increase in shiftworking numbers between 1954 and 1964— is frequently quoted, but mention is rarely made of the range of increases for different types of shift. The number of three-shift workers in fact rose by only 33 per cent whereas that of men on two-shift systems involving nightwork showed an increase of 63 per cent, and that of double-day and part-time evening workers one of 83 per cent (Appendix 4).

Expressed another way, the proportion of three-shift workers to all shiftworkers was lower in 1964 at 41 per cent than in 1954 (48 per cent). The proportions of workers on permanent nights, double-days and part-time evening shifts, on the other hand, all rose.

INTERPRETATION OF OFFICIAL STATISTICS

In current discussion of shiftwork, two features of the Ministry's work are popularly quoted. It is frequently stated, first, that the numbers on shiftwork have increased by 50 per cent "over the last 10 years." And, secondly, that one in every five workers is now engaged on some form of shift.

Although speakers on the subject are still (in 1970) happily referring to the "last ten years," it ought not to have to be pointed out that 1964 is rapidly receding into history. We really know very little about changes in the numbers and distribution since that date, and the Statistics Department of the Department of Employment and Productivity has no immediate plans for carrying out a further survey.

As regards the shiftworking ratio of one in five, it is often overlooked that this is based only on the $5\frac{1}{2}$ million employees included in the Ministry survey. But the overall working population of Britain is in the region of 25 million (16 million men and 9 million women), and the Ministry's shiftworking group of 1 million assumes rather different proportions when viewed against this greater total.

It is true that the Ministry's surveys were mainly concerned with workers in manufacturing industry. But in those sectors of the economy not covered by these surveys are many categories of worker engaged on some kind of shift basis or on nightwork—for example, coal-miners, police, prison officers, nurses, seamen, members of the armed forces, postal and transport workers, to name but a few. Also lying outside the scope of the Ministry surveys are those sections of the working population, referred to earlier in this chapter, who, while not engaged on shifts, have arrangements of working hours very different from the "normal," single-day shift of "9 to 5" or "8 to 4."

We know almost nothing about the length and arrangement of

working hours of the "missing 20 million" (about four fifths of the total working population) who lie outside the coverage of Ministry surveys.

While on the subject of official statistics, it should also be pointed out that there are some grounds for taking with a pinch of salt some of the figures supplied by employers on official returns. In at least two cases known to the writer there were considerable discrepancies between the information supplied by the Personnel Department and the existing state of affairs on the factory floor. In both these cases Personnel listed substantial numbers of operatives as working under an alternating day-and-night system. In practice, alternation had largely been replaced by permanent day and permanent night arrangements, through private swapping of duties between operatives with the agreement of the workshop foremen. The physical and social distance between "office" departments and factory floor often makes the former unaware of informal changes of this kind which modify established procedures through time.

Another point to remember is that the Ministry figures take no account of the extent to which overtime hours are worked in conjunction with formal shift systems. Where consistently used in this way, overtime working can effectively create new types of shift system out of an original system. The Ministry category "alternating day and night," for example, is likely to include, in addition to "normally" alternating eight-hour shifts, many examples of 2×12 working in which the day and night shifts are regularly linked by overtime hours. If one is concerned with, for example, the effects of shiftwork, then the 2×8 and the 2×12 ought not to be grouped together. Another common example of this type is found in the regular addition of 12-hour overtime shifts on Saturday and Sunday to a 3×8 discontinuous three-shift system from Monday to Friday. While this is still likely to be classified by an employer as "non-continuous work," overtime hours have effectively converted the original system into a continuous type of rota.

The Ministry's statisticians would certainly not claim more for their own figures than that they are approximations in an area of industrial activity about which nothing was previously known. The aspect of shiftwork which even the bare bones of the Ministry's tables succeed in bringing out quite dramatically is its tremendous variation. Variation by type of system, industry, sex, region; and, by implication, in the attitudes and degree of acceptance of different groups to different arrangements of working hours.

This element of variety is something which one can never forget for very long when considering shiftwork: it is a theme which will constantly recur in this book. In the pages which follow we shall be looking at the diversity which occurs within the main shift categories.

THREE

Description of Shift Systems

This chapter will briefly look at the main shift systems in use in this country under the following heads: systems not involving nightwork, two-shift systems involving nightwork, and three-shift systems.

SYSTEMS NOT INVOLVING NIGHTWORK

Shift systems which do not involve the shiftworker in spending a night away from home and out of his own bed consist of:

1   Part-time shifts of various kinds
2   Double-day work

Part-time shifts
Part-time work can be defined in a variety of ways. The definition provided by the Department of Employment and Productivity refers to "persons normally working for not more than 30 hours a week." In practice the weekly hours of many such workers are considerably fewer. For obvious reasons the bulk of part-time workers are female. Most, though by no means all, part-time shifts occupy the evening hours—and this type of shift has shown the most rapid increase in recent years.

Examples of part-time shifts during our own factory visits gave a good idea of their diversity and the range of needs which they serve. Twilight or evening shifts appeared either as a regular means of getting extra production or as a safety valve in cases of variable demand. Occupying up to 20 hours a week, they were spread over four or five evenings, with a variety of starting/stopping times. though 17 00 – 21 00 and 18 00 – 22 00 were commonest. Length of shift ranged from $3\frac{1}{2} - 4\frac{1}{2}$ hours, and personnel included clerical as well as production workers.

A few examples of male part-time evening shifts were found. For example, one firm in the food industry employs men in the evenings on lighter work. These men usually hold white collar daytime jobs and are regarded by management as working extra hours "to pay for the cost of running a car" and so on.

Of all types of shiftwork, part-time evening arrangements have proved the most popular among those who work them and the most successful and easiest to administer from management's point of view. They are popular primarily because they are worked by volunteers and, particularly in the case of the older married house-wife, because they provide a change of company and scene as well as supplementing income. From the employer's viewpoint the system is flexible in that it can be expanded or run down; training costs are minimal, particularly if former full-time employees can be re-cruited; part-timers are usually highly motivated to earn as much as possible in their short stint; and supervision, while sometimes presenting problems, is by no means as difficult as on night shift.

Part-time day shifts are often less satisfactory because, while the additional evening shift offers a means of getting extra production from existing machines, part-time daywork is often used simply because it is impossible to provide a normal full-time day shift cover. In an industry such as clothing, where recruitment of sewing machinists has been extremely difficult in recent years, many smaller firms have reported that it is wholly or partly by using part-timers that they have managed to survive at all, even though they consider the practice to be uneconomic (Belbin and Sergean, 1963). In some sections of the food industry in London the variety of part-time alternatives offered reflects the recruitment difficulties with which firms are faced. In addition to four-hour morning and afternoon shifts, arrangements include "short spell" shifts of $1\frac{1}{2}$ hours to cover breaks—worked mostly by older married women, ex-employees, living locally—and short day or "school shifts" from 09 30 – 15 30 for younger mothers. Some part-time morning workers also put in the odd afternoon, and some afternoon workers the occasional morning. Others are welcome to come in for their four-hour stint "whenever they are free."

While such varied shifts may still be popular among those who work them—because they can be fitted in to suit particular domestic and social circumstances—they often add up to a production supervisor's nightmare.

Nevertheless, in less feverish employment situations, part-time day shifts can be a useful supplement to the regular day shift.

Double-day shifts

With double-day shifts the work period is divided into two successive turns of duty—earlies or mornings and lates or afternoons—usually of eight hours each, inclusive of mealtimes.

Twenty-five cases of this type of shift which we examined yielded examples of double-working for both men and women; cover for weeks of 5, 6 and 7 days; and alternating and fixed working. Hours worked were most commonly 06 00 – 14 00/14 00 – 22 00, 07 00 – 15 00/15 00 – 23 00 or near variants of these. One example of 05 00 – 14 00/14 00 – 23 00 was found, while in another case where it had become necessary for maintenance facilities to be available to experimental equipment running out of normal working hours, fitters and electricians had been placed on a system providing craft cover from 07 00 – 16 00 and from 16 00 – midnight every day including weekends. In another instance, times were approximate since each shift has a set production target and leaves when this is reached.

Although some people may regard them as forms of staggered daywork we have also included in this category examples of two-shift daywork where there is shift overlap—for example, 08 30 – 16 45 and 15 00 – 23 00 (computer controllers); 07 30 – 15 30 and 10 00 – 18 00 (punched tape machine operators).

Reflecting the national picture, far more examples of double-day shifts of women than of men were found. In three firms, all in light engineering or metal work, where sizeable numbers of males worked on a double-day basis (200, 400 and 450), substantial numbers of women were also employed on this type of shift, and it is this fact which appears to determine the men's own arrangement of working hours.

Alternation between early and late turn on a weekly basis was by far the commonest practice. In two examples where women remained on the same shift, this was said to be by their own choice, younger unmarried women preferring the earlier, and older married women the later turn.

From the employer's point of view absence and lateness are sometimes reported as disadvantages of the early morning shift, and where alternation is not practised difficulty is said to be experienced in recruiting for the less popular afternoon shift. But this type of system again gives some flexibility. [In seasonal trades, for example, it is possible to operate double-day work during the busy spell with the help of temporary staff, while retaining permanent staff on day-work for the rest of the year.] It extends running time without involving the problems of supervision and liaison that often arise with systems involving nightwork.

In view of the undoubted advantages of the double-day system, it is surprising that more firms now operating alternate days and nights have not considered its possibilities. The alternate day and night system admittedly has greater flexibility: if necessary it can be extended by overtime working or a part-time link-up shift to give 24-hour cover. And it is possible to work more standard hours with this system than with double-days. Nevertheless, in view of so much management comment on the difficulties and disadvantages of running a night shift, to say nothing of all that has been written about the social and health consequences of nightwork, might not more double-day working for men be worth a bet?

The reason why more employers have not backed this particular horse could be that the double-day system is basically unpopular with men on the shop floor. Alternating day- and nightwork may be considered less socially disruptive even though it involves a stint on nights: the starting time of many night shifts does permit some evening social activity. Whatever the starting/stopping hours of double-days, work on late turns means loss of evening social life during that week: nor is time off in the earlier part of the day as great an advantage for most married men as for most married women who tend to use it for housework and shopping. Early duties under double-days may mean getting up at 05 00 for a 06 00 start, resulting in a possible reduction in sleeping time, and a feeling of being fatigued by the time evening comes. Day shift under alternate days and nights is likely to permit a somewhat later start, and to offer a more "normal" life during at least one week out of two. Under double-days a man may feel that no week is "normal," while at the same time his financial return for this type of shiftwork is minimal.

TWO-SHIFT SYSTEMS INVOLVING NIGHTWORK

Such systems consist of a day shift and a night shift with either:

1   Crews alternating between the two turns of duty
2   Remaining permanently on one or the other. Both arrangements may coexist in the same firm

Alternating days and nights
This highly flexible system allows (with overtime working) any daily period of coverage between 16 and 24 hours. Any interval between shifts can be used for maintenance. It includes arrangements where all daytime production activities are duplicated at night, as well as those in which only certain machines are run on the second shift. In the latter case the number of those alternating will be smaller than the number on days: or everyone may change shift, but at unequal intervals—for instance, three weeks on days and one on nights.

Firms in our own sample with alternate days and nights as their main, or only, shift system fall broadly into two groups. The larger of these consisted mainly of units in the engineering and allied trades where the system was operated by a sizeable work force, had been in use for some considerable time, and appeared to be generally accepted as a traditional pattern of work. Sometimes the system was found together with a smaller amount of three-shift working in sections (for example moulding, boiler room) where there were technical reasons for semi-continuous working; and in three firms engaged in motor vehicle manufacture the system was substantially supported by a permanent night force (300 permanent night men to 600 on alternate days and nights; 165 to 330; and 404 to 1171).

The second and smaller group of firms which had alternate days and nights as their main, or only, shift system was industrially more varied, for instance animal foodstuffs, asbestos, rubber goods, safety glass. A number of these had regular shift lengths which were much longer than normal, and perhaps because of this a characteristic of the group was that the shift system was regarded as unsatisfactory by management or by the shiftworkers themselves. In two cases management would have preferred three-shift working, but had either already encountered opposition to the suggestion or anticipated resistance. In a third (where shifts are of 12 hours' duration) a section of the plant had already gone over to three shifts at the men's request.

Considerable variety again characterised the detailed features of this shift system:

1 In fifteen cases where starting/stopping times were examined no two were the same. Departmental differences in starting/stopping times within the same firm also occurred

2 Examples of working weeks of 4, 4½ and 5 shifts on night duty were all found. A working week of fewer but longer night shifts is now increasingly preferred to five night shifts of shorter duration. Grouping together alternate days and nights and permanent night systems in our sample, working weeks of 4 or 4½ nights were found twice as often as those of 5 nights. This underlines the importance with which the traditional weekend is regarded by shiftworkers

3 As regards alternation, 16 recorded cases yielded the following as the main frequencies practised: on a weekly basis, 6; fortnightly, 7; monthly, 3. In one firm hourly paid operatives alternate fortnightly, but staff on a monthly basis. The general tendency appears to be towards shorter rather than longer spells on the same shift. Even where monthly changeover is the rule, more frequent alternation is permitted. One firm which lays down in its standing orders that "wherever possible a member shall not work on night shift for less than four calendar weeks at a time," does not too rigidly enforce this rule. In practice, variable production demands, as well as shiftworkers' own personal needs, mean that few alternate day and night workers are likely consistently to change duty at exactly the same, regular intervals for very long at a time

Permanent night duty
What the Ministry of Labour (1965*a*) categorised as "normal night shift" covers a wide range of night activity. It is as unrealistic to

think in terms of a single, uniform type of nightwork as to generalise about a single "type" of permanent nightworker. Consider only the following examples from our own sample by way of illustration:

1. "Straightforward" permanent night shift. Found in dominantly male factories and in use for a considerable number of years. It may be the only shift used outside ordinary daywork, or may be combined with an alternate day and night system, as in the engineering industry. Used to meet regular production demands that cannot be satisfied by single shiftworking, it consists wholly or substantially of men engaged on the same work as their counterparts on permanent day shift. Examples are engineering, plastics moulding and printing

2. "Straightforward" permanent night shift combined with other systems in production departments. For example, a firm with a large permanent night shift in motor vehicle manufacture uses three-shifts discontinuously in its grinding section and continuously in heat treatment

3. Permanent night shift balancing a permanent day shift of men on "male" operations in factories employing substantial numbers of women, for instance bakers and mixers in biscuit manufacture

4. Permanent male night shift doing "women's work," for instance in fine electrical assembly, and replacing, either wholly or in part, women on days or double-days

5. Permanent night shift as a relatively minor activity in a dominantly daywork firm, as in the case of an electrical engineering unit employing 2500 hourly paid workers, Although more than a hundred men are engaged on the night shift, the firm does not regard itself as a shift-working concern. The need for the shift arises from production demands on one department and its size tends to fluctuate

6. Permanent night shift composed of a number of elements. One firm's night shift is in part determined by variable production demands, and numbers fluctuate seasonally. In another section men on night shift take over from women on days. Elsewhere in the same firm, in a processing department where continuity of working is

necessary, this is achieved by using permanent nightworkers linked by overtime to a permanent day shift

Each of the types outlined above is likely to create its own particular administrative problems, and to feature specific attitudes and behaviour as regards shifts on the part of management, shiftworkers themselves and the rest of the work force. To take only one example, management attitudes towards the effect of night shift hours of work on performance, or towards problems of shift supervision and co-ordination, are likely to be very different in a factory where night shiftworkers represent half the productive labour force and one in which they form only a fraction of the total.

Variety again characterises the detailed features of such systems. In 30 cases where details of starting/stopping times were available, no less than 23 were different. Starting times ranged between 18 30 and 23 00, and stopping times between 05 30 and 08 00. Duration of shifts also varied considerably.

Some indications were noted during factory visits of a tendency for alternate day- and nightwork to be replaced by permanent day and night operation. Alternating day and night crews are always likely to include a proportion of men who are unable to adapt to this form of work, and for whom alternation between day and night modes of life means considerable physical discomfort. Those who have an unwilling sense of being conscripted to this form of shift-work are better off away from it: a volunteer permanent night shift crew is likely to give a better account of itself.

Particularly since the introduction of the 40-hour week, there has been an incentive in certain industries through the adoption of a four-night working week and an increase in the night shift allowance, for those who can adjust to nightwork to volunteer for it on a regular basis. Where night shift volunteers from the alternating day and night shift come forward in sufficient numbers, those who dislike nightwork can revert to the permanent day basis of work for which they are more suited.

At the same time, many employers and managers are strongly opposed to the idea of a permanent night shift, arguing that the disadvantages of nightwork are exaggerated if one crew is permanently out of their control. Admittedly, greater care may have to be taken over supervision and communication in the case of a team regularly working nights. Yet some degree of administrative cost and inconvenience would seem a reasonable price to pay for the benefits of having men working on the hours they prefer.

THREE-SHIFT SYSTEMS

Three-shift systems give complete 24-hours' coverage by a division of this period into three working stints. They consist of:

1   Discontinuous or non-continuous systems operating for less than a seven-day week with three crews
2   Continuous systems operating for the full 168 hours with four crews

Discontinuous three-shift work

So far only two-shift systems have been dealt with, in which the main reason for going outside normal dayworking is that existing plant capacity is inadequate for coping with required production. Putting on a second shift may begin in a small way—for example, in particular bottleneck sections—or as an occasional measure, to deal with a special or seasonal demand. A second shift will become a regular feature for the factory as a whole where production requirements are consistently greater than those obtainable from single-shift working.

Even where this applies, however, there may still be fluctuations in demand. If a firm is operating in market conditions which are to some extent unpredictable, the flexibility which a two-shift day and night system allows is of considerable advantage. There comes a point, however, if demand continues to be held at a high level, where it is uneconomic to use overtime in addition to the two regular shifts, and where the load upon shiftworkers in terms of total working hours becomes excessive. This was the point which had been reached, or exceeded, in some of the firms in the second group of alternating day and night examples mentioned earlier. It is the logical point for introducing a three-shift system: three-shift working presupposes regularity of demand at a much higher level than for two-shift working.

Exactly when to change over to three shifts in such circumstances is difficult to judge, although it is probably often delayed overlong. Many firms now operating on a day and night system ought logically to be working three shifts. The fact that they are not doing so may be due to delay in management decision taking, or to the reluctance of two-shift workers to give up their existing hours of work.

The advantages which the three-shift discontinuous system offers to the two-shift worker are a much shorter working day at a return not much lower than his previous earnings with overtime. The main disadvantage is the physical and social disturbance involved in having to follow three quite different weekly routines.

Where permanent day and permanent night arrangements have previously applied, the day man may be facing shiftwork for the first time, while the night man has the prospect of losing one of the main advantages of his shift, its regularity and stability. Those on alternating days and nights already have experience of changing duties, but the new system certainly doesn't improve matters in this respect. It involves two "socially dead" weeks out of three (afternoons and nights) instead of only one out of two, and may entail an earlier start on the day turn.

It is surely not surprising, then, that so many two-shift workers cling determinedly to their existing system in the face of management proposals for change. They have, of course, a nice moral point on their side. At a more primitive stage of demand, it was the company which decided when overtime should be worked: if demand fell, so did available overtime. As demand steadily increased there was company encouragement for overtime working: overtime opportunities may even have been advertised as a recruiting inducement. Now that overtime has reached such proportions that the company wants to replace it, it is hardly unreasonable on the part of two-shift workers to reject a new system which they find unattractive in favour of an existing system in which they can begin to assume some control over their premium hours and their free time.

So far we have been talking only about three-shift discontinuous systems adopted for production and economic reasons as an extension of two-shift work. There are many examples of three-shift discontinuous systems, of course, which are governed by technical considerations—where semi-continuous operation is called for, not because it is technically indispensable (as in the case of continuous process industries) but because it is technically preferable. Technical arguments are in general more acceptable to men on the shop floor than those based on the company's economic needs. And it is not unusual to see three-shift semi-continuous operation from, say, Sunday night to Saturday morning, in particular sections—for instance heat treatment—of factories where the principle of three-shift work has otherwise been rejected.

Turning now to the detailed features of discontinuous three-shift systems seen in our own factory visits, normal cover was for 5 days, although examples of $5\frac{1}{2}$- and 6-day working also occurred. Commonest shift starting times were 06 00 – 14 00 – 22 00 and 07 00 – 15 00 – 11 00. The computer software industry is a happy hunting ground for more unusual timings: 08 30 – 17 00, 16 45 – 00 45 and 00 30 – 08 45 (computer operators). At a bakery, different starting/ stopping times were laid down for different categories of worker: tablehands, doughmakers, ovenmen. In a six-day week starting on Sunday, shift times changed on Thursday and Friday to allow for greater customer demand at the weekend.

Equal eight-hour shifts were the rule, but a number of variations in shift length existed:

MORNING	AFTERNOON	NIGHT	
$7\frac{3}{4}$	$7\frac{3}{4}$	$8\frac{1}{2}$	
$6\frac{1}{2}$	$9\frac{1}{4}$	$9\frac{1}{4}$	(Outgoing shift works $\frac{1}{4}$-hour
$7\frac{1}{2}$	8	$8\frac{1}{2}$	overlap)
8	$6\frac{1}{2}$	$9\frac{1}{2}$	
7	8	9	

Such variations may be introduced to ease early morning travel or to reduce the length of the supposedly unpopular afternoon shift. These few examples (plus one of two found under continuous three-shift working) suggest that the tendency may be, where shifts of variable length are used, to make the night shift the longest. Since there is some evidence that this shift is the most demanding and the least efficient, the practice ought perhaps to be reversed.

Rotation was generally on a weekly basis (18 cases). Fortnightly change of shift was twice found and there was one instance of foundrymen spending a month on each shift. In one unusual case, there was no rotation, 24-hour cover being provided by the firm through the use of permanent morning, afternoon and night shifts. There was almost equal preference as regards direction of rotation, with nine systems which moved "forwards" (mornings, afternoons, nights) as against 11 in the opposite "backwards" direction. Both directions of rotation were found in different departments of the same firm. In one establishment the sequence was morning – night – morning – afternoon.

Continuous seven-day operation

All-the-year round, seven-day operation (using three-shift periods and four-shift crews) applies, first, in such industries as iron and steel, glass, chemicals and oil refining, where it is the nature of the process which demands continuity. In industries such as sugar refining, or paper and board making, where continuous working has been more recently adopted, technical considerations again apply: discontinuous three-shift working, with weekend shutdown, was previously possible, but the development and introduction of new plant has now made it economically as well as technically preferable to work continuously. In a range of other industries where continuous operation was not previously practised, the extent of recent capital investment in new machinery has meant that for economic reasons alone such machinery must be worked intensively. In the case of service industries such as water supply, continuity of operation is largely dictated by customer demand.

In traditional industries and areas continuous working tends to be accepted as a necessary way of life, although even here attempts are being made to find new arrangements of working hours which are less demanding than customary rotas. In firms changing to continuous operation for the first time, the shiftworker is faced with a quite new demand—the loss of Saturday and Sunday. Whatever the social disadvantages of other types of shiftwork, they do at least leave the weekend free for ordinary family and leisure activities. The supposed advantages of time off during the week are often eloquently argued, but for most men and their families acceptance of seven-day working involves a real social adjustment. Choice of a particular continuous rota is often largely determined by the number of free Saturdays and Sundays which it includes. [For a short account of the principles on which continuous three-shift rotas are calculated, and the way in which they are modified to suit different lengths of working week, see the relevant section in D C Powell (1966): "Flexibility of shiftworking—alternative methods" (in *The Benefits and Problems of Shiftworking*, Production Engineering Research Association of Great Britain, Melton Mowbray). Also,

D C Powell (1966): "How to plan a shift-rota." (Industrial Society).]

The chief difference in three-shift continuous patterns concerns the frequency of rotation between the three turns of duty. The traditional pattern in this country has been for spells of six or seven shifts of the same kind to be worked in succession before a break (of two or three days) is taken and a change made to the next type of shift. An example is shown in Figure 2. A common criticism of this type of rota, from the shiftworker's point of view, is directed at the boring and fatiguing nature of unbroken spells of seven shifts, and in particular at the "dead fortnight," the two successive weeks (on afternoons and nights) which allow little opportunity for social life.

An alternative which has gained in popularity in recent years is to make use of one of the "rapidly rotating" rotas such as the "Continental" or the "Metropolitan" system under which a man works only two or three consecutive shifts of the same kind, with a 24-hour break between shift changes, and a longer break of two or three days after the night shift. An example is shown in Figure 2. The advantages claimed for this type of rota are that it breaks up the monotony of the long weekly stint and permits men to join in normal social activities on at least two or three occasions each week. Nor is a man ever away from his home for more than three nights in succession. Although some success has been reported for this type of arrangement (Walker, 1966; Wedderburn, 1967), it is by no means every continuous shiftworker's cup of tea. Nor are the physiological advantages claimed for it, namely that it eliminates disturbance of bodily rhythms, yet established. It does seem likely, however, that sleep may be less affected under rapid rotation. Since sleep tends to be curtailed during nightwork, a stint of seven night shifts may be more demanding than a week of mixed shifts which does permit some opportunity for sleep at the "normal" time.

Rapid rotation has long been practised in the glass manufacturing industry. It was introduced a few years ago into the ICI organisation and into parts of the steel industry, and has been adopted more recently still by a number of other companies, though occasionally, it seems, for little better reason than that "it is the latest thing." No figures are available as to the number and size of firms which employ either "traditional" or "rapidly rotating" routines in this country, but in our own experience rapid rotators are still very much

TRADITIONAL "WEEK ABOUT" PATTERN

Shifts	Week 1 S	M	T	W	Th	F	S	Week 2 S	M	T	W	Th	F	S	Week 3 S	M	T	W	Th	F	S	Week 4 S	M	T	W	Th	F	S
Morning	A	A	A	A	A	A	B	B	B	B	B	B	B	C	C	C	C	C	C	C	D	D	D	D	D	D	D	A
Afternoon	C	D	D	D	D	D	D	D	A	A	A	A	A	A	A	B	B	B	B	B	B	B	C	C	C	C	C	C
Night	B	B	B	C	C	C	C	C	C	C	C	D	D	D	D	D	D	D	A	A	A	A	A	A	A	B	B	B
Rest Day	D	C	C	B	B	B	A	A	D	D	C	C	C	B	B	A	A	D	D	D	C	C	B	B	A	A	A	D

"RAPIDLY ROTATING" (3 × 2 × 2) PATTERN

Shifts	Week 1 S	M	T	W	Th	F	S	Week 2 S	M	T	W	Th	F	S	Week 3 S	M	T	W	Th	F	S	Week 4 S	M	T	W	Th	F	S
Morning	D	A	A	B	B	C	C	C	D	D	A	A	B	B	B	C	C	D	D	A	A	A	B	B	C	C	D	D
Afternoon	C	D	D	A	A	B	B	B	C	C	D	D	A	A	A	B	B	C	C	D	D	D	A	A	B	B	C	C
Night	B	C	C	D	D	A	A	A	B	B	C	C	D	D	D	A	A	B	B	C	C	C	D	D	A	A	B	B
Rest Day	A	B	B	C	C	D	D	D	A	A	B	B	C	C	C	D	D	A	A	B	B	B	C	C	D	D	A	A

FIGURE 2   EXAMPLES OF CONTINUOUS THREE-SHIFT ROTAS

in a minority. During our own visits traditional systems were used in mineral oil refining and water supply, and in the manufacture of photographic equipment, rubber products, refractory goods, pharmaceuticals and paper. Rapid rotation was seen in glass manufacture (3 × 3 × 3) and animal foodstuffs. In the paper and board making industry, which has comparatively recently gone over to continuous working, most mills are said to operate the traditional rota recommended in the industry's "National 4-shift Agreement" (1965) consisting of seven consecutive shifts of eight hours with forward rotation. At least one mill is operating a 3 × 2 × 2 system, while another has a routine based on its former three-shift discontinuous hours of work: 07 00 – 14 00 (7 hours); 14 00 – 21 00 (7 hours); and 21 00 – 07 00 (10 hours), with three-shift cover from Monday to Friday, plus two shifts of 12 hours each on Saturdays and Sundays. There is substantial weekly variation in the pay packet under this system, but two weekends out of four are free.

CHARACTERISTICS OF "SHIFTWORK"

These, then, are the main types of shift system. Many other arrangements exist, arising out of the particular needs of organisations or groups of workers, which do not properly belong under these headings. Anyone familiar with even a handful of shiftworking situations will be able to quote his own exceptions. To give just a few examples from our own sample:

1   Three-shift cover supplied by groups of two-shift workers alternating between either morning and afternoon, or afternoon and night, or morning and night

2   Permanent "late" shifts, for example 13 00 – 21 00, 14 00 – 22 00 and 15 00 – 23 00, worked in either maintenance or dispatch departments

3   A "link-up" shift, the function of which is to fill the gaps between permanent day and permanent night shift in a heat treatment department, thus giving the firm 24-hour cover. The "link-up" crew works four afternoons (13 00 – 21 00) plus one night (21 00 – 06 30) on Friday

4   An alternating two-shift system which cannot strictly be classified as either double-day or alternating days and

nights. In this, five early shifts (07 00 – 16 30) are worked, followed by five late turns (16 30 – 02 30). These unusual hours were the choice of the men themselves some years ago when a second shift was introduced, and they now insist on retaining them although the company is anxious to change to three-shift operation.

The variety of ways in which establishments combine the main types of shift system is another factor which deserves comment. This point was examined in 60 cases and, with the exception of 10 firms operating only a permanent night shift in addition to days, in no instance did more than five firms practise the same combination of systems. In over a third of cases the combination of systems was unique to the particular firm.

Diversity is the keynote throughout. No one who looks at data on the arrangement of working hours, and attempts to classify it, can fail to be impressed by the multiplicity of ways in which firms meet their shiftworking requirements and by the variety of routines to which groups of shiftworkers apparently adapt with some measure of success. This element of diversity is a feature which no statistical tables summarising numbers of shiftworkers according to broad shift types can adequately bring out.

Nor can such tables begin to convey the element of fluidity which is also so characteristic of the shiftworking scene.

In the short term this fluidity is mainly due to the extent to which firms use shiftworking flexibly as a means of handling variations in demand. The system itself may vary. For example, one small production group works on double-days or three-shifts discontinuously, five or five and half days, as required. Another team of 40 men works on alternate days and nights or on a double-day basis "according to machine availability and day-to-day circumstances." Numbers employed on shifts may be reduced or increased. In one firm making gramophone records the numbers on night shift fluctuate between 24 (in summer) and 100 (in winter). The system is kept going during the slack season because the company fears that it would be impossible to start it up again if it were once stopped completely. Instances were found, however, where a shift system was temporarily discontinued: in a furniture factory shifts had been "suspended for the present due to reorganisation involving redundancy." Recession in the car trade had caused one supplier temporarily to cut out double-day working for women. Another supplier to the car industry was working on a short time basis of three day and three night shifts per week at the time of our visit.

In the longer term, development in the type of system used (two-shift to three-shift; discontinuous to continuous) may come about because production, economic or technological considerations make it desirable. But, for various reasons, discontinuation of shifts or contraction in the amount of shiftworking also takes place through time. One firm had used the economic freeze of 1966–7 as an opportunity of getting rid of its permanent night shift. In another case fall in demand for a particular product had resulted in a reduction from 500 to 150 in the numbers employed on night shift over a three year period. In a company producing iron castings, where a two-shift system had previously operated in the foundry, new and improved plant now produced enough to feed subsequent departments from a single day shift. Group reorganisation is another factor which may in the long term influence the extent of shiftworking in a firm. In one concern, a permanent night shift of 200 in the London factory had gradually been run down (involving some redundancy and transfer to daywork) as part of a reorganisation within the group in which part of the firm's business had been transferred to a new factory in a northern development area.

Its diversity and fluidity are characteristics of shiftwork which cannot be too often emphasised. What is meant by "shiftwork," different "types" of shift system, "shiftworker," "a shiftworking firm," are variable concepts with meaning only in relation to particular contexts of place and time. It is important to bear this continually in mind when we come to consider at later points in this book the attitudes and responses of employers and employed to shift hours of work; the physical, psychological and social demands which shiftwork can impose; or its possible effects on health and on various aspects of performance.

Other Arrangements
of Working Hours

OVERTIME WORKING

No discussion of the arrangement of working hours can be complete without relating this to total hours worked. We have already seen that the progressive reduction in the length of the working week was a prime factor in the evolution of multiple shiftwork. And early research into shifts was closely tied up with the length of working week with which they were combined. Yet, curiously, shiftwork and its possible effects are now often discussed as though we all worked a week of standard length.

The subject of overtime in industry has received much attention since the end of the Second World War. More recently, an excellent research paper by Whybrew (1967) has served to underline the extent of the practice in Britain. More than 60 per cent of male manual workers, this report estimates, either work for more than 10 hours a day on 3 or 4 days a week, or know little or nothing of the 5-day week.

Much less publicised, however, is the extent to which overtime is worked in conjunction with shifts. This may be, of course, because shiftwork is often advocated as an alternative to overtime. One of the main encouragements held out to employers to get them to adopt or extend shiftwork is that it does away with costly overtime hours. And the chance of working shorter hours is a common inducement offered to workers to change from daywork to shiftwork. Some firms have managed to cut out excessive overtime in this way; and many shiftworkers are in fact earning the same as their daywork counterparts for fewer hours. (In an engineering concern on the Medway average weekly hours for permanent day and night workers were respectively 51 and 44, with average earnings almost identical.)

The Industrial Society's shift survey (The Industrial Society, 1966) showed that a majority of firms in their sample worked overtime together with shift work under *all* kinds of system, including continuous three-shift. This picture was confirmed by our own experience. Three quarters of the contributors to our own sample referred to the use of overtime, and of these two thirds spoke of the practice as a familiar and regular feature of their work arrangements. It was not unusual to find the amount of overtime described as "heavy" or "considerable."

Overtime in two-shift systems

Practically all our examples of overtime in conjunction with two-shift work occurred where permanent night and/or alternate days and nights were in operation. In these cases overtime was used in two ways: (*a*) by working an extra shift, for instance a sixth day-shift in addition to the normal five, or a Friday night shift on top of the usual four, and (*b*) to obtain complete, or virtually complete, cover for the 24 hours by filling the gaps between the customary day and night turns. In one extreme case, not only was 24-hour cover for five days obtained in this way, with day shift staying on late and night shift coming in early, but weekend turns were additionally worked when necessary.

Overtime in three-shift systems

The extent of overtime working here was more surprising: almost half the firms practising overtime in this sample did so in conjunction with three-shift systems. It is true that a lower proportion of such firms use overtime as a *regular* feature than is the case with two-shift units, but the proportion still seems high. Overtime here was worked in two ways: (*a*) under both discontinuous and continuous operation by bringing men in on their rest days, or by having them work on after their normal turn of duty, to deal, for example, with absenteeism; and (*b*) less moderately, and more regularly, by using 12-hour weekend shifts, on top of normal three-shift cover from Monday to Friday, and thus effectively converting a discontinuous into a continuous system with the same complement of men.

A number of firms commented that overtime was rare with them and that they actively discouraged it. In one concern where overtime had been "excessive," union and management had agreed that it should be eliminated, and an additional link-up shift had been introduced to fill the gaps between day and night shifts. Other companies claimed that they would like to do away with overtime but were unable to do so. One employer declared that he hesitated to try to introduce three shifts for fear that reduction of overtime earnings would mean loss of labour and difficulties of recruitment. Another reported that this did in fact happen whenever overtime opportunities were cut.

One informant who would have preferred a more systematic shift arrangement, less dependent on overtime, could see no likelihood of this in the immediate future. Not only was it impossible to increase rates sufficiently to compensate the high overtime worker for loss of earnings, but workers also resisted three-shift working on the grounds that "it restricts the individual's freedom of choice of working hours."

It is worth emphasising, however, that it is not only employees who cling to overtime practices. Retention of this method of working can result from management preference, too. On one large company, with manufacturing branches all over the country, a new model factory was in process of construction. The general manager was strongly in favour of operating the new unit on an alternate day and night basis, plus greater or less amounts of overtime, "because of the flexibility which this gives to management." Other members of the management team were highly critical of this attitude which they thought could only be interpreted as "indicating an inability on the part of management to plan its operations." It was absurd to think in these terms, they argued, in view of the size of capital investment in the new site.

There seems no doubt that in many situations where employee reluctance to forego overtime earnings is now an obstacle to the extension of shiftwork, management has made a rod for its own back by encouraging the practice of overtime in the past.

SHIFTS OF "LONGER DURATION"

By a shift of "longer duration" is meant here any single turn of duty which is substantially longer than 8 hours, but specially one which involves 12 hours or over at the place of work. Bearing in mind the progressive reduction in basic working hours over the years, the extent to which shift lengths of 12 hours or more are in use at the present time is of particular interest.

Often, of course, such longer shifts are used only as an occasional or temporary overtime measure to cover exceptional production demands, to meet contract dates or to cope with the holiday period or times of high absenteeism. In a food producing firm, for example, with a permanent night shift of 21 30 – 06 30, and where men "almost always" stay till 08 00 (10½ hours), they are sometimes asked to come in at 17 00, making a total shift length of 15 hours.

At the time of writing, over the summer holiday period, Air Ministry civilian staff at one station are putting in working weeks of 76 hours (that is, 36 hours' overtime), by attending on alternate nights in stints of 14 and 24 hours' duration, beginning at 18 30. This is even more hair-raising when it is realised that these men are engaged, sometimes in isolation, on watch-keeping operations in connection with the provision of radio navigational aids.

Another example which can be included under this head is that of Thames Estuary pilots whose hours of work (usually at night) are largely governed by the number and times of ships sailing from port. Much of the men's working time is spent in waiting for ships and in return travelling from the point of disembarkation. Their routine is extremely irregular and unpredictable, and can involve them in periods away from base in excess of 24 hours.

In other cases one finds long shifts regularly, though not exclusively, used—for instance, in the type of situation already quoted where 12-hour shifts are worked as overtime on Saturdays and Sundays in addition to 3 × 8 hour shifts from Monday to Friday. In another example, from a London printing firm, the Friday day shift regularly works on through Friday night. Compositors, who are "on their feet all the time," usually stop at midnight, but machine-men and warehousemen soldier on to 06 00 next morning (22 hours in the factory). Weekly hours at work equal 58.

Another instance of regular though not exclusive use of extended shifts is provided by deep sea trawlermen who work stints of up to 18 hours out of each 24 during actual fishing operations, when work goes on round the clock. On the old type of side trawler the job of handling the gear and catch, including gutting, takes place on open deck often in appalling weather conditions. The Holland-Martin report has recently made a series of recommendations concerning length of working stint, rest pauses, arrangement of working hours and breaks between trips in this hazardous and demanding occupation. (Holland and Martin, 1959.)

Elsewhere the regular *and* exclusive use of shifts of "longer duration" is found incorporated in rotas covering either part or the whole of the week. In many of these cases long stints of 12 hours and over are combined with working weeks of considerable length. For example:

1   Permanent night shifts (5 nights weekly). Textile workers: machine minding. (Ex-miners, retrained after pit closures). These men work 5×13 hours (18 30 – 07 30) Monday to Friday ($\frac{3}{4}$ hour break at 22 30 and three brief tea breaks at 01 00, 03 00 and 05 00). Sixty-five hours are spent in factory weekly. Management acknowledges these hours to be long but suggests that "money sweetens labour"

2   Permanent day and permanent night shift ($5\frac{1}{2}$ days; 5 nights). Bakers and mixers in a biscuit factory. Day shift (officially 07 30 – 17 00) is regularly extended to give 12 hours cover (06 00 – 18 00), that is 5×12 hours and Saturday morning work every other week. The night shift (officially 21 45 – 06 45) is regularly extended to give $12\frac{3}{4}$ hours cover (18 00 – 06 45). Time spent in factory weekly is 60 plus hours (day shift) and $65\frac{3}{4}$ (night shift)

3   Day and night shifts, alternating fortnightly (6 days; 6 nights). Men work in drying department of a factory producing electric cables: machine minding with some physical effort. Hours are 6×12 weekly, Monday to Saturday (1 hour meal break and 2×10 minutes tea breaks). Seventy-two hours are spent in factory weekly. Management calls these hours "rather excessive," but the operators concerned "do not seem to have deteriorated physically as a result"

In these illustrations the logical system would be 3×8 hour shifts discontinouusly. In fact, two-shift day and night working has been extended here by regular and heavy overtime to achieve semi-continuous operation. The firms concerned still refer to permanent day and night work or alternating days and nights, but these labels mean nothing without reference to the total hours involved.

Where the regular and exclusive use of 12-hour shifts is found in rotas which give continuous coverage over 7 days, the *average* weekly hours worked are likely to be less than in the examples of non-continuous cover just given. (They can still be well above standard, however; 56 hours is not uncommon.) But the total hours actually worked in any *one* week can be very high, as seen in the next two cases:

1   Continuous 7-day cover in 12-hour day and night shifts. Male workers in plaster board manufacture. Machine minding in most cases, but more physically arduous in section loading plaster board sheets. Three weeks' cycle: 7×12-hour night shifts (then 3 days off); 7×12-hour day shifts (4 days off). Weekly hours spent in factory are 84, 48 and 36. Average 56

2   Continuous 7-day cover in 12-hour day and night shifts with 130 chemical workers. Twelve weeks' cycle in which blocks of 4 day and 4 night shifts are worked alternately with 1, 2 or 3 days intervening. Actual hours average 56, with a weekly range of 48 to 72

What is happening here is that continuous cover is being achieved with three crews regularly putting in overtime. It is perfectly possible, however, to use 12-hour shifts with four crews so that a week of 40 or 42 hours is worked by each man. The use of shifts of "longer duration" within the context of an average working week of reasonable proportions is, in our experience, becoming increasingly popular.

The following are two examples of such 12-hour rotas where the average weekly hours worked are 42: both are illustrated in Figure 3.

1   This rota works on a 4 on/4 off basis, with 4 day shifts alternating with 4 nights. On any one day two crews are at rest. In a 16-weeks' cycle, weekly hours worked are either 36 or 48, with an average of 42

2   To avoid the working of four 12-hour shifts in succession as in (1), a rapidly rotating version can be used in which day and night shifts are worked alternately. Each day shift is followed by a 24-hour break, and each night shift

by a free period of 48 hours. In a 4-weeks' cycle 2 weeks
of 36 and 2 of 48 hours are worked, averaging 42

In our own examples of such types of rota, shift changeover was
at 06 00 and 18 00, though somewhat later timings might be preferable. One example of (2) was also seen in which a 10-hour day
shift and a 14-hour night shift were used, though the latter was
probably overlong. Version (2) is also reported to be working satisfactorily abroad, for example in the German chemicals industry
(Loskant, 1957; Noack, 1967).

To summarise, then, the ways in which shifts of "longer duration"
occur, they may:

1   Provide an occasional or temporary expedient
2   Be regularly though not exclusively used
3   Be consistently *and* exclusively used in rotas involving
     heavy total hours of work
4   Be consistently and exclusively used in rotas involving
     normal weekly hours of work

The attitudes of employers and management to shifts of longer
duration vary according to the way in which such shifts are used.
Where long shifts are a temporary expedient:

> It is obviously to our advantage to have employees will-
> ing to extend working hours according to production
> demands

But if the need for longer shifts persists:

> The employee may become accustomed to the higher
> earnings levels, and adjust his living standards accord-
> ingly, so that when slack periods come along he may find
> difficulty in making ends meet

The physical strain of working extended hours may also be felt, and:

> There then arises the dilemma of not wanting to lose
> money, but also not wanting to work such long hours,
> and claims arise for reduction in working periods without
> loss of pay

50

Cases where long shifts are regularly combined in rotas involving high average weekly hours are often hangovers from the past, surviving in conditions to which they are no longer suited. Sometimes they appear to persist simply because this is how hours have been traditionally arranged: because management has adopted a *laissez-faire* policy: "There is no pressure on us to make an alteration." In other instances management would dearly like to get rid of long shifts and heavy overtime, but is baulked because the 12-hour shift men strongly favour their retention.

As regards possible performance effects of longer shifts, the views of management informants were divided. In a pharmaceuticals firm (regular rota of 12-hour shifts, weekly average 56 hours) there was "no evidence that performance falls towards the end of a shift." Moreover, a number of men here had worked such shifts since 1940 "without any special evidence of performance deterioration," although "some men do ask to be relieved late in life." No adverse effects were said to have been noted in the cases quoted earlier of textile workers (65 hours weekly) or cable makers (72 hours weekly).

But there was no doubt in the minds of other managers that 12-hour shifts were too long, particularly when worked for any length of time. "Unless the job is semi- or fully automated," it was stated in a second cables factory, "operators cannot give of their best. There may be deliberate pacing, but in spite of this there is a drop in efficiency affecting both quantity and quality."

In a light metal working firm, which used 12-hour shifts seasonally, deterioration was noted after about a month. In the view of a company producing tiles and other building products, effects depended on the individual and the type of operation involved: "Where judgement or skill is required there tends to be a slight fall-off towards the latter part of the 12-hour shift, and the reject incidence is higher." At a sugar refinery there was a "definite tendency towards the end of the three-week holiday period, when 12-hour shifts are used, for quality and quantity to deteriorate." Moreover, "A combination of long working hours and a reluctance to abandon the social habits that go with eight-hour shifts results in a general fatigue at the end of the period." At a factory producing photographic equipment, which also used 12-hour shifts to cover the holidays, a "deterioration in mental alertness" was noted after a few weeks, resulting in a "falling off in the reporting back of incidents and in taking corrective action, while at the same time

"BLOCKS OF FOUR" CONTINUOUS TWELVE-HOUR SHIFT ROTA

Shifts	Week 1 S M T W Th F S	Week 2 S M T W Th F S	Week 3 S M T W Th F S	Week 4 S M T W Th F S
Day	A A A A C C C	C B B B B D D	D D A A A A C	C C C B B B B
Night	B B B B D D D	D A A A A C C	C C B B B B D	D D D A A A A
Rest Day	C C C C A A A	A C C C C A A	A A C C C C A	A A A C C C C
Rest Day	D D D D B B B	B D D D D B B	B B D D D D B	B B B D D D D

CONTINUOUS TWELVE-HOUR SHIFT ROTA WITH DAY AND NIGHT SHIFTS WORKED SUCCESSIVELY

Shifts	Week 1 S M T W Th F S	Week 2 S M T W Th F S	Week 3 S M T W Th F S	Week 4 S M T W Th F S
Day	A C D B A C D	B A C D B A C	D B A C D B A	C D B A C D B
Night	B A C D B A C	D B A C D B A	C D B A C D B	A C D B A C D
Rest Day	D D A A D D A	A D D A A D D	A A D D A A D	D A A D D A A
Rest Day	C B B C C B B	C C B B C C B	B C C B B C C	B B C C B B C

FIGURE 3 EXAMPLES OF CONTINUOUS ROTAS USING TWELVE-HOUR SHIFTS
The upper table shows the first four weeks of the rota which continues in the same pattern until the cycle is completed in sixteen weeks. The letters in the tables refer to the four shift-crews involved. In order to determine the sequence for any one man, follow one of the letters—for

people are less approachable." In the opinion of a number of informants a degree of strain upon operators was thought to exist even where no evidence of inferior work could be shown.

It is of interest to note that much of the comment on adverse effects of longer shifts comes from firms which use them temporarily. Workers in such firms are likely to be unaccustomed and unadapted to long hours, in contrast to the position in firms where extended work periods are a regular feature. In the latter case workers may also be said in some degree to have elected to work their long hours.

There also seems no doubt that in certain instances the reason why men can maintain performance during long shifts and long weekly hours is that their firms suffer from what has been called "the basic malaise of British industry," namely overmanning. This reduces the demand on the individual and may even afford some unofficial scope for rest and sleep on the job.

The type of work involved is another factor affecting the ability to maintain performance over a long period. A number of firms commented that long shifts were restricted to work "where physical effort is normally low" or which was "more in the nature of an attendant's job than anything else." For example, one such job involved minding machines producing plaster boards and making an approximate 5 per cent visual check on the edges of the product. Some degree of performance deterioration did not unduly matter, it was claimed here, since the process was a long one and a fault missed at one stage could be picked out further along the line. Twelve-hour shifts often featured in security departments where work was of an intermittent nature, or in maintenance where men were "on call" and again not necessarily involved in continuous activity. But, "12-hour shifts for normal piecework jobs would be entirely unacceptable to us," it was stated.

Twelve-hour shifts, regularly used, are certainly regarded as unsatisfactory in certain quarters, and efforts are being made to replace them. One of the case studies in the Ministry of Labour's shift survey (Ministry of Labour, 1967*b*) concerned the replacement in 1964 of a 12-hour system following criticism by the industry's Joint Industrial Council and by the main trade union involved. They are disappearing from some collective agreements, for instance in the cement manufacturing industry.

But much criticism of shifts of "longer duration" is confounded with objections to excessive weekly hours. Our evidence in the late

1960s does not confirm Downie (1963) in his view that, "Twelve-hour shifts are almost universally regarded as too long and too tiring by modern standards, and factories using the system have a high labour turnover."

There is, on the contrary, considerable interest at the present time in rotas using 12-hour shifts and average working weeks of 40–42 hours, examples of which have already been illustrated in Figure 3. This interest is developing in firms which have not previously used long shifts, and which are either already working continuously over 7 days with a traditional 3 × 8 rota or are going on to continuous work for the first time. The initiative in this comes sometimes from management, but mainly from shiftworkers themselves. It is tending more and more to be shown in situations where shiftworkers have the opportunity to devise their own rota.

It is not uncommon, of course, to hear of workers wanting to get on to 12-hour shifts, even where weekly hours are exceedingly long. "It is amazing how many men apply for employment on this basis," one personnel manager reported. "Eager" and "keen competition" were other terms used to describe the attitudes of such men. But this is purely and simply a matter of attraction by high wages; of lower paid workers seeking to boost their earnings by high overtime opportunities.

Interest on the part of continuous shiftworkers in 12-hour rotas within a normal working week is determined by something else altogether. It is concerned almost exclusively with the amount of a worker's free time and the way it is arranged. We have already seen one facet of this in the case of discontinuous two-shift workers, among whom there was a tendency to favour the concentration of working hours into fewer but longer shifts, thus giving a three-day weekend break.

The main advantage for the continuous worker of the kind of 12-hour shift system shown in Figure 3 is again that it concentrates the working session and therefore allows extended periods of free time compared with a 3 × 8 arrangement. This is a very real advantage to many men.

Such rotas have other advantages for the shiftworker. They eliminate the social disadvantages of the traditional 3 × 8 with its "dead fortnight," and they include more weekends which are either wholly or partly free. From the point of view of eating, sleeping and so on, it is less disruptive to have to adapt to two time changes than three. In the version of the 12-hour rota in which day and night shifts are worked alternately, each day shift is followed by a 24-hour break, and each night shift by a free period of 48 hours, and this allows reasonable recovery time from any effects of night work.

One disadvantage to the shiftworker may be that if there is no entitlement to sick benefit a day lost because of illness means a 12-hour loss of earnings. On the other hand travelling time and costs are lower in relation to total hours worked. The argument has also been advanced that this last point offers an advantage to the community in that there is less pressure on public transport, or, if the worker uses private transport, the traffic problem and the risk of road accidents is reduced (Loskant, 1957).

Worker enthusiasm for rotas of this type has been noted by a number of other commentators. Walker (1961) even cites [from an unpublished report by Wyatt and Marriott (1946)] examples of rotas involving 16-hour alternate night shifts which were greatly preferred to a 3 × 8 system by the men who worked them. And a contemporary 12-hour shift rota for control operators in the German chemicals industry has been "passionately defended by the workers for its many advantages, while the employers are well-disposed to such an arrangement of work" (Noack, 1967). Nor, "in spite of thorough investigation of the problem," has any objection to this system been raised by the medical department concerned.

In this country employer and management reaction to the possibility of introducing 12-hour shifts for the first time ranges from direct opposition—"We would consider it a retrograde step to increase hours by working longer shifts"—to actually proposing the idea themselves. A more common response is a willingness to consider such rotas if they can be shown to be workable, combined with some concern over possible adverse effects on health, output, quality, safety, absenteeism, etc. Sometimes one sees a division of opinion in management, with production and administration favouring the idea, and the medical and personnel people opposing it.

As regards trade union attitudes, shiftworkers and their official representatives may not always initially see eye to eye on this question. The unions, after all, have fought for an eight-hour day since the nineteenth century, and it may be a matter of principle to maintain it. [Note the prompt trade union response early in 1968 to the "Back Britain" campaign and its proposals for a voluntary additional half hour's work each day. For example, Mr Clive Jenkins, general secretary of the then Association of Supervisory Staffs, Executives and Technicians: "I think members of my union are all much too sensible to believe that longer hours result in more efficient production" (*The Guardian*, 4 January 1968).]

Official union reaction to the possibility of extending the length of the individual working stint (within the context of shorter weekly hours) was seen at the time of the introduction of the 40-hour week, when rank-and-file discontinuous shiftworkers favoured 4×10 rather than 5×8. "When we have been negotiating for shorter hours," declared Sir William Carron to delegates to the AEU national committee conference in 1965 (*The Times*, 17 May 1965), "one of the strongest arguments has been that it is not good for people to work over a given number of hours. If popular clamour is the reverse, that argument is denied us."

In the case of continuous shiftworking, an interesting illustration of management, union and worker attitudes was found in a London company late in 1967. In the words of the personnel manager here:

We have just recently had experience of reducing the basic working week of one department from 48 hours (4×12 hours) to 42 hours per week with somewhat surprising results. Our proposal to union officials and operators was that the working week should become one of 42 hours on the $3 \times 2 \times 2$ pattern. We had anticipated resistance from the operators because the change represented a loss of six hours earnings per week, but expected support from the officials in abolishing 12-hour shifts. In the event we had neither.

The operators accepted the reduction in the working week, but objected to coming to work on 21 days in 28 instead of 16 in 28, saying that this would unreasonably increase their travelling costs and reduce their free time. The union officials were interested only in agreeing with their members and voiced no objection to 12-hour shifts even though they had done so previously.

Out of the impasse created here a way was ultimately found in which it was agreed that operators should work alternate weeks of 3×12, and 4×12, averaging 42 hours.

Just how feasible is it to use shifts of "longer duration" in present day industry? A number of guidelines may be laid down:

1   First, no one should be expected to work 12-hour shifts unless he chooses to do so. This is not the type of rota to be worked by anyone to whom it does not appeal

2   Next, 12-hour shifts should only be used within the framework of the standard working week. It is comparatively easy to build overtime into this type of rota, by bringing men in during their free time, but this is a temptation to be avoided except in extreme emergency. The occasional "one off" type of marathon effort may be carried off without undue effects, but sustained performance over a sequence of such stints is altogether another matter

3   Finally, as regards the type of work involved, shifts of long duration are not suitable for work having a heavy physical content, or of a continuous and monotonous nature, for example, many industrial inspection tasks. Nor are they advisable in jobs having a prominent danger factor, or in which exceptionally high standards of quality or purity are demanded. But for many types of lighter and more varied work they are worth serious consideration in view of their undoubted social advantages for those who have to work shift hours

More information is certainly needed about the possible effects of long shifts (as indeed is the case regarding all arrangements of working hours). Much of the early research on 12-hour shifts was carried out when these were unrelieved by adequate intervals of rest, and when the working man had little choice in the matter. Working conditions, wages, health and general living standards were also vastly inferior to those of the 1970s. Further research, under existing conditions, is needed concerning such factors as:

1   The degree of possible performance decrement (quantitative and/or qualitative) during the later stages of a single long shift

2   The type of task which is vulnerable to such deterioration

3   The effects of the time of day during which the 12-hour shift extends
4   The effect of several long shifts worked in succession —that is, the possibility of decrement during the later stages of a spell of several such long shifts
5   The possibility of fall-off in performance as a result of a man working 12-hour shift rotas over a long period of time

Some of these topics can only be investigated in "real life". Others are amenable to study in the laboratory or in contrived field situations. Car driving is one activity which has been observed in this way over an extended session. Brown (1967), for example, has shown that "a virtually continuous 12-hour period of driving during the normal working day need not affect either perceptual or motor skills adversely." Not all studies of this kind have pointed in the same direction, however, and the same author has also demonstrated (Brown, Tickner and Simmonds, 1970) some impairment in efficiency over the last three hours.

All such research enables a more complete answer to be given to such general questions as "What is meant by a 'long' shift?" and "In what circumstances is a 12-hour shift 'long' or 'not long'?"

DOUBLE-JOBBING

We have talked about overtime and about shifts of "longer duration" combined with abnormally long working weeks. Another way in which a man may tot up a high weekly total of working hours is by taking a second job, or by working on his own account, during the time he has off from his main employment.

A common management objection to shiftwork, or to particular forms of shiftwork, is that it encourages double-jobbing, a practice which it is assumed has an adverse effect on the "main" job. Permanent nightwork in particular comes in for criticism on this score, as does any rota which permits extended periods of free time.

"You came here in a taxi?" the personnel manager at one firm asked. "Then the driver was probably one of our night shift men." "Probably" is the operative word here. Most managers can quote the odd example of a night shiftworker who has a daytime window-cleaning or milk round, or who works for a bookie or an undertaker in his time off. But few know the extent of such practices, and there may be a tendency to generalise from a few notorious cases. One manager estimated that a third of the firm's permanent night force of 400 had an additional part-time job. Another thought that weekend moonlighting might be the cause of high weeknight absenteeism.

Occasionally there is rather stronger reason to suspect seasonal moonlighting where workers are drawn from coastal or country areas—for example, in seaside holiday jobs, fruit picking, etc. And one firm claimed that the practice was quite prevalent because it had led to strong resistance when changes to existing shift arrangements had been proposed. But in the main there is no firm evidence from which to conclude that most night shift men also work part-time during the day.

A question on second-jobbing in this country was included in the 1966 10 per cent sample Census of Population, and some of this material has been analysed and presented by Alden (1968) with particular reference to Scotland. The same author later carried out a survey of double job holding in the county of Midlothian, although this was not specifically related to second-jobbing by shift-workers. As far as is known this is the only piece of empirical research undertaken in this country on the economic and social characteristics of double-jobbers.

This survey found a rate for double-jobbing in East Midlothian of 5.8 per cent, higher than the national average in the Census figures. A feature of particular interest was that one-third of these double-job holders put in between 41 and 60 hours on their main job, that is well above the average length of the basic working week. Alden stresses the need for further research into the activities and characteristics of "this significant and energetic category of the labour force."

As regards the effect of "spare-time" work on performance on the "main" job, there is really no direct evidence on which to draw. Much probably depends on whether additional work is undertaken out of necessity—because of a low wage on the main job—or whether it is seen by the worker as a form of paid hobby or a means of financing such costlier pleasures as holidays abroad and only-daughter's wedding. In the second case, there is no reason to think that performance on the main job should be affected to a greater extent than by more strenuous do-it-yourself activities in home and garden.

Another relevant factor is the number of hours additionally worked. In the Alden (1968) survey almost a quarter of the sample spent more than 10 hours a week on their secondary job. In a recent issue of a London evening paper a commercial security organisation advertised for spare-time guards and patrolmen for duties which included stints of 10 and 12 hours' duration. This advertisement specified that, "Applicants must be in full-time employment or doing shiftwork which leaves them free to undertake day, night or weekend duties."

As a variant on the performance theme, Downie (1963) raises the possibly more important point of efficiency in the *secondary* occupation. This, he suggests, is of particular concern in the case of those shiftworkers who drive taxis, coaches or other road vehicles on a paid part-time basis. "For reasons of road safety," Downie points out, "the law limits the number of hours for which a lorry driver, for example, may drive in one stretch. As the law stands, however, there there is nothing to prevent a man working a night shift and then taking a passenger or goods vehicle out on the road the following day."

The Industrial Society (1963) has published an interesting collection of papers on this subject by a personnel manager, an industrial medical officer and a trade union representative. These serve nicely to underscore the point that the line between second-jobbing and other unpaid spare-time activities is difficult to draw. They conclude that selective double-jobbing is not necessarily harmful, either from the point of view of health or performance, and that it can in fact provide relaxation from a monotonous daytime job (just as do other forms of unpaid activity).

The summary to these Industrial Society papers goes so far as to suggest that provided an employee maintains the required standard in his main work, "it does not matter to management if a man has two, three or more jobs."

Not every manager or employer would go along with this. Worker commitment to the company is something which a number of managements have been at special pains to try to develop in recent years. But many workers do not want to become "company men." They expect to put in a fair day's work, but their main interests lie outside the job and the workplace.

Certain forms of shiftwork may appeal to such men precisely because they give them greater control over the time they spend on the main job and the time they spend away from it. The arrangement of free time under a shiftwork rota may be particularly convenient for the pursuit of some leisure interest, whether paid or unpaid, and this leisure interest, shiftworkers would reasonably argue, is their own affair.

Consider, in this connection, the following rather startling example. The West German Ministry of Labour was recently reported (*Sunday Express*, 19 July 1970) as upholding the decision of a Cologne firm to deprive one of its employees of his holiday pay. So tired was this 48-year-old bookkeeper said to be after his mountain-climbing holiday that he was unable to concentrate on his work. "The holiday exists," a Ministry of Labour spokesman decreed, "so that workers and employees can draw new strength for the job." The legal department of the relevant trade union organisation also upheld the firm's action and agreed that there was no case to bring before the industrial arbitration court.

It is a view with which few British shiftworkers would concur.

Part Two
Management
Action on Shiftwork

FIVE

The Decision to
Introduce Shiftworking

From a purely management or employer point of view, "problems of shiftwork" are of four kinds, those associated with:

1 The decision whether to introduce multiple shiftworking at all
2 The choice of a particular type of shiftwork, and the detailed features of a particular rota
3 The introduction of shiftwork for the first time or of a major change in working hours
4 The day by day administration of shifts

The present chapter will concern itself with management rationale, with the questions "Why shiftworking?" and "If shiftwork, what sort?" Chapter 6 will be concerned with problems of introducing shifts and Chapter 7 and 8 with those of daily administration.

REASONS FOR USING SHIFTS

Whether or not to introduce multiple shiftwork at all is an exercise in costing and forecasting largely outside the scope of this book. In any event, the economics of the subject have already been excellently discussed elsewhere (Marris, 1964; Marris, 1966). The Confederation of British Industry has also produced a useful guidance sheet (CBI, 1968) on what shiftwork offers and the points to be considered by management before shiftwork is introduced into a company. The CBI leaflet is concerned not only with large capital intensive units, but with smaller more labour reliant companies. It sees the main advantages of shiftwork as a reduction of unit costs by the use to the full of existing plant and machinery; the reduction of the "costly practice of overtime working"; and the maintenance of an up-to-date factory since equipment can be written off and replaced more quickly. It concludes in general that "if depreciation and interest charges, plus overheads, amount to more than 25 per cent of labour costs the introduction of shift-work is worth while."

While it may to some extent be possible to generalise about the advantages of shiftwork, its introduction or extension is a matter of Individual judgement in each case. "Presumably," one author writes (Braddick, 1966), "each firm which introduces shiftworking calculates the cost and savings involved." But this optimistic view is not always confirmed in practice. For example, a report on shiftwork from the Dunlop Company (1969) observes that "too often vague estimates are made as to what the economic advantages are," and stresses that only a detailed costing exercise can establish accurately the results which any change may bring about.

This decision can never be straightforward. Likely increased costs may be set against theoretical benefits, but a number of imponderables are involved, not the least of which are those concerned with the human element—for example, availability of labour and employee performance under "abnormal" hours of work.

In 16 case studies of shiftworking undertaken by the Ministry of Labour's IRO's in 1966 (Ministry of Labour, 1967*a*), it was found that few of the companies studied had attempted full costing of their shiftworking proposals and that the few who were able to produce some estimates of costs had all set out "with the basic assumption that there was no doubt that shiftworking would provide the most economic use of their plant." Only one company had estimated the comparative costs of different shift systems.

A later report of this work (Ministry of Labour, 1967*b*), however, claims that this does not mean that employers and management were unaware of the impact of shiftwork on the profitability and operation of their businesses: "The management of the firms surveyed had satisfied themselves that overall, and according to each firm's particular set of circumstances, shiftwork would be beneficial either in terms of lower unit costs, or in increased production to meet market or technical requirements." On the whole, management were said to be satisfied with the results.

It is difficult to escape the conclusion, however, that companies commonly embark on shiftwork with a certain degree of blind faith about the consequences. Shiftwork is certainly no sovereign cure-all for economic ills either in the individual firm or considered nationally. Marris (1964) has warned against the view that a widespread extension of shiftwork will automatically improve economic efficiency and promote growth. On the basis of five years of research and reflection he goes on record as no longer believing that "a miraculous acceleration of economic growth could (or should) be achieved by knocking together the heads of managers and trade unionists in order to persuade them rapidly to convert us into a universal double-shift society."

As to why companies make use of shiftwork, it is clear that since shiftwork is itself many sided, the reasons for its use will be varied, too. This question is not a simple one, particularly where shifts have been in use for some time. To ask, for example, why shifts were originally introduced is to put a question which in many cases cannot be answered. In this, as in other cases where the inquiry concerns the development of company institutions, one is dependent on either minutes of meetings or memory. The first are usually either non-existent or inadequate, and the second unreliable. Moreover, in many of the factories we visited, shiftwork had been introduced before the informant joined the company, and sometimes prior to the working life of any present employee.

Again, the answer to why shifts were first introduced may not provide the answer to why they are still in use. A firm may continue to be a shiftworking unit, but its reasons change through time; shifts which were once used, for example, to obtain extra production from limited plant capacity may now be retained because the high cost of new capital equipment makes it economically desirable.

The reason for using shifts in any one firm may also be an amalgam of many factors—for example, nature of work, customer demand, economic necessity. It may also vary from one department to another in a firm.

The following results were obtained from discussion on this point in our own factory visits:

		TIMES MENTIONED
1	Nature of production process	27
2	Nature of customer demand	7

1 *Nature of the production process.* This group covers cases where the nature of the work makes some degree of continuity necessary. It includes examples (for example, glass making, mineral oil refining) where continuous working is essential by virtue of the process itself, as well as those (for example, sugar refining, flour milling, paper making) in which it is economically as well as technically preferable. While these examples are usually covered by continuous and discontinuous 3×8-hour shift systems, there are a number of cases where continuity is achieved by means of 12-hour shifts or through day and night shifts linked by overtime. Mention of this reason may refer to the total activity of the firm, or to some particular activity such as heat treatment.

2 *Nature of customer demand.* The smaller category of customer demand includes such activities as water supply, a round-the-clock service industry; printing, in a firm where the product has to be available daily by 04 30; and bread baking, where the shifts are governed by a customer demand for a fresh product fluctuating over the week. The transport section in one large organisation had organised a shift system to provide 24-hour coverage for varied transport needs within and outside the establishment.

3 *Cost of capital equipment,* and 4 *Maximum machine utilisation* are categories which could be grouped together in that the reasons given for using shifts are all concerned with economic advantage. However, it does seem worthwhile to make a distinction. In category 3 we seem to be concerned with high cost plant of fairly recent installation. For example, from the machine tools industry there is a reference to "almost fully automatic, high capital cost equipment in our new factory." Management in an engineering firm speaks of the introduction of a £60 000 machine for which the principle of three-shift working had been "grudgingly conceded" by the union. In category 4, however, capital investment may be more modest and the situation may have a longer history. A bakery, for example, gives as its reason for shiftworking that its small profit margin per

unit makes it economically necessary to make the best use of existing plant. In a rubber products factory, which was launched postwar on the strength of ex-service gratuities, shiftwork was initially used as a means of getting maximum production from the limited plant that could be afforded, and as a road to subsequent expansion.

5 *Greater machine utilisation,* from a production standpoint. This is a reason characteristic of firms with limited space and machine capacity, where demand exceeds the production that can be achieved from a single shift, either in the factory as a whole or in a particular section. Such firms describe their shift operation as "a variable with which to cope with work" and "an emergency means of taking care of bottlenecks." Shifts are used here "flexibly as a safety valve to meet fluctuations in production demand," and "as a buffer against production changes, and are reduced and expanded according to production needs."

It is interesting to compare these findings with those obtained from a postal questionnaire issued by the Industrial Society (1966). This questionnaire asked: "Was shiftwork originally adopted because of (*a*) the nature of the productive process, (*b*) the high cost of equipment, (*c*) the nature of service required by customers, (*d*) some other reason?"

Perhaps not surprisingly from this form of questioning the results showed reasons (*a*) and (*b*) as the commonest, with reason (*c*) coming a poor third. A few "other reasons" were mentioned, but there was no reference to the use of shifts as a means of meeting greater production demand, one of our own biggest categories.

What is of interest are the inferences which may be made from these two sets of results. If the main reasons for shiftworking were the nature of the process and high capital costs, a simple and progressive increase in shiftworking practices might be inferred, since capital investment is likely to increase as technology develops (although whether actual numbers of shiftworkers would increase at the same time is debatable). But this is to ignore the not inconsiderable category of firms in which, on the evidence of our own survey, shifts are used on a fluctuating basis to cope with demand.

A different management attitude to shifts is indicated here. The employer who says that he uses shifts to obtain *greater* machine utilisation is in a different category to one who gives *maximum* machine utilisation as a reason. The former is using shifts as he might use overtime, to obtain greater room for manoeuvre. He may well be using shifts reluctantly and he ready to give them up if the opportunity offers: "We would like to cut out the night shift but couldn't get the production if we did."

In firms in our own sample where a permanent night shift is operated as the main system, "production demand" is the reason most commonly given for using shiftwork, and it is probably not coincidental that this type of shift is also the most unpopular among managers.

Of the 23 systems reported in the Ministry of Labour's 1966 survey (Ministry of Labour, 1967b) the major reason put forward for introducing shifts (mentioned by two thirds of firms) was "the need to make greater use of machinery." In this category are included what we have called maximum machine use as well as greater machine use. For example, in two cases in the Ministry's survey, shifts had been introduced in industries of rapid technological change "to obtain maximum output from new plant before it became outdated," whereas five firms saw shiftwork as a means of raising output with existing machinery.

REASONS GOVERNING
DIFFERENT SHIFT ARRANGEMENTS

To some extent the decision whether or not to work shifts is governed by technical and economic factors outside management's control. Such considerations may also determine the broad form of arrangement of hours—extended daywork, continuous work over part of the week, continuous work over seven days.

But beyond this there is considerable scope for choice over such shift features as stability or change of hours, the number of shifts to be worked continuously without a break, the duration of free time, starting/stopping times, length of shift, frequency of alternation, frequency and direction of rotation, frequency with which free weekends occur under a continuous system, variations in weekly hours and weekly wage packets. How is such choice determined?

The decisions governing shift features often appear to "just happen." One firm admitted that the process was "all very accidental." Particularly where shifts are of long standing it is extremely difficult to get at a logical account of how they came into existence. Reasons for particular aspects of a shift system may be lost in time and their effectiveness not queried. Habit plays as powerful a part in the functioning of companies and organisations as with individual shiftworkers. Weekly alternation or a 06 00 start may be practised simply because this is how shifts have always been used in the firm. In a factory operating a continuous 3 × 3 × 3 system it was reported that this began before the war, but that no one now remembered where it came from, how it was introduced or why. "But," added the informant, with a touch of pride, "we believe it to be unique." In another organisation the starting time of the morning shift was thought to have been fixed on the basis of the old tram timetables. The trams had long since been replaced.

In a factory with a discontinuous three-shift system, it was de-clared that whatever might have been the original reasons for the firm's particular shift arrangements, their retention was now dictated by an old hard core of workers who preferred to stick to the system they knew. Even where change is effected, as in the case of the paper industry's switch to three-shift continuous working, old habits may persist. One mill had rejected the National Agreement's recom-mended rota in favour of a pattern based on the hours worked (07 00 – 14 00, 14 00 – 21 00, 21 00 – 07 00) under the previous dis-continuous system.

Local or industrial tradition is an important factor. "You have to fall in with the accepted pattern," was one comment. Similarly, "The whole has developed by custom and practice," and, "It's traditional in the area." In the case of one discontinuous three-shift system in heavy engineering, detailed arrangements had been taken over direct from those in use in existing plants in the group.

But widely differing practices are found in different factories in the same organisation. A firm of cablemakers in Kent had practised alternate day- and nightworking for many years, although a Lancashire company in the same group, producing the same kind of product, operated a permanent night and day system.

One or two interesting examples were found of shift arrangements, formerly in use in independent manufacturing units, which had survived subsequent amalgamation and change of location. A manu-facturer of domestic electric appliances had two distinct discontinuous three-shift rotas dating from an earlier stage in the company's development (06 30 – 14 30, and so on with forward rotation, and 07 00 – 15 00 and so on with backward rotation). A firm making plastic products had a variety of departmental hours of work, shift lengths and directions of rotation, which originated when these departments were on separate sites, and which were maintained after a merger.

In contrast to all these examples of traditional behaviour, many shift features are quite rationally decided upon and accounted for. Legal control over the hours during which it is permissible for women and young persons to work, for instance, lie behind the usual 06 00 – 14 00 and 14 00 – 22 00 limits of double-day work. Hours of work are also often logically related to transport facilities and to starting/stopping times in neighbouring factories. Starting/stopping times may also be linked to production and market factors—for instance, in the bakery industry the National Agreement has been revised to permit greater flexibility in starting times and shift lengths to cope with the daily fluctuations in customer demand which occur during the week.

Logical explanation is also forthcoming over the type of shift itself. One firm introduced three-shift work in place of 12-hour days and nights when it discovered that its permanent night team of security officers was working for a commercial security agency during the day. It also expected greater alertness as a result of the reduction in shift length. Other firms produced reasons for *not* changing from two- to three-shift systems. One was very dependent for its production on a large permanent force of nightworkers drawn from nearby seaside towns, and was afraid of losing this. Another firm also feared labour turnover and recruitment difficulties if three-shift working were introduced. A third considered that the likely increase in output from three shifts would not be worth the cost of extra maintenance on its old machine presses.

Permanent night shifts were in some cases accounted for in terms of labour availability. Two firms engaged in dominantly "women's work" (manufacture of biscuits and electric light bulbs) put on a male night shift as the next logical step beyond double-day and twilight shifts of women. Shortage of full-time women workers in the food industry also accounts for the variety of part-time shifts found there, as well as for permanent male night shifts whose crews have ranged over the years from ex-Polish army workers in the late 1940s to the coloured immigrants of today. At an east Kent factory where no part-time women cleaners were available, a permanent night shift of men was recruited—reluctantly regarded by the Personnel Department as "an anti-social but necessary step."

In a printing firm alternating day- and nightwork had gradually been eliminated, and replaced with a permanent system, since the nature of the work performed on the two shifts differed, and it was considered an advantage to let crews specialise.

Many managers are opposed to permanent nightwork and are fluent with arguments in support of their attitude. Permanent nights have been variously condemned to the writer on grounds of medical undesirability, as encouraging moonlighting, as making men less flexible, leading to reduced management control and attracting an inferior standard of worker. All these claims can be challenged. Certain alternating or rotating systems, for example, may well be more demanding in terms of physical adjustment than a permanent night arrangement. And as regards the quality of nightworkers, greater resource and responsibility may be required of them since they are usually cut off from supervision and normal supporting services. The fact that none of these claims of management critics of permanent nightwork has been systematically established does not, of course, reduce their force for those who hold them.

Stereotypes of nightwork and the nightworker are often built up from a limited number of cases. These sometimes achieve press publicity. For example, under the dramatic headlines, "Night shift caught napping—door forced as factory chiefs swoop at 3 a.m. the *Daily Mail* (3 March 1967) describes how three night shiftworkers were found asleep at a Dagenham plant while one of their colleagues was surprised playing the canteen piano. From the London *Evening News* (10 July 1968) comes the headline, "Vice squad drops in on the night shift," over an account of a police raid on an allegedly blue film show in a Southend workshop. Such cameos of life on the nightshift are hardly the best grounds for selecting an alternative system.

Choice of shift features is thus determined by a variety of elements: rational factors as well as habit and tradition, prejudice and irrational fear. Some features of shift routines, of course, are not the result of management decision at all, since it is common practice to allow for employee preference in these matters and within certain limits to accept a majority vote. In the remainder of this chapter we shall look at examples of such employee preference.

STARTING AND STOPPING TIMES

As has already been seen in an earlier chapter the commonest times for double-day shifts are 6–2 and 2–10 (largely governed by legal control over the hours on which women and young persons can be employed). Common starting times are 06 00, 14 00 and 22 00 in three-shift work, but 07 00, 15 00, 23 00 and 08 00, 16 00, midnight are also frequently used. Starting/stopping times for night duty under both alternating and permanent arrangements show a much wider variation.

Account is usually taken of employee preference in this matter, the most extreme case of this being in a food factory where it was said to be "so difficult to recruit women that we let them work at any time of the day which suits them." Management–union disagreement occasionally occurs, as in the factory where management wanted to change from a 06 00 – 14 00 to a 07 00 – 15 00 sequence, but met union objection. In another factory, the start of the morning shift was put back half-an-hour because the union contended that the men could not arrive by 06 00.

Objections to the 06 00 – 14 00 – 22 00 routine stem mainly from the early 06 00 start on the morning shift. This may cause difficulties to those who find it a struggle to wake and get up early in the morning, physiological "late starters," those who have longer distances to travel to work and those who rely on public transport. Women on double-days, particularly where a walk to and from work is involved, may find travel in the dark a disincentive.

On the social side, under three-shift working, the 06 00 – 14 00 – 22 00 routine breaks into the evening on both afternoon and night turns. With the 07 00 – 15 00 – 23 00 and 08 00 – 16 00 – midnight routines the night turn is preceded by a relatively clear evening. They also permit a later start on the morning shift. An 08 00 – 16 00 – midnight rotation is said to be much commoner in the United States where social amenities are in general available to a later hour than is usual here, (Cook, 1954).

It has been shown that a change from 06 00 – 14 00 – 22 00 to 07 00 – 15 00 – 23 00 may not only be more acceptable socially (Oginski, 1966), but may result in fewer accidents (Wild and Theis, 1967). In a study on West German mineworkers the accident rate fell by 6.8 per cent when the start of the morning shift was altered from 06 00 to 07 00. In a second experiment part of the morning shift clocked on at 06 00 and the remainder at 07 00. It was found that the accident rate for the former was 4.8 per cent higher and for the latter 23.8 per cent lower than usual. It has also been suggested on evidence from the steel industry in this country that short term absence on the morning shift may be reduced by a later start (Shepherd and Walker, 1956).

Although a fair amount of research has been carried out in recent years into time-of-day effects on performance, this would seem more likely to effect duty times in military and para-military situations than working hours on the average factory floor. Starting/stopping times in industry are likely to continue to be controlled more by social and technical factors than by physiological considerations. This is not, of course, to rule out such possibilities as a rearrangement of work within orthodox industrial hours, for instance, where a high degree of accuracy or safety is called for, so as to concentrate certain critical operations or types of task into times in the shift or day when the human organism is at its most efficient.

LENGTH OF SHIFT

Under three-shift working it is usual to have shifts of equal eight hours' duration, but where variants of this occurred in our own sample it was commonest to find the longest stint being given to the night crew. While there are good social and administrative reasons for this, there are some physiological grounds for suggesting that the night shift ought to be the shortest.

As early as 1916 the Health of Munition Workers' Committee (1916), commenting on two alternating shifts of unequal length (06 00 – 17 00 and 17 00 – 06 00), regretted that "the strain of the night work should be increased by these additional hours," and recommended that "wherever practicable the night shift should not exceed the day shift in length." More recently it has been suggested from both Scandinavian and United States sources that the night shift should be reduced in length so as to allow the worker some opportunity for sleep during "normal" night hours. But any physiological advantage for the night man derived by getting to bed earlier would be offset by the social inconvenience of an early start for the worker on the following morning shift.

PERMANENCY VERSUS CHANGE

Fixed or stable versus alternating or rotating arrangements must be decided upon. In one engineering firm it was claimed that the "average person" preferred permanency and that there was less difficulty in introducing a permanent than a rotating system. This was also the case in a metal-working firm where a three-shift discontinuous system had replaced permanent days and nights. The new system had been accepted only on a non-rotating principle, the previous night men taking the new night shift, the previous day men taking the new day shift, while the afternoon shift was manned by new recruits.

But how far this general contention holds is arguable. It is not difficult to think of situations where men would be unwilling to be condemned to what they would see as the hard labour of a permanent night shift, or a work schedule in which it is "always afternoon." A liking for change for its own sake may characterise some workers who report, for example, (Shimmin, 1962) a horror of travelling to and from work at the same times each day. Another reason for wanting change may be a fear of being permanently on a "bad" turn in situations where the nature of the work is not constant from shift to shift.

In this connection it is interesting to look at the Ministry of Labour shiftworking figures for 1964 in which alternate day- and nightworkers outnumber those on permanent nights by two to one (237 000 to 119 000). But the proportion of permanent nightworkers to all shiftworkers rose from 9 to 12 per cent between 1954 and 1964 (Appendix 4) while that of alternate day- and nightworkers remained steady at 23 per cent. Moreover, these figures take no account of those who have elected for permanency on a day basis in situations where their jobs are matched at night by permanent night men. For some dayworkers the attraction of permanent day work is its element of permanency as much as its quality of normal work in hours of daylight.

Evidence of worker preference on this issue in the literature is in favour of stability. In answer to the question, "If regular days were not available, would you prefer permanent nights or rotating shifts?" McDonald (1958) found that 56 per cent expressed a preference for permanency. De la Mare and Shimmin (1964), in a situation in which preferred duties were achieved by the swapping of unwanted duties, found that the chief characteristic of this exchange was an avoidance of mixed day- and nightworking. In a later study on the same working population de la Mare and Walker (1968) found that 27 per cent elected to work permanent nights as against 12 per cent who preferred a rotating shift arrangement.

The remainder of the work force was engaged on a permanent day basis.

A study from the USA (Mott *et al*, 1965) quotes evidence to suggest that men who worked on a permanent night shift basis were more likely to have a favourable attitude towards their hours of work than those who alternated between night and day. A Ministry of Labour report (1967*b*) refers to the favourable attitudes to shift-work of married women who had been able to select the particular non-rotating routine best suited to their domestic circumstances. Most men and women on double-days in the study by Brown (1959), however, preferred to alternate than to remain permanently on one shift.

Much of the criticism that has been levelled at permanent shifts refers to permanent *night* arrangements. Teleky (1943) concluded that continuous nightwork ought to be abolished as far as possible on "hygienic as well as social considerations." The Health of Munition Workers' Committee (1918) considered continuous night-work to be less productive than alternating day and night arrange-ments (based on studies of women on repetitive tasks) and attributed this to a failure to get proper rest and sleep during the daytime. The criticism of permanent nightwork on grounds of in-adequate daytime sleep has also been more recently made (Brandt, 1969; Morioka, 1969).

On the other hand, recent research on human performance under different systems of shiftwork carried out on Royal Navy volunteers by the Medical Research Council's Applied Psychology Unit at Cambridge suggests that people adapt better to a stable pattern of activity which permits them to sleep at approximately the same time each day (Wilkinson and Edwards, 1968), thus confirming an opinion given in evidence 100 years earlier before a Government inquiry to the effect that "probably people can sleep better if they have the same period of rest than if it is changed." [Children's Employment Commission, 4th Report, 1865.] It has also been sug-gested that ulcer rates are higher for rotating shift workers than for fixed shift workers (Pierach, 1955).

Once again, there is a need to be more specific when talking about the effects of, or worker preference for, permanency or change. Does permanency refer to nightwork or to some other kind of fixed shift arrangement? What is meant by a permanent night routine—5 × 8-hour shifts, for example, or 4 × 10, or a 12-hour shift on alternate nights on a permanent basis? One type of permanent night arrangement may be acceptable and another not; one may result in sleep loss and another not. What is meant by change—every other night, each week, every three months? We have to remember all the time that permanency and change are themselves blanket terms.

FREQUENCY OF CHANGE

Where alternation and rotation are practised the position today does not appear substantially different from that described over 50 years ago in the Final Report of the Health of Munition Workers' Committee (1918). The Report found no uniformity of practice, although week-about was commonest. There was no legal requirement, the matter being left "to the individual employers to settle with their workpeople." Choice was said to be largely influenced by the social conditions under which the worker lived and worked.

In our own survey weekly changeover was the general rule where double-days and three-shift work applied. Under alternating days and nights a greater proportion of fortnightly and monthly changes was found, but the tendency was towards shorter rather than longer spells on the one shift.

Where weekly alternation was practised the explanation most often given was the unpopularity of nightwork, for example, "one week on nights is enough." Another management informant said: "Our long 12-hour shifts and weekly changes may be contrary to medical opinion as to what is best, but our operators wouldn't stand for longer than a week on night shift."

The supposedly medical argument for better adaptation was occasionally quoted in favour of alternation at monthly intervals: "It takes you about a fortnight to get used to the change." In the case of one firm where supervisors alternated four-weekly, this was to enable them to see both operative shifts, which changed fortnightly.

Fortnightly systems of change often seem to have been arrived at as a compromise because of disadvantages seen in weekly and monthly arrangements. Weekly change, it was said in such cases, doesn't allow men time to settle down. The imbalance between day and night shift pay packets was a factor sometimes quoted as a disadvantage where monthly alternation applied.

There is no consistency in the reports of worker preference from studies in the literature.

Brown (1959) found weekly changeover to be almost unanimously preferred by women on double-days. Marriott and Denerley (1955) compared factories using a day and night system with alternation at different intervals, and encountered less satisfaction in the case of monthly turnabout. Nor did the idea of rotation at monthly or longer intervals appeal to most of the workers interviewed by Mott and his colleagues (Mott *et al*, 1965), but these authors point out that the men's arguments were in the abstract since they had never actually worked on such a schedule.

By contrast, among McDonald's (1958) night workers who preferred alternation to permanency, the choice of frequency was weekly 6 per cent, fortnightly 17 per cent, monthly 69 per cent and longer 8 per cent. Even among those who preferred changing shifts, this author concludes, "there was an aversion to the upsetting effects of too frequent changes."

Brown (1959) found that fortnightly change emerged as the most popular spell for nightwork. In Wyatt and Marriott's (1953) experience the existing system was the most popular, irrespective of length. Attitude to shift change was determined more by custom and habit than by the system's intrinsic merits or defects. Among those preferring weekly change it was thought that a longer period would be too tiring. Those preferring fortnightly change considered that this period was better than a week from the standpoint of digestion and sleep, and the same reason was given by those who liked to alternate on a monthly basis.

In the case of women on three-shift rotation Wyatt (1945*b*) found fairly high percentages satisfied with weekly change, though few had experience of other arrangements. In this study attitudes seemed to be influenced by specific dislikes which were associated with each shift. Particular discomforts and disadvantages were tolerable for a week at a time but the prospect of putting up with them for longer periods could not be faced.

Many of the arguments in favour of less frequent change which have been put forward on physiological grounds have been tempered by the recognition that it might be difficult to reconcile these with personal and social preference (see the reports of the Health of Munition Workers' Committee, for example). In the case of double-day work, in the experimental period between 1920 and 1935 [following the Employment of Women, Young Persons and Children Act, 1920] the Home Office generally imposed conditions that shifts should alternate weekly. Some witnesses before the 1935 Committee (Home Office, 1935) recommended that longer periods of alternation, say a month, would give workers a better chance of becoming accustomed to altered hours and habits. But since worker preference was overwhelmingly in favour of weekly alternation because it caused least interruption to social life, and "in the absence of any evidence of injury to health," the Committee was not prepared to recommend any general modification of Home Office practice. The employer was allowed discretion in the matter, however, so far as the individual worker was concerned.

Considerable interest has been shown in recent years in rapidly rotating systems of three-shift operation, where more than three shifts of the same type never occur in succession, and where the physiological argument is that disturbance caused to bodily rhythms is minimal. One study has shown a preference by shiftworkers for this type of rota over the more traditional week-about system which was formerly used (Walker, 1966). Reported advantages were that breaking up the sequence of six or seven shifts of the same kind in a row reduced monotony and a sense of fatigue. Frequent breaks provided an opportunity each week for the enjoyment of domestic and social activities. A slight preference for the $2 \times 2 \times 2$ system over the $3 \times 2 \times 2$ was stated on the grounds that rotation of shifts was easier to follow. The $2 \times 2 \times 2$, however, permits a free weekend only once every eight weeks, compared with every four weeks under the $3 \times 2 \times 2$ routine. Nor is the break between shifts ever longer than two days under the $2 \times 2 \times 2$.

DIRECTION OF ROTATION

The Ministry of Labour's experience in its survey of shiftworking firms (Ministry of Labour, 1967b) was that in the introduction of three-shift work the order mornings-afternoons-nights (that is "forward") had usually been initially adopted. In all but one case, however, workers had requested a change to "backwards" rotation (mornings–nights–afternoons), on the grounds that this gave a long weekend between their hours on the morning and night shifts.

In the case of three-shift discontinuous systems in our own sample a "better" weekend arrangement of free hours was given as an explanation for both forward and backward movement. Under a five-day working week arrangement (with the first shift of the week being the Monday "morning" turn) the actual weekend hours off are:

Forward rotation: 72, 72 and 48 hours
Backward rotation: 80, 56 and 56 hours

It is difficult to label one or other of these alternatives as objectively "better," though one may well be subjectively so. Both can be criticised on the grounds that the night shift is followed by the shortest amount of time off in which to recover.

Direction of change in the case of shift foremen may be with the shift crew or in the opposite direction. In the former case the argument is against splitting up a production team. The latter course is favoured by firms which believe that a change in leadership is a way of keeping both foremen and shift teams "up to scratch" and helps iron out inequalities in foremen's abilities. Rotating in reverse directions still means, however, that the same crew has the same foreman whenever its turn for night duty comes round, and the only way of avoiding this is for foreman and crew to change shifts at different intervals.

ATTITUDES TO
PARTICULAR TURNS OF DUTY WITHIN A SHIFT SYSTEM

The particular advantages and disadvantages which are perceived by shiftworkers in different turns of duty will help determine their preference for such features as stability/change and frequency of change.

The afternoon shift is often quoted as the most unpopular in the three-shift system. One report (Downie, 1963) claims that the highest incidence of disputes in coal-mining is at the beginning of the afternoon shift, and attributes this to dislike of this turn. Taylor (1968) quotes the following figures for oil refinery workers:

06 00 – 14 00 shift preferred by 213; disliked by 72
14 00 – 22 00 shift preferred by 49; disliked by 157
22 00 – 06 00 shift preferred by 60; disliked by 103

Although these results show the afternoon shift as the least popular, what is more striking is the preference for the morning shift over both afternoons and nights.

An inquiry dealing with workers in South Wales (St. David's Diocesan Evangelistic Committee, undated) indicated that the 15 00 – 22 30 shift was "cordially disliked," especially by young men, because it deprived the worker of "all cultural life, social activity and entertainment." On the other hand some men worked this shift regularly: middle-aged and older men in particular preferring it because it did not demand early rising and also allowed nighttime sleep.

A wartime study by Wyatt (1945b) of women three-shiftworkers found an overwhelming preference for the morning shift (76 per cent), with proportions of 29 and 18 per cent preferring the night and afternoon turns respectively. The morning shift was more popular among married women, and the night shift among those who were single.

Studies which have examined short term absence (if this is taken as a measure of dislike) have not confirmed the unpopularity of the afternoon shift. Under a 06 00 – 14 00 – 22 00 routine short absences were found to occur predominantly on the morning shift among men in the steel industry (Shepherd and Walker, 1956). In another study (Sergean and Brierley, 1968) of metal workers on a 08 00 – 16 00 – midnight routine both short term absence and permitted days of leave occurred most frequently on the night shift.

Brown (1959) has provided a very full account of worker preference on early and late turns within double-days. The early turn had the advantage of leaving the afternoon and evening free, but made it difficult to organise meals. It was also more tiring because of the early start and shorter hours in bed. The afternoon turn made the day more leisurely, and women felt they had more energy. But social and domestic life was difficult on this shift. The early turn increased in attraction in the summer, and the late turn became more tolerable in winter.

It is of interest to note that in one of the factories in this study nearly all women preferred the afternoon shift, while in another the majority favoured the morning turn. Brown relates this difference to factors of age, family composition and shift experience, a classic illustration of what has been argued throughout this book, namely that generalisation is only possible within specific situations.

INDIVIDUAL PREFERENCE ON THE PART OF SHIFTWORKERS

Allowing for the preferences of shiftworkers operates in two ways. The first, as we have seen, is by taking account of majority wishes over such matters as starting times or frequency of rotation. Some highly original arrangements of working hours can result.

Mott (1965) quotes an example of "the ability of management personnel to meet the needs of the workers in some rather ingenious ways when they set their minds to it." In this rota workers took only one day off between each weekly turn of duty, in return for which they earned 10 consecutive free days every 13 weeks. A continuous rota in a London brewery included a complete week off at the cost of a solid block of fourteen night duties.

The second way of meeting worker preference is by permitting individual variation within the general rule. A number of cases occurred in our own sample, for example, where workers could choose to work days and nights alternately, or on a permanent basis (provided that pairing with an opposite number on day shift could be arranged). Permitted individual variations as to frequency of shift change were commoner. At a factory where monthly alternation between day and night shift was the general practice, weekly, fortnightly and six-weekly changes also occurred. Variations in starting/stopping times were also found: in one instance of three-shift discontinuous working on a 06 00 – 14 00 – 22 00 pattern, a 07 00 changeover was also permitted by mutual agreement. Shift breaks could also be varied: in one example the half-hour night shift break was normally timed at 01 30, but could be taken "whenever the working group wants, provided the whole team breaks together."

An interesting example of taking individual preference into account has been reported (Marks, 1970) from the Messerschmitt-B-B research and development headquarters near Munich. In 1967 the company introduced a flexible working day, the essence of which is that, within certain limits, each of the 3000 employees can decide for himself when he starts work in the morning and when he goes home. Previously hours were 07 20 to 17 00. Employees may now arrive at any time between 07 00 and 08 00 and leave at any time between 16 00 and 18 00.

Each employee must complete an agreed number of hours per

month, but he now has a degree of control as to how they are put together. Moreover, he has the option of working up to 10 hours a month over the norm, which can be balanced out by more free time in the following month. Or he can lag up to 10 hours behind and make up the balance at a later date. This experiment is reported to have been highly successful. Similar arrangements are being adopted by other German companies.

Many firms can be fairly easily classified as exhibiting either a permissive or a rigid attitude to this question of accommodating the individual worker. The former is illustrated by such comment as: "Provided we have sufficient cover they can arrange it how they like," "Individual variations and pairing are allowed as long as the machine lines are manned," and: "Variations are permitted, and relatively easily arranged, provided the work gets done." In an organisation working continuously it was reported that "the men sometimes spell each other for naps during the night, and sometimes knock off half-an-hour early on the afternoon shift to get a drink before the pubs close. We turn a blind eye to this provided it doesn't affect the work."

In contrast are situations where much stricter discipline is imposed regarding adherence to shift patterns, and where individual variations are frowned on—for instance: "It is made clear at the outset what is expected of them and changes are discouraged." Change in such firms is regarded as a concession reserved for occasions of illness or domestic crisis. At one factory each individual request had to be submitted via the nursing sister and "good evidence" such as a doctor's certificate was usually required before permission was granted.

These differences are to some extent determined by the type of production and the type of shift system in use. In general there is greater room for manoeuvre under a two-shift than under a three-shift system and changes are less difficult to arrange. Under some three-shift systems it may be important not to break up production teams by allowing "shift swapping."

But while the "permissive" group is largely composed of firms using two-shift patterns, and the "rigid" group of firms using continuous three-shift systems, this is by no means exclusively so. One often has the impression of something more in these firms, an impression of different styles of management which show themselves either in a strict "going by the book" and adherence to standing orders, or in a readiness to bend the rules to meet current needs.

Allowing for individual preference does not, of course, imply confusion in the arrangement of working hours. At the same time management does need to remain in control of the situation: changes not infrequently appear to take place without management knowing very much about it. This was clearly brought out during factory visits, when information given in personnel and work study departments about shiftworking in the firm failed to square with what was subsequently found to be shop floor practice. The clearest case of this was an engineering firm in which permanent day and permanent night working, informally arranged, had largely replaced the official system of alternating days and nights thought still to be in operation by Personnel.

One of the Tavistock Institute's reports on the coal-mining industry contains an interesting example of this sort of thing (Higgin *et al*, 1957). Two teams manning composite longwall panels at one colliery were themselves responsible for the details of rotation of team members through the various tasks. The report notes not only the way in which the two rotational arrangements developed quite differently although the teams were in close physical proximity, but the extent to which both management and lodge were largely unaware of changes and modifications made by the men in what had originally been agreed in management–Lodge discussions.

GROUP POLICY

While most of the manufacturing units in our sample were members of larger companies or groups, the apparent influence of group policy on the ordering of shift arrangements appeared to be small. Even allowing for the fact that most informants held *plant* management positions and that they may have wished to stress their freedom of action, it did seem that most unit managements had the authority to take their own decisions on shifts, and that arrangements were largely determined—whatever the basis—on each site. Such comments as, "Conditions are dissimilar in member companies so there is no rigid personnel policy," and, "Practices grow up as needed in response to specific situations," were confirmed by evidence of different shift practices in other parts of the company.

Only one instance was found, a company with eleven manufacturing units in various parts of the country, of a genuine group policy on shiftwork. Double-day work was practised in ten of the units, and the main reason for this appeared to be that large numbers of women workers were employed. The tendency in the company, however, was to use more and more male labour and gradually to reduce the numbers of women. Shift arrangements were likely to change, it was said, "in accordance with group policy."

Apart from this, one manager mentioned that his company was in fact against the use of permanent nights, and another, while confirming that shift arrangements were a domestic matter, indicated that his freedom of choice was curtailed by the industry's national agreement. A number of informants where firms had recently been taken over or incorporated into larger groups commented that changes might be expected in the future. Merging with a larger group may lead to some rationalisation of shift arrangements as production and manning are themselves reorganised.

THE ROLE OF THE INDUSTRIAL MEDICAL OFFICER

Although the industrial medical officer may be involved in the initial selection of shift personnel, and in the decision as to whether or not a man shall continue on shiftwork, he rarely appears to be consulted on the choice of shift systems or the design of rotas.

Nor are the decisions of management and of individual shift-workers often modified by an interpretation of medical or psycho-physiological evidence. Where these decisions are not apparently a matter of historical accident, they are most likely to result from a combination of administrative convenience and social acceptability.

As research evidence becomes clearer and better publicised, the medical implications of shift hours of work may come to be better appreciated, and the industrial medical officer will play at least as important a part as personnel, work study and production staff in the arrangement of working hours.

SIX

Introduction of Shiftwork

OPPOSITION TO SHIFTWORK

Introducing shiftwork for the first time, or making a major change in an existing shift system, can cause far greater problems for management than the day-to-day administration of shifts. Some workers will not tolerate any disruption of this kind, and may be prepared to change their job rather than their hours of work.

Overcoming resistance to change was seen as a major difficulty by many management informants. In part this resistance was regarded as opposition to change as such. References were made to *"natural* objection to change" and to *"inherent* opposition." "Any alteration in a well-established system," one manager said, "is always extremely unpopular."

Apart from resistance to change "as such," the first barrier to be broken through is clearly that of dislike for nightwork. Rotas which involve work during "normal" hours of recreation and sleep are those which are seen by the traditional dayworker as making the greatest and most dramatic demands for adjustment upon him.

But resistance on the part of dayworkers to work at night by no means forms the only main area of opposition. Difficulties at least as great can be encountered when proposals are made to change from one kind of shift system involving nightwork to another. A number of cases have been found where opposition of this kind was so strong that the companies concerned have given up their plans for change. For instance, in the North-East, where the alternation between day- and nightwork often appears to be accepted as a "fact of life," a third firm found its suggestions for change to discontinuous three-shift work strongly resisted, although, in its view, "the social and disturbance factors are not significantly greater with three-shift work than with our existing day and night shifts."

This kind of example points to what is contended elsewhere in this book, that opposition to shiftwork is not opposition to shiftwork *per se,* but to particular forms of shiftwork which have specific disadvantages, real or supposed, for those concerned.

Examples of opposition to change from those already working some form of shift system appear to fall broadly into two groups:

1   Where change from a two-shift system (with nights) to a three-shift system is proposed
2   Where the change involves giving up a discontinuous for a continuous shift system

Change from a two-shift to a three-shift system
In this case there are two main grounds for employee opposition. One concerns possible loss of earnings, and there are many informants who would argue that this is the only real obstacle to change. There are certainly a number of cases on record where negotiations regarding shift change have broken down because it has not been possible to reach agreement on the "compensation" to be paid to workers who have grown accustomed to considerable amounts of overtime. There is the additional problem, particularly where the previous two-shift system has largely been worked with permanent day and night crews, of persuading workers to accept rotation through three shifts. Both these difficulties were faced by one engineering firm which manufactures components for the motor trade. This firm had worked a permanent night shift since the war, but decided to try to regularise a shift system dictated by lack of machine capacity by the introduction of three shifts, thus cutting out the excessive amount of overtime which had been worked in recent years. Only after protracted and difficult negotiations was this achieved, and then only by making compensatory payments over and above the normal night shift allowance. In addition, the firm had to agree to a non-rotating system in which the previous permanent night men took the new night shift, the previous day men took the new day shift, while the new afternoon shift was manned by fresh recruitment from outside.

In a further case of change from two to three shifts the development was said to have taken place more smoothly in spite of considerable initial resistance. In the Lancashire and Midlands branches of this company there had been a long standing tradition of three-shift work for men, but at the London factory only a two-shift system had previously been known. Considerable overtime had been the rule at the London works: four hours on every shift—that is 5 × 12, plus Saturday working and occasional Sunday shifts. There was also said to have been considerable overmanning.

Three-shift working over five days was introduced here late in 1965 at a period of recession, a piece of timing which may have contributed much to acceptance of the change. Management attributed this success, first, to realism in dealing with financial compensation for the disadvantages of three-shift work and loss of overtime earnings. "My managing director told me not to scrimp over a few pence one way or the other," the works manager said here, "and this is the basis on which I negotiated." He added that the offer had, of course, to be realistically related to current rates and earnings in the vicinity. Men's earnings in the firm are now said to be "within striking distance" of old earnings with overtime.

The second factor stressed by management here as making for success was the extent of advance information given to those concerned and the way in which the need for change was presented.

Adopting a continuous shift system

As regards the negotiation of change from a non-continuous to a continuous seven-day system of shifts, the problem of weaning operatives away from old overtime habits may again arise. Under a 24-hour system over five days, overtime opportunities can still be considerable, either through men voluntarily working additional Saturday or Sunday shifts, or by an extension of the length of normal turns of duty between Monday and Friday.

For example, in a metal-working factory in the North-East, attendance records showed that a fifth of the work force had average weekly overtime figures in excess of 10 hours for the whole of the year 1967. One man's weekly average was over 18 hours during this period. In this company, management regarded the possibility of changing to a seven-day week as a silly question. The men "just wouldn't entertain it." And it is reasonable to suppose that many employees who have grown accustomed to excessive amounts of overtime earnings will regard with dismay any proposal to get rid of overtime, even where a financial inducement is to be paid in the form of an amended shift allowance.

But change to continuous working may still be resisted even where there is no fear of financial loss. This was the case in a company which wanted to transfer 170 workers from a three-shift, five-day system, with voluntary weekend overtime, to a seven-day continuous system with rotating days off during the week. No loss in total earnings was involved, and the number of hours worked would have been reduced. Yet this move was "extensively resisted on the grounds that rotating days off during the week were of little or no value, and that voluntary weekend overtime was a preferable system in that it allowed individuals to opt for a greater or lesser amount of time off at weekends according to their domestic circumstances." Two-thirds of this group finally accepted the new system. The remainder continued to hold out, and a compromise agreement was finally reached in which they continued with their old five-day system, but undertook to work a fixed number of weekends per year at a modified shift allowance.

An even more striking case was found in a bakery which had previously used 12-hour shifts to give continuous cover over five days. The management proposal here was to switch to a seven-day system, using four crews on 8-hour turns of duty. But the operatives themselves would agree to no more than a 3 × 8-hour arrangement over five days, and were prepared to accept a cash loss to keep their normal weekend free. "Saturday and Sunday off," it was forthrightly declared in this factory, where 35 per cent of the labour force was Pakistani, "is an Englishman's right."

The experience of other companies confirms the difficulties that can arise in persuading men to adopt shift arrangements in which the customary weekend break is lost, and time off during the week is offered in lieu. In a Lancashire factory where management planned to extend operations from five to seven days, little difficulty was anticipated since continuous working was the almost universal pattern in the area. But fierce opposition was encountered the moment the firm's proposals were made: it was realised too late that over the years the factory had in fact become a local haven for refugees from the seven-day system. Since the company was determined to persevere with its plans, considerable labour turnover was experienced.

Probably the best publicised example of rejection of a seven-day system in recent times has been that at the coal industry's "£18 000 000 push-button showpiece" at Bevercotes, Notts, where miners voted by a majority of nearly three to one to end a two-year experimental agreement for continuous operation. "Miners there will be losing some £9 a week in wages," according to a writer in *The Times* (27 February 1970), "but they apparently prefer this to loss of leisure hours which seven-day working entailed." In some newspapers this action on the part of the miners was somewhat flippantly reported as being due to their inability to keep their regular football eleven together. But objections obviously go deeper than this.

One manager who was interviewed spoke of the weekend as a "sacred feast," and Saturday sport, the "rush to the seaside," and wives' expectation that husbands accompany them on Saturday shopping expeditions, were all referred to by others as "set patterns of life."

If the abandonment of "normal" dayworking is the first hurdle to be crossed in the acceptance of shift practices, sacrifice of the traditional weekend proves an equally difficult barrier for many. The arguments which management quote in support of the supposed advantages of rest days off during the week fall mainly on deaf ears. No doubt there are instances where shiftworkers' fidelity to the traditional Saturday and Sunday break is used as a convenient bargaining point. But far more often objections appear to stem from a genuine attachment to the weekend and what it represents.

"Wednesday isn't Saturday," one boilerman (and Aston Villa supporter) objected when offered time off during the week. Another worker claimed that he and his wife had been to bed together every Sunday afternoon in 15 years of marriage, adding that "it just wouldn't be the same in the middle of the week."

But Saturday sport and Sunday sex are not the only appeals of the traditional weekend off. There is a "feel" about a Saturday and a Sunday that is lacking about a Tuesday or a Wednesday. It is a feel built up of a lifetime of weekend bathnights and Sunday dinners; of leisure to turn over in bed, of the *News of the World*, of a shave and a clean shirt; of the pub and racing pigeons and allotments and checking the football coupon; of a collection of familiar weekend sounds and smells.

Banks (1956) noted this kind of association with the weekend when, in the 1950s, she studied the reactions of the wives of steelworkers who had changed from a non-continuous to a continuous shift system. After discussing a number of quite practical, objective factors from which antipathy to weekend work can spring, she writes: "Yet underlying and reinforcing such difficulties is what can only be described as an attitude of mind, an attachment to the weekend as the 'proper' time to be at leisure. . . .'

It is this sense of propriety which seems to lie behind much of the resistance from the factory floor to proposals for the extension of continuous shiftworking. One can point, of course, to firms where shiftworkers have adapted with apparent composure to schemes involving rotating days off during the week, with only infrequent Saturdays and Sundays free. Many such cases, however, occur in industries where continuous working is technologically determined and is therefore accepted as inevitable by those concerned. Here men have grown up, and may have spent their whole working lives, within a tradition of rotas involving weekend work.

The position is very different in firms where, for reasons of economic advantage, a policy change from a five- to a seven-day system is proposed. Here men are being expected to act in a way that is not only at variance with their own past, but, in a non-traditional shiftworking district, in a way which is at odds with that of the rest of the working population.

There is a growing demand for continuous seven-day working dictated by the need to use costly and sophisticated equipment intensively. Running counter to this, however, is a development of a different kind. This consists of an entrenchment of the traditional weekend by an extension of the period which it covers. There is growing evidence, for example, of a preference, on the part of operatives on permanent night or alternating day and night systems, for a working week for four longer night shifts rather than five shifts of shorter duration: or a short night shift may be worked on Fridays, as in the motor car industry, where an agreed four and half-night week enables employees to leave at midnight.

One firm visited has introduced a 17 30 – 21 30 shift on Fridays at the request of its employees, and this is said to have made shift-working generally more acceptable by ensuring an entirely free weekend. Of 39 two-shift (day and night) firms visited in London and the South-East, two-thirds were found to be operating working weeks of four or four and half nights.

Also relevant is a tendency, under continuous five-day working, for the bulk of casual, single-shift absence to occur on Mondays and Fridays, again creating a three-day weekend. At one factory where this question was examined, Mondays and Fridays jointly accounted for 67 per cent in 1966 and 64 per cent in 1967 of absence of this kind. In the same company employees also qualified, with increasing length of service, for additional paid "rest days" to be taken when they chose. During 1967, 66 per cent of such rest days were taken on either Monday or Friday.

Evidence of this kind suggests that there is a limit, whatever some enthusiasts may claim, to the extent to which more intensive machine usage can be achieved by the employment of human operators on a seven-day basis. The weekend as an institution—and perhaps as a particularly English institution—hardly seems in danger of withering away while it can claim so many protagonists on the factory floor.

THE PROBLEM OF INDUCEMENTS

"Quite clearly," one management informant declared, "if equivalent pay were available in this area for normal day work the men concerned would jump at it."

If men and women don't want to work outside normal hours, how does an employer encourage them to do so? Hard cash is the answer usually seen by management. Shiftwork is only made palatable, it is thought, by the increased rates which apply.

High rates are necessary, it is argued, to compensate men for the inconvenience of putting up with unconventional times of work. Such high rates can certainly be an aid to recruitment, even in non-shiftworking areas. For example, a firm in the vehicle building industry reports fewer difficulties in recruitment and fewer applications for exemption from shifts since its night turn became payable at time and a third instead of time and a fifth. "Money," as is said in the North, "sweetens labour."

The financial inducement, however, has its limitations. As has already been seen from examples quoted, some workers prefer to forego financial advantage, and even to take a cut in earnings, in order to retain preferred hours. In 1968 Nottingham tobacco workers rejected a double-day system negotiated by their Union which would have brought them immediate lump sums of £100 for men and £80 for women as well as increases in the hourly rate (*The Times*, 6 December 1968). The wage packet is only a foundation on which an acceptance of shiftwork can be built, rather than a simple answer in itself.

It may in certain circumstances be possible to use other incentives

—for example the prospect of promotion leading to related work not involving shifts. This is illustrated in the case of computer operators and certain supervisory grades. But such appeal is likely to be limited among hourly paid manual workers.

To some the prospect of shorter hours and greater leisure may be an attraction. But leisure is unlikely to be a generally acceptable substitute for "hard cash" in all situations, particularly among lower paid workers and where the introduction of shiftwork means a reduced pay packet through a cut in the number of overtime hours worked.

The rearrangement of work and leisure hours which shiftwork offers is in itself a possible incentive. Free time at unusual times of the day and on unusual days of the week—"advantages" commonly played up in advertisements for shiftworkers—may appeal to some but are likely to deter more.

Longer holidays and earlier retirement for shiftworkers have both been advocated as additional benefits by some trade union spokesmen, on the grounds that shiftwork imposes physical demands not faced by dayworkers.

Some managers believe that the provision of incentives to work shifts is not a problem which ought to be tackled by management alone, but one in which government and local authority should help. They argue that recruitment could be made easier if public transport, shopping facilities and licensing hours were designed to meet the needs of those working outside normal hours. (Although this might create fresh problems in transport and in the retail and licensed trades!)

Appeals for more television time for the benefit of those working unusual hours have often been made. "We should like to provide programmes in the afternoon for workers on the night shift," said the chairman of the Independent Television Authority, commenting on an application to the Postmaster General for more hours of broadcasting. (*The Times*, 1 December 1967.) Some effort was made during the 1970 association football World Cup in Mexico to provide coverage for viewers coming home after a night shift.

The income tax position of shiftworkers was mentioned as early as 1953 by Hutton (1953) when he spoke of high wages and high night rates only being effective if unaccompanied by "penal rates of tax." More recently it has been argued that, since wage differentials after tax no longer appear to provide the necessary incentives in certain areas, men on shift deserve some special recognition in the overall national tax structure. For example, the chairman of a large Midlands' company writes that "... continuous manning and operation of capitally intensive plant should be encouraged by differential tax rates for night shift working" (Brookes, 1968).

With few exceptions, informants in our own factory visits always returned to the conclusion that in the face of factors discouraging the introduction or extension of shiftworking—shortage of labour, lack of amenities, unfavourable community attitudes, alternative day job opportunities—it was difficult to see "what persuasive alternatives there can be to acceptable shift premiums."

But reaching agreement on the financial compensation to be paid was seen as a major difficulty, particularly in companies where shiftwork had been recently adopted or a major change had been made from one system to another. A number of other companies, which would have liked to develop shiftworking further, agreed that the size of inducement necessary would be such as to neutralise the advantages of shifts from the company's viewpoint. A furniture manufacturer, for example, commented: "The cost of making shift operations attractive, or even acceptable, tends to put it out of court in our particular case." And in an engineering concern it was stated that the idea of introducing double-day work would not be pursued "because the effect of full employment on bargaining power would swallow up any financial advantage there might be in operating the system."

Uneconomically high inducements may be necessary where previous earnings have been considerably inflated by excessive overtime. One personnel director observed that he had had to negotiate higher premiums than would otherwise have been the case because of the size of the premium paid for emergency shiftworking in other parts of the company.

Limitations may be placed upon the amount which a firm is allowed to pay by way of shift allowance by agreement within a trade association. Such a figure, if agreed nationally, may be insufficient to attract workers in a particular area. A similar situation arises in the case of an organisation made up of a number of separate establishments where rates of pay are negotiated centrally for the organisation as a whole.

The negotiation of change in the arrangement of working hours is not always just a matter of securing acceptance of one system in place of another, and agreeing a financial settlement for this. It may be made more difficult by having to negotiate change in other directions at the same time. In the case of one large organisation, shrinking export markets in recent years had resulted in a company decision to streamline activities by cutting out certain plant and using the remainder more intensively. It was proposed to run down one factory completely and to continue in the remainder on a seven- instead of a five-day basis. Two years of negotiations over such other questions as reallocation of jobs, new places of work, new working methods and redundancy did nothing to make the adoption of a new shift system any easier.

Interviews in this company suggested that some breakdown in communication in the early stages, in which there was a manage- ment failure to make clear just who and what were involved, was at least partially responsible for the "mulish resistance" said to be encountered from the trade union side.

PAYMENT FOR INCONVENIENCE

The case for shift allowances, as set out in one trade union hand- book (NUGMW, 1969), is that "payment for shiftwork is essentially compensation for inconvenience." This source lists possible dis- advantages to the shiftworker under three heads: health, social and financial. Shiftworkers, it is said, may experience sleep difficulties and digestive troubles; their family and social activities may be curtailed; and they may suffer loss of earnings through the elimina- tion of overtime and payment-by-results.

Little systematic examination of premium payments for shiftwork appears to have been made. One recent analysis was carried out by workers at the London School of Hygiene's Institute of Occupational Health (Sergean, Howell, Taylor and Pocock, 1969). They compared the percentage shift payments for double-days, permanent nights and discontinuous three-shift work in 138 national collective agree- ments in the United Kingdom. The distribution of these percentage rates is shown in Appendix 5. The analysis showed:

1   A very high degree of consistency from one industry to another in the order in which the three types of shift system were ranked, with permanent nights the highest,

and double-days the lowest paid
2   A wide range of differences across industries in the actual size of payment for any one type of shift system
3   A wide range of differences from one industry to another in the differentials between types of system

At first glance it is tempting to regard the shift pay structure which emerges from this kind of analysis as a reflection of the way in which different groups of employers' and workers' representatives perceive shiftworking "inconvenience" relative to that of day-work, and the hardship of different shift systems relative to each other.

Unfortunately the situation is not as straightforward as this. In practice the levels of shift payment in the agreements of different industries are largely a product of the state of the market economy, relative bargaining positions and the availability of labour.

At the same time negotiators do appear to have in mind some scale of values about the demands which are made upon the worker by different types of shift system. It is not suggested that this is a matter of open debate during negotiation. But rather that negotiation takes place against an accepted background of values about what is "normal" and "abnormal" in hours of work. The uniformity in ranking of payments for different types of system suggests overall agreement as to order of abnormality.

Final judgement on an order of inconvenience or hardship cannot be made in the absence of any objective scale against which to measure the demands made by different forms of shiftwork. But certain features of the present pay structure invite comment. For example, while there is fairly general agreement in industry that regular nightwork warrants a payment far higher than that for any other type of system, it would not be difficult to make out a case to suggest that three-shift work, (or even alternating day- and night-work), with its rotation between different periods of duty, is more exacting in terms of physical and social adaptation.

Discontinuous three-shift work often seems to be under-assessed in the premiums that are specified for it in collective agreements. In particular, the differential between payment for this type of shift and that for double-day work hardly seems to discriminate adequately between the demands for these two systems, or to provide a real incentive to transfer from two- to three-shift work.

There is also the point, bearing in mind the high rate for permanent nightwork, that many employees on this type of system are likely deliberately to have opted for it. Admittedly some of these men will have volunteered for nightwork simply because of its high premium payment, but others will have elected to stay on this system because, socially and physically, it suits them best. One may therefore have the anomalous situation in which those shiftworkers best adapted to their hours of work are also the most highly remunerated.

In the not-too-far distant future it should be possible to compare the assessments of shift inconvenience which appear in national, local and company agreements with those made on the basis of medical and psycho-physiological tests and measures. Research leading towards this end is already under way, and may result in some surprises for both employers' and workers' representatives at the negotiating table.

METHOD OF CALCULATION OF THE SHIFT PREMIUM

Although shift payments may be expressed in a variety of ways, there are basically only two ways of making the calculation. One is by adding a fixed amount to the basic hourly rate—for instance $1\frac{1}{2}$p an hour—the other is by using a proportion of this (for instance time and a quarter).

The method of calculation is of interest to shiftworkers in various ways. For example, where the fixed method applies, shift payments will be devalued when increases in the base rate take place unless the shift element is itself raised. Again, while calculation by the fixed method reduces differentials between grades of employee, the proportional method tends to maintain these differentials. Since shift premiums are ostensibly paid to recompense shiftworkers for hardship and inconvenience, which in theory at least are the same for all, it is perhaps surprising that trade unionists should so often have accepted a method of calculation which compensates their more highly-paid members more liberally.

The methods of calculation used in the collective agreements referred to in the previous section are summarised in the table below. This shows that, of the three types of system, only permanent nights are predominantly reckoned by the proportional method.

METHOD OF CALCULATING PREMIUMS FOR DIFFERENT TYPES
OF SHIFT SYSTEM IN NATIONAL COLLECTIVE AGREEMENTS

	FIXED METHOD	PROPORTIONAL METHOD	TOTAL
Permanent nights	31 (26%)	87 (74%)	118 (100%)
Three-shift discontinuous	37 (66%)	19 (34%)	56 (100%)
Double-days	39 (56%)	32 (44%)	71 (100%)
	107 (44%)	138 (56%)	245 (100%)

No satisfactory rationale has been uncovered as to why industries calculate their shift premiums in one way or the other. Or why both methods sometimes appear in the same agreement. Or why an industry changes its method of calculation through time.

It is interesting, however, to note that the proportional method appears to work to the advantage of the employee in that shift payments calculated in this way are on average higher than those in which the fixed method is used. The mean value of premiums for permanent nights, proportionally calculated, is 26.7 per cent as against 16.2 per cent by the fixed method. For discontinuous three-shift work it is 16.4 per cent (against 10.1 per cent), and for double-days 14.3 per cent (against 7.2 per cent).

CONSULTATION AND CHOICE

No discussion of incentives for shiftworkers would be complete without returning to a subject which was touched on in the last chapter, that of taking account of the worker's own wishes in the arrangement of the hours on which he is employed.

In seeking to rearrange its hours of work it is improbable that a firm will be dealing with a uniform body of opinion. Rejection or acceptance of shiftworking is a matter of individual response to particular features of a particular type of shift system, and to the way in which the advantages and disadvantages of a particular system have a personal application. The wide range of employees' individual differences on the one hand, and of possible arrangements of hours on the other, underlines the importance of offering opportunities for consultation and choice when initiating change.

Only one management informant was outspoken enough to lament the legal onus placed upon his company of holding a ballot when shift changes were proposed, arguing that this had made management's task more difficult. But a number of others were satisfied that consultation had benefited the organisation as well as the individual worker. "In all instances of change," wrote the production manager of one Midlands firm, "operators themselves have had an opportunity to suggest how the required period could best be covered." In a Yorkshire engineering firm employees were offered a choice between permanent nights, alternate days and nights or a double-day system. Voting showed that the first two of these systems were preferred to the third, and both were accordingly introduced. In the textiles industry, three neighbouring mills belonging to the same company each had different shift arrangements made at the request of the employees themselves. One operated a permanent night system of four longer shifts per week. In the other two a system of four shorter night shifts was preferred, with an additional part shift on Friday evening: different starting and stopping times had been chosen.

FLEXIBILITY IN SHIFTWORKING ARRANGEMENTS

Beyond the provision of initial consultation and choice when introducing or altering a shift system, there is still room for flexibility. Even after a general rule had been agreed by ballot, fair allowance was made by many firms visited for particular needs and preferences of employees, as the following examples illustrate:

1   Regarding type of shift worked. Two companies agreed to retain under existing hours of work a minority of operatives who were not prepared to make a change. In the first instance, where alternate day- and night-working was being introduced for the first time, this entailed accommodating the men concerned on normal day shift. In the second, where change from three-shift discontinuous to continuous working was involved, a minority of operators were allowed to remain on a discontinuous basis, though receiving a modified shift allowance

2   Regarding length of shift and changeover times. One firm which failed to secure general agreement when first introducing three-shift working was now able to report: "The problem has been overcome by allowing certain

shiftworkers to extend or reduce certain shifts within reasonable limits on the understanding that they are paid on an equal shifts basis to reduce administrative difficulties." Another stated: "In practice we allow, though we do not encourage, variation of changeover times to suit the convenience of operators"

3   Regarding rotation. A Lancashire engineering firm made the comment: "There is no hard and fast rule with regard to the frequency of rotation. Some operators work night shift regularly. The remainder change round once a month and a few once per fortnight. We have found no great difficulty with this arrangement"

The extent to which such flexibility can be used will vary with the nature of the process and the type of shift worked. A process industry, for example, engaged exclusively on continuous shiftworking has less room for manoeuvre than an engineering concern operating a two-shift system.

The larger concern, with a varied production and a variety of shifts, has an advantage here. Although the use of a variety of shifts can give rise to administrative complications, it does give more scope for accommodating individual preference. The general manager of a Lancashire paper mill, for example, wrote: "We are fortunate that, in having other systems of work in the same mill, we can often help employees who wish to change from three-shift work because of domestic difficulties or ill-health." Similarly, the personnel manager of a large electrical engineering concern said that his department was quite often asked to transfer to a more convenient system employees whose domestic circumstances had changed, "and this we do wherever possible."

Additionally a firm may sometimes find it necessary for its own purposes temporarily to transfer certain workers. If production demands make it necessary to put a section normally on double-days on to three shifts, and some of the men concerned do not wish to work these hours, they can be transferred to double-day shift areas elsewhere in the plant. "I do not want to over-simplify the difficulties involved," one informant added. "We experience the usual and natural reluctance of men to change jobs. But the fact that alternative work is available, with the hours of work to which they are accustomed, is a great help."

The greater the choice of rotas and the more varied the alternatives, the easier it is for the employee to fit in with company planning. Flexibility in arrangement of hours helps individual adaptation. The principles of consultation and choice, variety and flexibility, must involve additional administrative chores for the company, but these are likely to be repaid in terms of improved employee morale. This morale derives in part from the satisfaction that comes from participating in a scheme which one has helped devise oneself. Secondly, from a sense of acquiring some degree of control over the way in which ones's hours at work and hours away from work are arranged.

Allowing for individual variation could be extended much further than is the case at present. To take an extreme example, even on a continuous seven-day rota it ought not to be impossible to accommodate those who value their traditional weekends as well as those who see an advantage in time off during the week. Is it really beyond human planning and resource to visualise working rotas in which everyone gets more or less the arrangement they want and to which they are best suited? Planning to take account of individual differences works out much better in practice than is often feared by management. The devising of a system of working hours by shiftworkers themselves implies that these men also exercise a degree of control over its operation. Timekeeping, for example, may be more punctilious if it depends on reciprocity.

RECRUITMENT, SELECTION
AND ENGAGEMENT OF SHIFT PERSONNEL

Bearing in mind possible resistance to change in new shiftworking situations, a number of firms recommend the taking on of new staff, where this is possible, rather than the transfer of existing personnel. Older employees may subsequently come to accept the new arrangement of hours when they see it in operation. "Our experience of introducing a new shift system," one works manager commented, "has been to introduce it in a new department and engage new labour on this basis from the start, because present employees usually feel strongly about having a change in a shift system. After a reasonable length of time, however, it has been noticed that operators on old shift systems do request transfer to the new department when a vacancy occurs."

The recruitment and selection of shift workers, however, may present more difficulties than the taking on of dayworkers. As with the recruitment and selection of supervisors, it is not only that the number of volunteers may be fewer, but that the possibly greater demands and responsibilities involved in the job may narrow the range of choice. Particular care in selection is thought to be necessary in the case of men without previous shiftwork experience, and in the case of continuous shiftworking systems. Such selection involves some estimate of a recruit's likely adjustment to interruption in his normal daily pattern of living. More careful medical checks may also be necessary. "High blood pressure, epilepsy and heart conditions," and "duodenal ulcer or any digestive complaints," are among the reasons quoted as making a man unsuitable for employment on nightwork, as also are "chronic bronchitis, diabetes, or a strong history of recent or recurrent psychosomatic symptoms." While these may be valid reasons for not engaging a man on shiftwork for the first time, they should not be regarded as automatic grounds for taking an experienced man off shiftwork.

Reference to shiftworking as a condition of employment was quite often made by management informants, and not only in firms exclusively engaged on shiftwork. A number of problems were mentioned as arising through its not having been made clear at the time of engagement that a man might later be required to work on shifts. In one company this had necessitated the accommodation of a substantial number of men on permanent days when a night shift was introduced.

A special form of this problem existed in another firm where earnings under the previous daywork system had been inflated by overtime. Difficulty was experienced in getting agreement to new shift proposals because total earnings would fall, even though substantially fewer hours would be worked. The workers in this situation maintained that they had been engaged on a day job known to require high overtime—up to 16 hours a week—and that they had geared their standard of living to this level and could not lower it. Agreement to the new shift hours was only secured here by paying these men the shift rate plus a "lead" to bring the total wage acceptably nearer to former earnings. Newcomers to the scheme were paid at shift-rate only and it was hoped that the "lead" would gradually die out.

The danger of problems of this kind may be reduced where

agreement to work shifts, if required, is made a condition of employment, although it will not be entirely eliminated. One firm, for example, when first considering the need for specialist operators, decided to engage staff initially on days for training, their terms of contract stating that they would eventually be required to work shifts. "Even so," this firm reported, "when the time came to institute shiftwork, considerable reluctance and misgivings were apparent." Nor is it an uncommon story for firms to find youngsters leaving their employment as soon as they are old enough to go on shifts at the age of 18.

CHANGES IN ATTITUDES

While a wealth of management comment was encountered on resistance to change by employees, evidence is not lacking of modification of attitudes and behaviour on the part of operatives who are now said to be working well under changed shift arrangements. A firm which met considerable initial reluctance when it introduced a double-day system for craft maintenance workers now reports that, having established the shift, ". . . the staff who have transferred recognise the advantages in having time off at periods different to the majority of the working population."

The experience of another firm which introduced shiftwork for its professional and technical staff has been that ". . . once the pattern was established the majority were quite happy to continue." In an organisation where continuous working on a $3 \times 2 \times 2$ principle was adopted, it is now even claimed that ". . . the men would be unwilling to change back to any other system." In such cases we appear to have reached a situation where opposition might be expected to altering a system the introduction of which was itself strongly resisted only a short time earlier.

Reference should also be made to one or two quite dramatic examples, notably from the North-East, of adaptation not only to new shiftwork systems but also to quite different work. Miners made redundant by pit closures, for example, and accustomed to heavy manual work on a rotating three-shift system, are now to be found working a long permanent night shift on jobs requiring a high degree of manual dexterity in the textiles industry. "These men have adapted themselves extremely well both to this type of work and to our shifts," one personnel manager reports.

There is also some evidence to show that social, as well as individual, habits and attitudes change, although such change may hinder as well as favour the spread of shiftwork practices. Although shiftwork may come to be accepted in a non-traditional shift area, it may also become less popular in areas where it has been traditionally accepted, if improved daywork opportunities increase.

SEVEN

Day-to-Day
Administration of Shifts

"Departments which have been working on a shift basis for any length of time present few problems to management." This comment on the day-to-day administration of shiftwork is typical of many. Where a shift system has become hallowed through years of use, the teething problems that accompanied its introduction may have been forgotten. Alternatively, any daily problems involved in administering shifts may seem of minor importance compared with those that arise from their introduction and change. Certainly, management informants do not appear to talk or write with such strong feeling about events in the former category.

One type of comment, however, does deserve special mention because of the sheer frequency with which it was made. This concerns the extent to which the working of shifts can increase problems of communication and/or management and supervision. In a few extreme cases difficulties of communication and coordination were said to have led to the abandonment of night shift working altogether.

"ISOLATION" OF SHIFTWORKERS

Lack of normal contacts that are available to dayworkers was often thought to produce a sense of isolation and remoteness in certain groups of shiftworkers. They were said to feel themselves "an inferior race," "a race apart," "second-class citizens" and to show a tendency to develop "a separate group identity" as a result.

Where such feelings exist they may stem in part from shiftworkers being at a disadvantage so far as the community at large is concerned. They may be neglected in terms of travel facilities, entertainment and other social amenities. They are odd men out in a society geared to a daywork economy. It has even been suggested that in certain areas there is still something of a social stigma about being a shiftworker. Not only may those engaged on unusual hours make inconvenient lodgers, for example, but an association between shiftwork and "dirty" work lingers on, a throwback to the days when continuous working was confined to such industries as coal, iron and steel. Lack of opportunity for outside social contact, especially in the case of permanent nightworkers, was put forward as one reason for present pressure towards a four-night week. Certain shiftworkers may also be at a social disadvantage in some unexpected directions: for example, they may run up against some old anomalies when claiming unemployment benefit. [An interesting account of this problem, by David Steel, MP, "Nights of madness," appeared in *The Guardian*, 23 February 1970.]

But within the factory, too, shiftworkers may be regarded, and regard themselves, as less of an integral part of the firm than is the case with day staff. Permanent night staff again appear to be particularly vulnerable in this respect: "There is a tendency for them to regard themselves as not quite so much a part of the organisation as the day shift." A number of informants admitted that there might be some justification for "this feeling of being forgotten."

There are several areas in which communication may break down. Men on night shift can be deprived of opportunities of social contact with friends on daywork unless they stay on at the end of their shift. A tendency is often reported for nightworkers to associate off the job only with their own workmates, and this reinforces the exclusiveness of the shiftwork group. The standing orders of one company specifies that "Managers shall make ever endeavour to aid members working on abnormal shifts to participate as fully as possible in the social life of the company."

What one informant called "the manager's involvement with the shiftworker as an individual" may suffer. This increases the manager's problems in assessing the performance of shiftworkers and in recognising and rewarding talent. In one engineering concern it was observed that few promotions were made from among night shiftworkers. Opportunities for promotion may certainly be more limited on the night shift "since the line of contact with management stops at the level of the foreman" (Pigors, 1944). On the other hand it can be argued that the proportion of permanent night men seeking promotion is lower, because either such men have elected to work this shift out of a desire for a quiet life, or with their higher shift earnings there is less financial incentive towards a supervisory job. [In one London organisation permanent day and permanent night rates for the same work were £27 against £33 respectively (at the top of the grade) and £23 against £27 (at the bottom).]

By no means all shiftworkers feel themselves deprived in this respect. Of one group of permanent nightworkers in a Midlands factory who had expressed an interest in promotion, only 9 per cent considered their chances of advancement would be improved on the day shift: "You've got to be on days among the men who really matter to be noticed," one said. But over half thought that shift made no difference (McDonald, 1958). Workers who considered that there was less competition for promotion on nights gave as their reasons a higher labour turnover rate on that shift and a smaller proportion of workers interested in promotion.

Shiftworkers may be overlooked in industrial relations matters. "Until someone remembers to say, 'What about the night shift?' "; this comment comes from a predominantly dayworking firm with a small, ancillary night shift. Because shiftworkers are restricted in their access to higher management, adequate two-way communication is harder to achieve. "Finding out what shiftworkers are thinking about conditions and so on is a good deal harder than when one is dealing with a single labour force," commented the personnel officer of a firm operating three-shift working. Management–union dealings are more difficult to organise and may depend on off-shift negotiation for which night shift respesentatives have to come in specially during the day. In such case arrangements may have to be made to release shift personnel from duty. For instance in one London organisation permanent night staff attending union liaison meetings are released from night duty immediately after attending afternoon meetings, and in the case of morning meetings are not expected to work the preceding night shift.

The distribution of production and technical information necessary for the job is another aspect of communication which may be regarded as inadequate under some shiftwork arrangements.

Whatever the basis of such feelings and whether justified or not, they often reflect a deterioration in relations between shiftworkers and "the company," or between groups of workers on different systems of hours. Typical references were to "a feeling of 'them' and 'us' " and "a tendency for the shift teams to develop into two opposing forces."

This shows itself in overt behaviour. In one company the "insularity of our shiftworkers from the dayworkers with whom they have little contact results in a rejection of the idea of dayworkers standing in as temporary shift reliefs." In an engineering firm where considerable friction existed between shifts, and between daytime supervision and the night shift, faulty work was always blamed on the other crew. In another engineering establishment, permanent night shift shop stewards, numbering nine out of a total of 30, were said to vote always in a solid block to try to force through decisions, and to resent the ability of the day shop stewards to outvote them. The permanent night shift in this last firm was described as "a cut-off community with strong feelings of solidarity."

Examples of human problems of shift operation of this type are also to be found in the literature. Reid (1961), for example, talks of the tendency of some night shiftworkers to develop "the tight-knit internal loyalties and sensitivities to criticism characteristic of minorities." This can lead to continuous warfare with the daytime crew, with mutual buck-passing and recrimination as the weapons. An interesting characteristic of such situations, mentioned by Reid, is for a man to become extremely possessive about his working equipment: "*my* grinder, *my* turret lathe, *my* truck": this reached such proportions in one factory that men were found to be taking tools home with them at the end of the working day.

Clanishness of this kind on the part of shiftworkers may arise as a direct response to attitudes known to be held by dayworkers. De la Mare and Walker (1968) suggest that it may have been dayworkers' opinions about men who had chosen permanent nights—for example, "You have to be mad to go on nights," and "You wait until you see the night men, they're a queer lot"—which contributed to the unanimity of response which they found on the part of nightworkers in defence of their hours.

Closing of the ranks in the face of real or imagined outside attack may make for good morale and satisfactory relationships within the working group, but only at the expense of disharmony in the organisation as a whole.

But the picture of shiftworkers as comprising minority groups in a hostile daywork world by no means portrays the overall state of affairs. De la Mare and Walker's (1968) nightworkers had no real sense of social isolation. Asked to rate themselves on a middle-class–working-class scale, they felt themselves to be significantly more middle-class than did dayworkers.

So far from feeling themselves at a disadvantage, Taylor's (1967) three-shift oil refinery workers saw themselves as an industrial élite, with degrees of job satisfaction, responsibility and identification much higher than those for day shift men in the same plant.

In one section of a large London corporation, where work was carried out with permanent day and night crews, the view was expressed that "if anything it is the day group which gets left out in the cold." Morale was "surprisingly high" among the night men, and "there was a real spirit of comradeship"—facts which were attributed to their having been recruited to the organisation at about the same time, low turnover, good supervision and the knowledge that they had the option of transferring to daywork. This last fact is important: it is worth noting that in the last three examples the shift men were all volunteers.

The computer software industry is another field where shiftworkers often see themselves in a position of advantage, and are so seen by others. There is no social stigma about being a shiftworker here; no sense of being overlooked within the company. There is, on the contrary, often something of a cachet about being a shiftworker in this type of work situation. "They are the glamour boys," it was said of computer staff in the insurance field, enjoying rates of pay and privileges denied to those with whom they worked. Of computer staff in banking it was wistfully observed: "They're the ones who can stroll into the bank wearing a pink shirt and floral tie."

The status of shiftworkers and their position in the communication structure are clearly topics about which it is again impossible to generalise. "How they are seen" and "how they see themselves" relate to many factors. They relate to shiftwork pay, compared with that of dayworkers and levels locally, and to shiftwork perks, shorter hours, longer holidays, paid mealbreaks and so on. The shiftworker–dayworker ratio is obviously important: attitudes will differ in companies which are predominantly run on a shift basis and those where shiftwork is only an appendage to daywork operation.

The type of shift itself is also relevant: this is one area in which the man on an alternating or rotating system may have an advantage over the stable or permanent shiftworker. One engineering firm at present operating a permanent night shift is proposing changing to double-day shiftworking, an arrangement which it sees as overcoming most of the objections to shiftwork. "In this way the dayworking managerial staff can be in touch with both shifts, and shiftworkers can maintain contact with their friends on day shift."

The type of work on which the shiftworker is employed is also a factor to be taken into account. There is a growing tendency for shiftworkers to be engaged on jobs calling for special skills or in which they are responsible for costly and sophisticated equipment. The more this is so, the less likely they are to be overlooked or neglected. Occupational status has been shown in one United States study (Bohr and Swertloff, 1969) to be related to the way in which day and night shift workers perceive their own jobs and those of the people they work with. Non-supervisory nightworkers attributed less prestige to their own and co-workers' jobs than did their counterparts on the day shift, whereas no differences were found between the ratings of day and night supervisory personnel.

As the number of shiftworkers increases, and as shiftwork spreads into industries, occupations and locations where it was previously unknown, old perceptions and prejudices are likely to diminish. Lack of information and lack of opportunity to those on unusual hours should become less of a problem as unusual hours themselves become normal. But there is still a long way to go. As one works manager put it: "In spite of all we can do to avoid the shiftworker feeling that he is isolated and denied access to normal employee services, communication does remain a problem."

MANAGEMENT CONTROL AT NIGHT

Many of the kind of problems discussed above derive, of course, from the absence of more senior managerial staff on duty outside dayshift hours. "Little is known about what happens at the start and finish of the double-day shift," it was said at one factory, "and even less about what happens during the night." This lack of contact between senior management and the night shift is one reason for the development of management stereotypes about nightworkers' motives and behaviour. [See also Marris (1964), pp92–4, on the management function in shiftworking establishments.]

Lack of standard terminology regarding grades of supervision makes inter-firm comparison difficult, but many firms appear to be content to leave the responsibility of the night shift to charge hands or leading hands. One often feels that little progress has been made in this respect in the half century and more since the Health of Munition Workers' Committee (1916) wrote that "not infrequently fewer and less experienced foremen are employed at night." Downie (1963) suggests that the lack of authority vested in night shift supervision, resulting in the shelving of problems until more senior supervision can deal with them on the following day shift, may be one reason for an allegedly lower productivity at night.

Such criticisms by no means apply universally, of course. One firm which uses only first line supervision in the case of its double-day and three-shift discontinuous departments, raises this to second-line supervision where continuous working applies. At another firm, night supervision duplicates that on days up to, but not including, factory manager level. In a third case, three grades—leading hand, assistant foreman and shift foreman—are on duty at night.

The need for more senior staff on shift duty has been recognised by a number of other concerns because of either the extent of shift-work operations or the cost of equipment and material involved. One high capital cost plant reported that no nominated supervision was originally appointed for its workshop and inspection staff, but that "... it became apparent that a senior member of the staff was required to be present, and an overall night superintendent has now been appointed for the whole factory."

Another firm which previously had only limited supervision for its permanent night shift of 140 has, as a result of recent reorganisation, also appointed a night shift superintendent and raised the number of its foremen to seven, one of whom has been promoted to senior foreman. In addition, the factory manager, senior superintendent and each departmental superintendent take it in turns to come in the evening and stay until about 23 00. This is aimed at giving night foremen the backing and contact they need. The reorganisation resulted from an unsatisfactory night shift situation in which "an atmosphere of careless abandon" was said to prevail, with low productivity and a high rate of scrap.

It is of interest that in the cases just quoted management has obviously thought it economically and productively worthwhile to invest more in shift supervision. This contrasts with other situations in which firms appear to try to balance the extra cost of nightwork by economising on supervisory and supporting services.

It may be argued, with some justification, that it is difficult to get senior supervision and management to work shifts. One solution here might be to attempt to raise the status of shiftwork and shift-work management. One firm in our sample, with an American parent company, claimed that in the United States men are "promoted" to the night shift and that night supervision is carried out with higher calibre staff of "managerial" status. In the British subsidiary, on the other hand, no member of management set foot in the factory between 18 30 and 08 30 next morning.

OTHER STEPS TAKEN TO MAINTAIN LIAISON

Apart from the appointment of more senior staff on non-daywork shifts, various other steps are taken to try to overcome communication difficulties. One works manager makes a point of visiting the night shift at least once a week so that shiftworkers can have an opportunity of raising any problem. Elsewhere, all levels of supervisory staff up to works production manager were said to come back at times "just to walk around and have a word with the night shift."

At one factory, one or other of the day managers usually stays on late so as to have the opportunity of talking to the night foreman. In another example, permanent night foremen are periodically switched to daywork for a spell to keep them in touch and, it was said, "to maintain their standards." In yet another firm regular twice-weekly "coffee mornings" were held where factory foremen and shop stewards met for informal discussion. Each group participated as it rotated on to days under a three-shift system. In addition, the senior shop steward worked on a permanent day basis (though paid at shift rates) in order to keep in touch with all shifts.

In matters of communication and liaison first line supervision often acts in a go-between capacity, in both personnel and technical matters, for the men in their shift crew. In one firm in the computer software industry, for example, the shift for each machine reports to a shift leader, who in turn reports to one of two chief operators who are graded as monthly staff and work on days. Elsewhere the supervisors of the two shifts overlap; either the man going off duty stays for an extra half-hour at overtime rates, or the man coming on duty arrives early.

In other examples, however, there is no personal meeting, contact being maintained by having a "communications book" in which the foreman makes a note of queries. These are then dealt with by the day people and the replies written in the book—a procedure described by one informant as "cumbersome and time consuming." The use of written notes and logs itemising decisions and action taken during the shift are common, but this remote and impersonal method is likely in itself to give rise to misunderstanding and communication difficulties.

Similar efforts are also made to improve personal contact between day and night operators on the same machine, either by the dubious use of notes, or by allowing night personnel to work overtime to link up with the dayworker. Examples of overlap by outgoing and incoming shift operators were found under most kinds of shift system. Length of overlap ranged from five minutes to an hour, and longer periods were usually paid for at overtime rates. In one establishment, working on a seven-day continuous basis, a more informal arrangement applied: "Some departments arrange a small overlap at shift changeover, but this is a purely personal measure."

Another firm uses a financial incentive to encourage cooperation between day and night operators on the same machine. On some of this firm's bigger machine tools, which are paid on piecework, and on jobs which extend from one shift to the next, an additional payment is made to the two operators in the form of a "mate allowance." Until this system was introduced, the firm found it difficult to double-shift these heavy machines because an operator wanted to have the machine to himself and to retain complete control over his bonus earnings. The new allowance provides an incentive to an operator to get a replacement if his existing mate leaves. The additional payment amounts to something between $2\frac{1}{2}$ and 4p an hour for every hour the operator works on the same job as his mate.

THE ROLE OF FIRST-LINE SUPERVISION

The problems, to which shiftwork is likely to give rise, place an additional responsibility on the foreman. As one member of this hardworking and much-tried fraternity put it: "As usual, it's yours truly who's got to cope."

This makes care in supervisory selection especially important, a point which was forcefully set out by the director of a research and development establishment:

The existence of a high level of shift activity has placed considerable responsibility on shift supervisory staff, and the selection, training and calibre of personnel for shift supervision duties has been found to be of paramount importance in the operation of an effective shift system. The personnel who find themselves in charge of shift-workers must show qualities of leadership, tact and understanding and be prepared to accept responsibility for urgent decisions which may have to be taken without reference to middle management, to a degree which would not normally be required of a day supervisor

The problem of finding such supermen is made additionally difficult since the range of choice is likely to be limited by the reluctance of many possible candidates to work hours different from those to which they have been accustomed. Such a higher grade of supervision, in the experience of one Midlands manager, "has to be bribed to work nights." But even higher pay, in the opinion of others, is not always successful in attracting the "right type of man" to positions of shift supervision. In large organisations it may be possible to deal with the problem on a temporary basis by making a stint on the night shift a necessary step up the promotion ladder.

Choice may also be limited by the scope of job and career opportunities elsewhere and by a lowering of the standard of intake into an industry. From the paper industry it was reported that shift supervision is now upgraded from the shop floor as entrants at other levels do not favour shiftworking. In the past this presented no problem to the firm:

> Lack of mobility and lack of alternative employment meant that people of all levels of intelligence entered the industry and it was possible to make suitable selection for promotion. Nowadays the more able man can go elsewhere, probably on a day job, and the selection of people who will make good foremen and supervisors is more difficult

This firm reported trying to meet this need by introducing a training scheme, which although well-supported initially was now foundering for lack of recruits.

As regards the supervision of coloured and/or immigrant night shifts, our own factory visits confirmed the finding of a report in the *Observer* [16 March 1969, "The night shift from Pakistan"] that as yet management is not in the habit of looking for foreman candidates within the coloured group itself, even in the case of 100 per cent coloured night shifts. "Lack of experience" and language, according to the report, are held up as the main barriers to promotion. Exceptions, of course, occur: the author worked as part of a mixed British–Polish–West Indian factory night shift crew under a West Indian foreman as long ago as 1951.

Supervision is widely reported as a problem in the unit with only a few shiftworkers, for example, on a small evening or permanent night shift. This is related, of course, to the economics of small shiftworking and is part of the wider problem of what supporting services to provide when the numbers employed on shifts are limited.

On the whole, the evening shift appears to present less of a problem than the small night shift. In some cases evening supervision is carried out in turn by daytime foremen and chargehands as an overtime task. In another, "We find it best to have a supervisor who works from 14 00 to 22 00, who assists with daytime supervision and is then able to follow straight through with the evening shift." Elsewhere, suitable people are found within the part-time group itself, the re-employment of personnel with previous experience in the firm helping in this respect.

In the case of units operating very small permanent night shifts (usually to obtain extra capacity from particular machines) attempts may be made to deal with the problem by getting a senior hand to take responsibility. But while it may be argued on economic grounds that the use of full-time supervision is not justified, the outcome may be unsatisfactory. An engineering firm in the Home Counties which had less than a dozen night shiftworkers controlled by a chargehand, subsequently abandoned night work, giving as its reasons lack of suitable supervisory staff, difficulty in communications between shifts and increase in the amount of faulty work. A similar firm in the same area with a night shift of 15, considered that it was not worth while to employ high grade supervisory personnel or technical staff, but conceded that "work occasionally goes awry or a job has to be stopped until the day shift arrives." A Midlands engineering concern, on the other hand, provided both a foreman and toolsetter on a night shift varying between only 10 and 15. But in this case the firm was a large one with, presumably, a larger supervisory group on which to draw. Supervisory problems of this kind are less associated with small night shifts as such, as with small night shifts operated by small firms.

It may be relevant to include at this point the comment of one personnel manager on the greater responsibility given to shiftwork operatives themselves in the absence of senior supervision and management outside normal day working hours. In the opinion of this informant this factor increases job interest and satisfaction, and is one of the features which influences men to remain on shiftwork. Perhaps this is where part, at least, of the answer to the problem lies: in devoting much greater care to the recruitment, selection and training of night shiftworkers themselves.

THE PROVISION OF SUPPORTING SERVICES

Apart from difficulties of communication and supervision, the administrative problems most often mentioned were those concerning the provision of ancillary services to production crews working outside normal daytime hours. The question of transport for shift-workers was the first of these. This was particularly seen as a difficulty in certain country areas and smaller provincial towns, and among firms operating three-shift systems. A number of companies arranged their own service to replace or to supplement public transport, and while this has the advantage of more effectively controlling timekeeping, it is not always an economic proposition for the smaller firm.

The provision of various support services in the evening and night hours is very much a matter of economics. What steps should be taken to provide separate facilities for medical and first aid treatment, for a canteen and for the payment of wages? At what point does it become profitable to bring in on a shift basis technicians, toolsetters, maintenance men, quality controllers, inspectors and security staff? "Shiftwork," writes Marris (1964), "creates considerable additional burdens on management, whose weight increases proportionately as the size of the firm reduces."

A number of firms in our own sample were operating shifts on a large enough scale, for example, 200 production workers per shift on a four-crew three-shift system, to find it clearly worthwhile to bring in a fairly complete team of indirect workers with each shift. Such firms go to considerable lengths to ensure that their shift production teams are adequately catered for and supported. Others, in business on a smaller scale, make do with a skeleton supporting service.

It should be remembered that many firms with shift problems are very small indeed, with no more than a handful of shiftworkers. Small engineering concerns, for example, limited by plant capacity, may find the use of a small night shift on bottleneck sections the only way to cope with increasing demand. Yet for such small units even the cost of heating and lighting, or the expense of running air compressors for the whole factory in order to supply a few machines, may have to be taken into account in deciding whether or not to run the extra shift.

Lack of technical staff in such cases may mean that errors occur in night shiftwork or a job may have to be held up until the day shift arrives. This is one factor which makes shifts of this kind expensive to run, although, in the view of one manager, "The marginal costs of such operations are considerably less than the 'bought-in' price of such work if subcontracted."

TAILPIECE ON COMMUNICATION AND COORDINATION

Although interviews revealed a great awareness of problems of the kind discussed in this chapter, not every management informant recognised shift employee relations as an area of special sensitivity. One personnel manager, for example, produced the conversation-stopping comment: "The personnel department isn't in contact with the shop floor, anyway: so there's no less contact at night than during the day."

Poor management, as an Industrial Society speaker once observed, becomes even more vulnerable with the introduction of shiftwork.

EIGHT

Shift Arrangements and Performance at Work

We come now to the question of how different arrangements of working hours may affect performance on the job. The types of question with which we shall be concerned in this chapter are these: Do shiftworkers tend to produce more or less than their daytime counterparts? Do shiftworkers on one type of rota make more errors than those on another? Do particular groups of shiftworkers take more time off, have higher labour turnover, experience more accidents? An attempt will be made to review what evidence is available on these questions, although the information is limited, variable in quality and often appears contradictory.

ANECDOTAL EVIDENCE

Little information was collected from employer and management informants on these topics. Out of the correspondents from 76 companies who wrote to the author on the subject of shiftwork only one or two attempted to discuss the question of how shift hours may affect a man's performance at work. Output was twice mentioned. In the opinion of a rubber manufacturer in the Home Counties: "A continuous nine-hour shift gives a higher hourly production rate than a 12-hour shift with a one hour break because the fatigue factor is more apparent." And from a Yorkshire textiles firm came the view that "It is always more difficult, and in many cases nearly impossible, for night workers to obtain the standard—a fact which may have some bearing to either lack of supervision or fatigue owing to long hours." Errors at night were also twice mentioned: "general increase in the amount of faulty work" (engineering firm/Home Counties), and "a greater tendency for mistakes to be made on the night shift" (engineering/Lancashire).

Readily available views on this topic as a result of visits to firms were also few, and hard and fast facts even fewer. It is perhaps understandable that management may not normally think in terms of individual variations in performance as a man works his way through the shift cycle. But information about the overall comparability of different shifts in terms of performance or profitability might have been expected. This was seldom forthcoming. It is true that in certain situations the work done on different shifts—for example, day shift and night shift—is dissimilar, thus making comparison of performance difficult. But even where comparison was possible many informants appeared to be considering this topic for the first time when asked about it during their interview, and were unable to do more than hazard a guess about the position in their own firm. In general, what information was forthcoming was impressionistic and conflicting: "If anything, production may be greater at night," "There are possibly more errors on the night shift," and so on.

One reason for this apparent lack of interest and lack of information could be that management in many cases is prepared to accept a lower level of performance on certain shifts. This could apply where a night shift is used to secure extra production which cannot be obtained from the normal day shift, either in the factory as a whole or in certain bottleneck sections. Such extra production may be necessary to the firm irrespective of whether unit costs are heavier than on day shift. In such circumstances only extremely gross differences would presumably be considered relevant by management.

Another possible reason is that in most semi-skilled machine operations in industry the operator may be working well within his capacity. This was in fact suggested by a number of informants— for instance, "On few jobs is the individual really extended," and, "They are not hard pushed here to reach the required output." If these statements really describe the existing state of affairs, such measures as are available within the firm will not be true indicators of performance. In such circumstances performance differences from one shift to another would neither occur nor be expected.

In cases where some performance difference between shifts was suspected, this was usually attributed to other factors in the working environment rather than to the effect of actual shift hours. A higher scrap rate at night was in one instance ascribed to less favourable lighting conditions on that shift. In another case, difficulties of manning and organising a department at night were thought to be responsible for lower performance. By reorganising the work so that each man would be responsible for a complete, instead of only a partial, assembly, it was hoped to cut out waiting time and achieve greater efficiency. Lack of maintenance facilities was mentioned as leading to greater delay when breakdowns occurred at night, and the effect of the quality of supervision and leadership upon group performance was also referred to on a number of occasions.

The kind of conflicting and unsupported evidence produced by informants in this area is illustrated by the examples of two manufacturers in the confectionery trade. In each case the informant had no qualms about comparing the performance of a male night shift with that of women daytime workers. One considered that night shift performance was better, and the other had the "impression that it was worse." The former gave as his reasons that men were more "machine-minded" than women, that a lower level of performance was acceptable to women workers, and that the firm paid a night packing bonus for 70 per cent efficiency. The latter claimed that the male night shift was not so well trained or organised, that the men were doing jobs "more suited to women" and that night time maintenance and supervision was inferior.

Similar lack of hard and fast information, and of positive views, was encountered in relation to lost time. There was little spontaneous comment from management concerning differential rates of absence between, or within, different types of shift. There was occasional mention of high labour turnover, particularly at times of change in the arrangement of working hours, and the problems of recruitment and training attendant on this. But such comment was counter-balanced by claims that labour wastage directly attributable to shift-working was very small. Views of the kind have to be considered strictly in relation to particular circumstances.

A number of other surveys have been carried out of management opinion as to the effect of shift hours upon various aspects of performance. On the basis of visits by its Industrial Relations Officers, the Ministry of Labour (1967a) refers to an "alleged lower productivity among shiftworkers," suggesting this as a factor which might have to be offset against any savings in capital charges through the introduction of shiftworking. But the industrial study groups reported by Downie (1963) differed considerably in their views as to the effects of day and night work.

Two or three of these groups stated categorically that performance, in terms of both quantity and quality, was better on days. Poorer nighttime performance was attributed to such administrative difficulties as linking up with workers on the previous shift and inadequate authority given to supervisors on night shift. Difficulties of adjustment and the "natural reluctance of the body to function as effectively during the night as during the day" were also mentioned as reasons. Other groups reported by Downie took the opposite view, claiming a superior performance at night due to freedom from interruption, a more relaxed atmosphere and a greater sense of teamwork. [Of interest in this context is a report from Victor Zorza in the *Guardian*, 25 February 1970, under the heading, "Disgruntled workers a threat to Kremlin." Zorza quotes *Pravda* to the effect that in the Soviet Union "the night shift is much less productive and more troublesome, for both workers and management, than the day shift."]

An Institute of Personnel Management survey (Cook, 1954) found that in the opinion of 30 firms (out of a total of 38) shiftwork had no material effect upon sickness absence. A similar number considered that shiftwork did not lead to any increase in the number of accidents or in the time lost as a result. Rather fewer, 23 out of 38, thought that absence due to reasons other than sickness or injury was unaffected by shiftwork. The association between shiftwork and labour turnover was thought to be more marked, these firms being more or less equally divided in their views on this point.

Anecdotal evidence on these questions, then, is contradictory. In the paragraphs which follow it is proposed to look at what measure of agreement exists in the findings of those field investigations which have attempted to relate arrangement of working hours to different aspects of performance.

FIELD STUDIES

In the investigations reviewed in subsequent sections the types of comparison made are threefold:

1   Performance on daywork with that on some kind of shift rota

2   Performance on some kind of shift rota with that on another kind of shift rota

3   Performance on different turns of duty *within* an alternating or rotating type of shift system

The methods used for such comparisons include:

1   The use of matched groups on different types of rota

2   The use of "before and after" studies in which the performance of the same group of workers is compared before and after a change in working hours, or in which an experimental group which changes its hours is compared with a control group which continues under the former system

3   The use of "follow-through" studies in which the performance of the same group of workers is observed as it moves from one turn of duty to another within an alternating or rotating shift system

Such studies can also be classified according to the broad form of performance measure which is used:

1   Firms' own records—of output, productivity, errors, scrap, absence, lateness, labour turnover, accidents and so on—usually, though not always, collected on a retrospective basis

2   Performance on various physiological and psychological tests—for example, reaction time, vigilance, memory, association—and the use of various physiological measures —for example, heart rate, oxygen consumption—carried out on the job before, at intervals during and after a particular shift

3   A combination of 1 and 2, supported perhaps by interviews or questionnaires dealing with subjective impressions of fatigue, leisure activities, sleep, etc

The duration of such studies varies according to a number of factors, for example, availability of records, or what is practicable in a real-life situation. Investigations using various physiological measures and tests have usually been restricted to a limited number of trials for a small sample of workers. The period over which a company's own records have been studied has varied enormously. In an early Industrial Fatigue Research Board investigation, for example, a report of hourly output under two systems of working hours covered periods of only one week on each (Osborne, 1919). At the other extreme, in a retrospective study of Swedish gas-workers on a three-shift system, Bjerner (Bjerner, Holm and Swensson, 1955) followed through their production records for the whole of the period 1901–43. (Not all organisations keep past records for so long a time!) He found that it was possible to distinguish the handwriting of different workers, whose job it was to read and record figures from meters, and so was able to identify errors in relation to the time of day at which they occurred.

The investigations reviewed here will be grouped according to the aspect of performance with which they are chiefly concerned:

1   "Production performance": output, errors and the like
2   Lost time: absence, lateness and labour turnover
3   Accidents

1 *"Production performance" in relation to shifts*
As far back as the Health of Munition Workers' Committee report (1918) on investigations comparing performance on continuous night work with that under alternating day and night arrangements, and concluded that the former was less productive since workers on this type of shift were unable to get proper sleep and rest in the daytime. But the bulk of research under this head consists, not of comparisons between one type of shift system and another, but of "within shift" studies in which the performance of the same group of workers is traced through the different turns of duty within a particular system.

(a) *Studies comparing performance on day and night shifts within an alternating day and night system.* A number of earlier examples of this type are recorded. The Health of Munition Workers' Committee (1917), for example, reporting on investigations with women workers engaged on such repetitive tasks as cartridge-making, found no significant difference in rate of output on day and night shifts. Similarly, an early Industrial Fatigue Research Board study (Osborne, 1919), using as subjects women on war work under an alternating 12-hour system, concluded that: "No evidence of detrimental effect of night work in comparison with day-work is traceable."

In the Second World War, Wyatt (1944) obtained results that were "in agreement with those recorded during the last war," that is very little difference in hourly output for the same workers. This investigator's conclusions were based on studies of from 12–28 weeks on 1500 male and female operatives in nine factories. But in a slightly later investigation of men in three large manufacturing establishments, Wyatt and Marriott (1953) found a slightly reduced output at night in comparison with days, this difference being equally noticeable whether shifts were changed weekly, fortnightly or monthly. However, although most of the men produced more on the day shift than on the night shift, the authors point out that some "worked just as well or even better on the night shift."

Turning to more recent studies, de la Mare (1967) compared the night and day performance of operators on asbestos board making machines under an alternating scheme. Observing units produced, scrap and machine stoppage time over four months, she was able to detect no difference in performance between the two shift periods. A report from India, however, notes that production and departmental efficiency were lower on the night shift of an alternating day and night system (Pradhan, 1969). But a Czechoslovak study of railway dispatchers on alternating 12-hour shifts found errors to be more frequent during the day (World Health Organization, 1969).

In Poland an investigation of 17 glass workers, alternating on a two-monthly basis, found that working speed was the same on both day and night shifts (Makowiec-Dabrowska *et al*, 1967). But this study also made use of various physiological measures and concluded that night time performance was maintained only at the cost of greater energy consumption. These measures confirmed the men's subjective impressions that work at night was more tiring.

(*b*) *Studies comparing performance on different turns of duty within a three-shift system.* A number of early investigations are again reported. In a 1924 study of different shifts in the Yorkshire glass bottle industry, Farmer (1924) found an order of efficiency (from greatest to least) of *A, N, M* (afternoon, night, morning), and concluded that "Night work in the three-shift system does not appear to put a markedly greater strain on the men than day work." The same order was also reported by Wyatt (1944) for working rate, on the basis of studies of 6–12 weeks' duration on 326 men and women on manual work in four factories. The only exception was provided by one factory group in which the placing of the night and morning shifts was reversed.

Browne (1949) describes a study of women teleprinter switchboard operators engaged on a three-shift system, in which the turns of duty were of unequal length, 08 00 – 16 00, 16 00 – 23 00 and 23 00 – 08 00. The measure used here was the time taken to respond to a flashing call light, and on this basis the order of efficiency (greatest to least) was *A, M, N.*

Errors in recording the figures read from dials was the measure used in Bjerner's (Bjerner, Holm and Swensson, 1955) long term study of gas-workers in Sweden. The task here also involved simple addition and subtraction, which were subsequently checked and corrected. On the basis of a detailed analysis of three men over the period 1912–31, the authors found "The greatest number of mistakes were made during the night shift, the next greatest during the afternoon shift, and the lowest during the morning shift." (Order of efficiency *M, A, N.*)

Turning to examples which combine physiological measures with the use of production records, Oginski (1966) studied three-shift workers engaged on an inspection task in a Polish hot strip rolling mill, and found nothing to choose between the three turns of duty in terms of performance on the job. But on the basis of various tests of fatigue (increase in tremor, simple reaction time and so on) concluded that the afternoon shift placed the lowest load on the organism, while work on the morning shift was the most fatiguing and dangerous. In Rumania, Pafnote and his associates (1967) investigated 25 assembly operators on semi-automated tyre production. The use of various performance measures such as hourly production rate gave an order of efficiency of *M, A, N.* Various psychological and physiological tests were also used in this study to assess the degree of adaptation taking place during the week in which men were on different turns of duty. Adaptation occurred in each case, but was incomplete during the week on nights, even though work speed and output by the middle of the week on nights reached the same level as on the morning shift.

Another Rumanian study (Gavrilescu *et al*, 1966) used physiological and psychological tests only (tests of attention, memory and association; reaction time to auditory and visual stimuli), for 110 control board operators in two power stations on a rapidly-rotating $2 \times 2 \times 2$ system. On the basis of these tests, carried out at intervals during the various turns of duty, the morning shift was the most, and the night shift the least, efficient (*M, A, N*). Using similar measures with glass cutters, Polish investigators (Rzepecki and Wojtczak, 1969) also found night shift performance to be inferior to that on mornings or afternoons. Night time performance was slower, although quantitative effects were less marked.

The order of efficiency (best to worst) from these "within" three-shift studies may be summarised:

	"PRODUCTION" MEASURES			PHYSIOLOGICAL: PSYCHOLOGICAL MEASURES
Farmer (1924) UK	*A,*	*N,*	*M*	
Wyatt (1944) UK	*A,*	*N,*	*M*	
Browne (1949) UK	*A,*	*M,*	*N*	
Bjerner (1955) Sweden	*M,*	*A,*	*N*	
Oginski (1966) Poland	*M = A = N*			*A, N,M*
Pafnote (1967) Rumania	*M,*	*A,*	*N*	*M, A, N*
Gavrilescu (1966) Rumania				*M, A, N*
Rzepecki (1969) Poland				*M* and *A, N*

To the extent that it is possible to combine so varied a collection of studies, it would appear that, overall, the night turn tends to be the least satisfactory of the three shifts in terms of efficiency, while the afternoon shift (although often reported to be the most unpopular turn of duty) may have a slight edge over the morning turn. [Smith and Vernon (1928) also found, though on limited evidence, that output was higher on the afternoon shift of a double-day system.] These results are of interest in that they are what one would predict from the fluctuations of the normal body temperature curve: there is little evidence of adaptation. The evidence, such as it is, concerning the relative merits of day- and nightwork within an alternating day and night system does not permit even such tentative conclusions as this.

One point of interest lies in the divergence of conclusions reached on the basis of "production" measures and those based on psycho/physiological measurement in the factory situation. An observed order of efficiency of *A, N, M,* using firms' records of output, led Farmer (1924) to conclude that three-shift working did not appear to put a greater strain on the men concerned that did daywork. But the studies from Poland (Makowiec-Dabrowska *et al,* 1967; Oginski, 1966) and Rumania (Pafnote *et al,* 1967), quoted above, which additionally used psycho/physiological measures, make it clear that conclusions about demands upon the shiftworker cannot be reached on the basis of production performance alone.

In the study of Polish glass workers on a two-shift system (Makowiec-Dabrowska *et al,* 1967) working speed was the same on night and day, but night time performance was only maintained at the cost of greater energy consumption. Among Polish rolling mill inspectors on three-shift (Oginski, 1966) the different turns of duty could not be separated in terms of the work done, but were found to vary in the degree of fatigue which they produced. In the case of Rumanian tyre assembly operators (Pafnote *et al,* 1967), although working speed on nights reached day shift level by the middle of the week on nights, no adaptation took place in such bodily functions as heart and pulse rate.

Equally, of course, it cannot be assumed from production measures which show that output on the night shift is lower than on days, that the night shift *necessarily* places a greater strain upon the workers concerned. This point is made by Wyatt and Marriott (1953). Figures collected by these investigators suggested that working rate tended to be higher on the day shift. But does this mean that night work is more fatiguing? Such may be the case, but the lower night shift figures could also be due to the ability of workers to control their output and earnings. Wyatt and Marriott wrote: ". . . many workers aim at a fixed weekly wage and regulate their output accordingly. Such workers could afford to reduce their rate of working on the night shift and yet earn the same weekly wage because of the higher basic rate."

What does emerge is that considerable care has to be exercised in arriving at conclusions from investigations of the type briefly reviewed here. As Wyatt (1944) himself reminds us: "Factory output records must be interpreted with the greatest caution."

2   *Lost time in relation to shifts*

(*a*) *Studies comparing absence in dayworkers and shiftworkers.* In a study, Smith and Vernon (1928) compared women dayworkers with double-day workers on the basis of sickness and other absence, lateness and labour turnover, using two "parallel groups" in the case of one factory and, in four other factories, groups of women who had changed from daywork to shifts or vice-versa. As regards sickness absence they found no difference between day and double-day workers, but the evidence of two years' records in one factory suggested that time lost through lateness and absence other than through sickness was greater on double-days. Turnover was also slightly greater in departments which had always been on shifts than in those always on days. But turnover was considerably greater in departments which had experienced a change in rota, whether from daywork to double-days or vice-versa.

Wyatt (1945a) in his wartime study of certified sickness among women in industry looked at the effect of the shift pattern among various "miscellaneous factors" associated with absence. To the extent permitted by his data he compared the attendance of women on day shift with those on two-shift work (unspecified as to whether double-day or alternating day and night) and with those on three-shift. In both cases he found that absenteeism on the day shift was lower. While this difference, based on comparatively few women in two factories, was only suggestive, Wyatt points out it becomes more significant "when it is remembered that the workers on a permanent day shift included a higher proportion of women who, because of minor ailments or inferior physique, might be expected to be more prone to sickness."

In a French investigation (Jardillier, 1962) the shift system was considered as one of 14 possible factors affecting absenteeism among factory workers. Groups of women on double-days and of men on three-shift work were reported as having more absence than non-shiftworkers. A reduction in weekly hours for women workers resulted in an overall drop in absence, but this improvement was minimal for those on two-shift.

In a recent East German study (Brandt, 1969) which compared daytime sickness absence in men with that on double-days and on three-shift, the lowest absence was found on the day shift and the highest on the three-shift system. This was particularly marked in the case of men in the youngest age group, both as regards occasions and duration of absence. In Japan (Mayeda *et al*, 1969), on the basis of a year's study of 42 000 workers in various industries, the arrangement of hours was considered to be "remarkably influential" in its effects upon absence. The order, from highest to lowest, in incidence rate quoted here was alternating day and night, daywork, three-shift and double-days. In the 45–54 age group daywork replaced alternate days and nights as the arrangement with the highest incidence.

A recent study comparing the absence experience of permanent day- with permanent night-workers was carried out by Walker and de la Mare (1970) in three industrial situations, but without consistent differences appearing. In two cases, however, more long term absence (four days and over) and more lost time occurred at night, although the average duration of absence per spell was rather less on this shift. No consistent trends for short term absence were found.

Aanonsen (1964), in his studies on shiftwork and health, analysed a year's absence behaviour for more than 300 continuous three-shift workers and more than 300 dayworkers in the Norwegian electro-chemical industry. In addition to this he carried out a 13 years' retrospective analysis of the 50–65 age group in his sample. As a whole, his continuous shiftworkers had 30 per cent fewer days absence from work both in the special one year study as well as in the 13 years' study of the oldest age group. Aanonsen believes that the reason for this lay in the fact that the shiftworkers initially comprised a highly-selected group with a capacity for adaptation to this type of work, and that a further process of selection had taken place through time by transfer to daywork of the less adaptable.

Perhaps the most carefully conducted and convincing study comparing dayworkers with those on three-shift work in this country is that of Taylor (1967) who analysed the sickness absence, lateness and other absence behaviour of male oil refinery workers over a period of four years. This author found that the shiftworkers had consistently and significantly lower rates of sickness than did dayworkers in similar occupations and when allowance was also made for age. Age-related lateness and other-reasons absence were also measured and found to show similar wide differences between the two groups. These differences were not due to initial medical selection, or to an excess of any one type of ailment in the day men. Taylor suggests that the main reason lies in the degree of personal involvement in their work on the part of the shift men, and in the social structure of their working group.

The same author also quotes a study at a Baltimore refinery

[L Wade (1955) *Arch. Industrial Health,* 12, 592] which, although it does not give rates standardised for age or occupation, found that the number of men going sick within the period under review was 11 per cent lower in the case of shiftworkers. He adds that similar differences in sickness rates between day and continuous three-shift workers have been found in a number of other continuous process plants in this country and abroad.

(*b*) *Studies comparing absence on different types of rota.* Perhaps the most interesting studies of this kind are those in which are compared "traditional" types of continuous rota (in which periods of about a week are spent on each turn of duty) and the rapidly-rotating type of continuous system (in which no more than two or three turns of the same kind are worked in succession).

Walker (1966) examined the attendance of 88 men at a chemical plant who had changed from a traditional seven-shift cycle to a $3 \times 2 \times 2$ system, matching them by age with men in a control group who had continued under the old system. Absence from work and lateness were checked for two periods of five months before and after the change by the experimental group. No evidence of a difference in absence behaviour as a result of the change was detected.

Similar results were obtained in a Czech chemical plant (Jindrichova, 1960) in which the absence of 38 men was compared over a period of three years under a traditional three-shift continuous system and a four year period under a $2 \times 2 \times 2$ rota. Workers who had remained on the original system were again used as a control. No change in the causes of absence or in the duration of incapacity due to illness was found as a result of the new arrangement of working hours.

Very little work has been carried out on the relation between frequency of change and performance under two-shift alternating systems. In an early study, Vernon (Health of Munition Workers' Committee, 1917) found output to be slightly higher and absence less during the first week on nights than on the second. Corresponding figures for the day shift pointed to the opposite tendency. Wyatt and Marriott (1953) also found absence on the night shift to be higher in the second week than in the first, with an opposite tendency on day shift. When shifts were changed every four weeks the amount of absence in successive weeks also tended to increase during time spent on night shift and to decrease during time spent on day shift. The tentative conclusion of these authors is nevertheless that fortnightly change is the most effective compromise in the case of alternating days and nights from the viewpoint of "health, efficiency and personal satisfaction."

(c) *Studies comparing absence on different turns of duty within shift systems.*

(i) *Within double-day shifts.* At one pit in his survey of coalminers' attendance at work, Buzzard (1958) found that fitters who worked alternate weeks on early and late turns had fewer absences during the former. The increase in absence on the afternoon shift was due to the behaviour of the youngest and oldest groups. But when on early turn these men worked a voluntary Saturday morning shift, and Buzzard suggests as a possibility that "the week-end attendance before the week on the afternoon shift was the cause of the increased absence in that week."

(ii) *Within alternating day and night shifts.* In their study on nightwork and shift changes Wyatt and Marriott (1953) suggested that factory records will be likely to show more absence on daywork than on nightwork, mainly because of the employment on the former of men who are unfit for work at night. But when they examined the records of men in their sample who worked days and nights in alternate periods little difference in absence was found.

In an Indian factory (Pradhan, 1969), however, more absence of all kinds on the night shift of an alternating day and night system has recently been reported. Absence was also greatest on the night shift when the firm changed to a three-shift system of work.

(iii) *Within three-shift systems.* A number of studies have also looked at comparative absence on the different turns of duty of three-shift systems. Wyatt and his colleagues (1943) traced the absence of random samples of women on war work in two Royal Ordnance factories over a period of six weeks (two complete cycles). Absence for both married and single women was found to be highest on the morning shift: this was particularly marked for short term absences. These authors write: "Casual absences of one to two shifts per week are often due to personal needs or desires, and their frequency is usually a measure of the extent to which the needs conflict with hours of work. Longer absences, on the other hand, are often associated with sickness: hence they are likely to be distributed more evenly over the morning, afternoon and night shifts."

Shepherd and Walker (1956) obtained similar results in their study of short term absence in a large iron and steel works. About three quarters of single-shift absence without permission occurred on the morning shift. Single-shift absence *with* permission was distributed more evenly over the three periods of duty. These authors demonstrated that the concentration of short term casual absence on the morning shift was not due to workers showing a preference for particular mornings of the week or to a large amount of casual absence by a few men. They conclude that absence of this kind was largely unpremeditated and resulted from the early (06 00) start on the morning shift.

In contrast to these results Sergean and Brierley (1968), in a two years' study of 200 + men on discontinuous three-shift work in a light metal working unit in the North-East, found most absence of all kinds on the night shift and least on the morning shift. As would be expected, this trend was least marked in the case of certified sickness absence: there is no reason why genuine illness or injury which prevents a man from attending work should occur on one shift rather than on another. In the case of absence for reasons other than certified sickness (consisting chiefly of single-shift absence without permission) a greater element of personal choice is involved and, in consequence, liking for or antipathy towards particular shift periods becomes more clearly shown in the variable amounts of absence taken on mornings, afternoons and nights.

Whereas in the Shepherd and Walker study no night shift differential existed, in our own case a differential of four hours was paid and this could be considered as an incentive to maintain attendance on the night shift. But the effect of this was outweighed by greater opportunities for overtime on the morning shift, and to a lesser extent on the afternoon shift. On such evidence it is quite impossible to determine the extent to which better morning shift attendance was due to the attractions of overtime, and how far it resulted from a dislike for work during nighttime hours. To decide this question it would be necessary to have a situation in which both overtime opportunities and premium payments were equal on the three shifts. In such circumstances, it could then be argued, any differences between the three shift periods in time lost would be attributable directly to varying degrees of preference for morning, afternoon and nightwork.

There remains the question of the effect of different starting/stopping times. Shepherd and Walker's shift times were 06 00 – 14 00, 14 00 – 22 00, 22 00 – 06 00: in our own study they were 08 00 – 16 00, 16 00 – midnight, midnight – 08 00. The possibility that later starting times of shifts may be associated with lower absence has been discussed by Buzzard (1958). Evidence which he produced from the coal-mining industry suggested that this was the case in certain areas, although no effects could be demonstrated in others. Buzzard makes the point that a later start to the morning shift implies that other shifts will be later, too, and that this may create fresh problems. A late finish to the afternoon or evening shift, for example, can cause difficulties of transport. Manipulation of shift starting/stopping times may merely cause a redistribution of absence over the 24 hours, and leave total lost time unaffected.

Tailpiece on studies of lost time in relation to shifts. As was the case with investigations of "production performance," the evidence produced from studies of lost time in relation to the arrangement of working hours is far from clear, and much more research is needed in this field.

So far as comparisons of dayworkers and shiftworkers are concerned, some evidence is beginning to accumulate that men on continuous seven-day rotas tend to lose less time from work than their counterparts on days. The distinction between dayworkers and those on two-shift systems is less consistent. This may be due in part to the fact that discontinuous two-shift systems are often more varied in their nature and more unstable through time than continuous three-shift rotas.

The evidence of the two studies which showed no increase in lost time as a result of a change to a rapidly-rotating system of continuous work may be of interest to those who are contemplating the introduction of this type of rota.

The results of "within-shift" comparisons of absence behaviour, and particularly of short term absence, are likely to be closely dependent on such factors as starting/stopping times, and different premium payments and overtime opportunities on the various turns of duty.

3 Accidents in relation to shifts

Various writers have specifically dealt with the question of whether nightwork results in more accidents than daywork. A number of these report negatively.

A French report (Andlauer, 1960), for example, claims: "As far as industrial accidents are concerned, the findings do not warrant the conclusion that nightwork is more dangerous. Statistics for various industries... have shown that accidents in a number of firms have not been more frequent and have sometimes even been less." This view is qualified, however, by the suggestion that accidents at night tend to be more serious.

On an inspection-type job in the Polish steel industry, most accidents occurred on the morning shift of a three-shift system and fewest on night shift, with a slight tendency to greater severity at night. The report on this work (Oginski, 1966) considers that: "The work in the morning shift, probably the most fatiguing and dangerous, is related with the shortest time of sleep and rest."

There is also some evidence from the Health of Munition Workers' Committee and from the Industrial Fatigue Research Board to support the view that nightwork is not likely to produce more accidents. Vernon (1918) in the First World War analysed 50 000 accidents in four munitions factories. For men and women on a roughly 2×12 alternating day and night shift, accidents at night were overall considerably fewer at each factory than during the day. On average night shift accidents were 15 per cent fewer in men, and 16 per cent fewer in women. Differences were found, however, in the kind of accident on each shift. Eye accidents, probably due to defective illumination, were 7–27 per cent more numerous by night than by day. The better safety record at night was not due to output being lower on this shift: at one factory it was considerably higher. Vernon considered that the reason lay in the night shift workers "settling down to a calmer mental state than the day shift worker, and so becoming less careless and inattentive."

This investigator found the curves of accident incidence for day shifts to be quite different to those on nights. Day shift accident curves usually showed a rapid rise during the morning spell, and a fairly steady incidence during the afternoon spell. The night shift accident curves, on the other hand, showed a fairly steady fall throughout the night, except for a small rise at the end. These results were unrelated to lighting or temperature.

For women on a three-shift system (06 00 – 14 00, 14 00 – 22 00, 22 00 – 06 00), Vernon reported fewest accidents on the night shift. There were considerably more on the morning shift, and most during the afternoon.

During the 1920s Newbold (1926) as part of a study of the human factor in accident causation in 13 large firms, looked at the effects of night- and daywork in men engaged in chocolate manufacture. Groups of permanent day and permanent nightworkers doing the same kind of work were compared over the same period. She found "no significant difference between either the mean number of accidents per person or their variability." When age was taken into account—men on days were eight years younger on average—a very small increase during the night was found, but Newbold calls it "not large enough to be of any importance."

Wyatt and Marriott (1953) found a similarly slight but statistically insignificant increase in accidents at night when they analysed the accident records of 14 000 men in five factories.

Quite different results have been reported, however, in other studies. Among mine-workers in Poland (Wanat, 1962) the highest incidence of accidents was found on the night shift and lowest on the morning shift. At the 1969 symposium in Tokyo on occupational health aspects of shiftwork, Brandt (1969) reported on an East German study in which accidents were compared on days, double-days and a three-shift system (including work at night). He found the "accident hazard is the highest in the three-shift system," and that this higher incidence was not restricted to incidents occurring at the place of work. At the same conference a paper from an Indian contributor (Pradhan, 1969) reported more time lost through accidents on nights than on days under a two-shift system. When the firm in question changed its working hours to a three-shift pattern, the night shift still yielded most accidents. In a sample of German railway workers on a three-shift system with starting times of 06 00, 14 00 and 22 00, accident frequency was found to be greatest between 22 00 and 02 00—that is, at the beginning of the night shift (Menzel, 1950).

As with "production performance" and lost time, studies of accidents in relation to shift hours present some apparently conflicting results. Only with more detailed information about the local conditions and influences applying in each case would it be possible to account for this seeming conflict.

DIFFICULTIES OF
STUDYING PERFORMANCE IN THE FIELD

Many difficulties are involved in attempts to measure, in the factory situation, performance in relation to shift arrangements. After listing the field research requirements necessary for their study of night-work and shift change, those painstaking Medical Research Council investigators, Wyatt and Marriott (1953), observe briefly that in three large factories "very few of the processes were found to satisfy these conditions." Only those who have trodden the same frustrating path in field investigation will know just how many laborious hours of research donkey-work lie behind this short sentence.

The difficulties involved arise partly from *the nature of the work itself*. Comparisons between shiftworkers and dayworkers, or between shiftworkers on one rota and those on another rota, are frequently not possible because the work done by the two groups is quite dissimilar. This applies particularly in the case of direct production workers. It is not uncommon in a factory of several hundred to be unable to match even one pair of workers who are employed on different shift hours, but on the same task.

Nor, in the case of "within-shift" studies, is the work performed always constant at all times in the 24 hours. Differences may be particularly marked as in coal-mining, where various types of work —coal getting, maintenance of roofs and roadways, and preparation of the seam—are largely reserved for the three different shifts. In an industry like light engineering, although the type of work may be similar, "difficult" jobs may be given to the day shift and the longer, more straightforward runs reserved for the night shift.

Even with a "before and after" study, in which performance is compared after a change in working hours, other changes may take place at the same time in the job and working conditions, which invalidate the comparison. It is rare for a change to be made from daywork to shiftwork, or from one type of shiftwork to another, without some accompanying change in type of equipment used, or organisation of work or method of payment. At the time of writing, for example, a change from daywork to double-day working is being negotiated in the London docks, but only as part of a package deal involving changes in working methods and payment. In such circumstances any behavioural changes which may be noted can hardly be attributed to alteration in hours of work alone.

Even assuming similarity of work, *the conditions in which this is carried out* can never be held completely constant in the real-life situation. In comparing day- and nightwork, for example, the level of supporting services such as maintenance is invariably lower in the case of the latter. Even though production may be pre-planned for the night shift so that work can have a clear run, unforeseen circumstances may arise which will cause delays and so reduce production. Dealing with breakdowns may have to wait for daytime maintenance staff, or may take longer to rectify than during the day.

Level of supervision is also likely to be lower at night and this, too, may have an adverse effect on production, although, contrary to expectation, it may achieve precisely the reverse result. Marris (1964) includes a nice quote from a pieceworker: " 'I always choose the night shift because you can earn more then. You don't get so much messed about at night. You are rarely kept waiting for material, because the dayworkers leave behind a good supply, and the machines are left ready set up for us. There are no women and no supervisors in the factory at night; that speeds up production a lot.' "

Apart from the nature of the work and its accompanying conditions, *sampling of workers also presents problems*. Comparison between dayworkers and shiftworkers may be difficult, for example, because the latter comprise a selected group. "Men are frequently excused shiftwork and remain on daywork on grounds of ill-health and age. Others who are unfit for or disinclined to work shifts find employment elsewhere" (Walker, 1961). Even where this problem does not arise, as in "within-shift" studies (where the comparison is between a worker's performance on one turn of duty with the same worker's performance on another) there may be difficulties in locating an adequately sized sample of men or women who regularly and consistently rotate through the stages of a working schedule, and over an adequate period. This is particularly so in the case of two-shift systems which tend to be unstable in their composition. Any one who has tried to follow, shift by shift, the performance of a group of, say, 100 men, will know just how rapidly such a sample can be reduced to half its size by temporary transfers or absences, private arrangements or swapping of duties, which affect the strict order of rotation. In reported studies of this kind it is not always very clear just how rigorously this standard of consistency is applied.

Finally there is the question of *measurement*, and the possible limitations of firms' own records for this purpose. In many cases individual measures of output from factory records are not possible simply because the work is carried out on a group basis. Ideally the type of work should be such that output is affected in a fairly direct and continuous way by the operator himself, but in manufacturing output is frequently governed more by the pace of the machine.

Even where individual measures exist, it may not be possible to rely on these as satisfactory measures of the effect of hours of work. Take individual piecework performance figures, for example. Apart from the "overbooking" and "downright fiddling" by operators which is often suggested by management, the consistency, shift by shift and week by week, which one finds in the output and earnings of many operators suggests that loose times on jobs and too slack prices permit men to set themselves fairly definite production targets that lie comfortably within their own capabilities. Such considerations can "entirely swamp any physiological changes in performance such as can be demonstrated in the laboratory" (Browne, 1949).

In the case of accidents there may well be differences of recording on different shifts. At one factory a young and attractive nursing sister ran the surgery during the day shift and there was certainly no reluctance to report to her. The night production team included a number of trained ambulance men who were called on in case of necessity. Not unnaturally men were less inclined to report minor casualties, preferring to deal with them themselves, or to save them for the nursing sister when she came on duty. In such circumstances accident records cannot be relied on to give an accurate picture either of the incidence of accidents or of the time of day at which they occur. Absence data, too, may often be suspect.

In part because such figures may be no more than an approximation, which serves a company's purpose, it is unfashionable to suggest their use for research purposes. Nevertheless, company records are not suspect by their nature, any more than, say, direct observation or the use of psychological tests are by their nature to be relied upon. There seems no reason why company information should not be used, or adapted, as a yardstick, provided that some check can be made upon its validity and reliability.

VARIETY, AND APPARENT
INCONSISTENCY, IN THE RESULTS OBTAINED

The characteristics of each particular work force, the nature of the work done, and the conditions under which it is performed, will all vary from one context to the next. There is a sense in which each situation is unique. No two factory set-ups are ever precisely comparable.

The fact that, as we have seen in this chapter, apparently conflicting results are reached in field investigation, does not mean that shiftwork and output/absence/accidents are unrelated, but that they may be related differently in different situations. The reason for these differences can only be found by detailed studies in each factory. Performance on shifts will vary along a number of dimensions:

1   The particular composition of the work force or sample concerned. Differences in their age distribution, attitudes, physical characteristics, capacity to adapt and so on

2   The nature of the work involved. This has been demonstrated under laboratory conditions and will apply also in the real-life situation. Different results may be anticipated for tasks which are physically or mentally demanding, repetitive or varied, simple or complex. Performance may vary if men in one situation are working well within themselves and in another are being pushed to the limit

3   The precise aspect of performance investigated. "Absence" and "accidents" and "job performance" are themselves broad labels. Quantitative and qualitative performance may be differentially affected by shift hours. Casual absence may be susceptible to shift changes, but certified sickness absence remain unaffected

4   The conditions under which the work takes place. This includes not only physical/environmental and organisational conditions, but motivational factors. Taylor's (1967) continuous three-shift workers saw themselves as an industrial élite, and had high morale and low absence. But other groups of shiftworkers in situations predominantly geared to daywork may see themselves as "odd men out," and here shift absence could well be high

5   The exact nature of the hours-of-work schedule. Similar "types" of shift system are not necessarily comparable. Results can be affected by such "minor" differences as starting/stopping times, direction of rotation, frequency of rotation, etc. "Continuous seven day working" is in this country mainly operated by four crews; in Japan it is common to find only three

6   The broader social/cultural environment against which an investigation is carried out. In this chapter studies from Britain, Scandinavia, Eastern Europe and the Far East have been quoted. To what extent are they comparable, bearing in mind the different backgrounds of these areas? To what extent can one compare studies carried out in time of peace and war, in the years of the depression and those of full employment?

Any, or all, of these factors can affect "shift performance." Multi-causation is a phenomenon referred to by many investigators in the field. "... variations in output," wrote Wyatt, (1944) "are rarely, if ever, due to a single outstanding cause." And recently, workers from the National Institute of Industrial Psychology (1969), investigating errors on one industrial job, were able to identify nearly 70 contributory factors.

Isolating the effects of any one factor in the field situation is unlikely except under the most unusually favourable circumstances. What we are likely to be observing in any situation, then, are the combined effects of a number of features associated with a particular shift routine. Since such combinations are unlikely to repeat themselves exactly, it is hardly surprising that variety and apparent inconsistency in results should occur.

Apart from "situational uniqueness," results may to some extent differ according to the way in which particular studies are carried out. Differences in methods of determining the composition and size of a sample, duration of the investigation, research design, the degree of scrupulousness observed by the investigator may also account for differences in reported results.

For both these sets of reasons there is a very real need for further carefully-controlled and carefully-reported investigations in the field.

Part Three
Shiftwork and
The Individual Employee

Employee
Attitudes to Shiftwork

——————————————————————————————————————

Examining the fairly limited conclusions of European and American writers about the psychological effects of shiftwork, Mott (1965) found general agreement that "few workers like shiftwork, many dislike it strongly, and many others have learned only to live with it."

Certainly there has been a tendency to emphasise dislike of shifts. Two Medical Research Council investigators (Wyatt and Marriott, 1953) in the 1950s reported that almost all the men in three large undertakings preferred daywork to nightwork because it was believed to be better for health, output and social life. And a report of a survey carried out by the Industrial Relations Service of the Ministry of Labour in 1966 (Ministry of Labour, 1967a) in 16 factories in different parts of the country states that "Almost all the workers interviewed . . . disliked shiftworking."

It is not difficult to find companies in which the tide of opposition to shiftwork is running strongly, and where employers have been compelled to modify, and even abandon, plans for introducing or changing a shift system. But to what extent is this opposition to shiftwork or opposition to change?

RESISTANCE TO CHANGE

"The chief problems associated with shiftworking are experienced in the introduction of a new shift system rather than in the day-to-day operation of shift arrangements." This management comment is a fair reflection of the situation across a wide range of British industry. Day by day administrative headaches may occur, as in any other sphere of business operations, but in the main, departments which have been working on a shift basis for any length of time present far fewer problems to management. It is when a department becomes involved in changing from a regular dayworking basis to shiftworking, or when an existing shift arrangement is radically altered, that the major difficulties are encountered.

Studies of attitudes to shiftwork which are carried out in advance of, during or immediately after changes are likely to indicate adverse comment about working hours. But there is much evidence to show that once shiftwork has become established, attitudes become more favourable, and that proposals for further change would themselves result in opposition. The practice of shiftwork may of itself result in greater acceptability (Griew and Philipp, 1969).

As long ago as 1928 evidence was produced (Smith and Vernon, 1928) to suggest that the longer the time on shiftwork the greater the degree of satisfaction. From this it appeared that "the most potent factor in producing a preference for day or shift work was habit ... if the shift system was kept going steadily for some length of time ... the workers became accustomed to it, and it ran smoothly." Similarly the Brierly Committee on double-day shift-working (Ministry of Labour, 1947) observed that the reluctance to accept this form of shift was based on an objection to the changes necessitated at the outset, and that the system was not unpopular with workpeople when they were accustomed to working it. In her study of the effects of shiftwork on social and domestic life Brown (1959) included examples of companies where shiftwork was of long standing as well as where it was of recent origin, and found that the "proportion in favour of shifts was much higher where shift work was not a recent innovation."

This effect of habit also applies to particular aspects of shiftwork. Thus, dealing with groups of male workers who were all employed on an alternate day and night system, but who changed shifts at different intervals, Wyatt and Marriott (1953) found large majorities (66, 78 and 68 per cent) preferring the existing system of change. This they call an example of the general principle that people tend to like what they are used to.

Another relevant piece of research (Smith and Vernon, 1928) indicated that while labour turnover was only slightly greater in departments continuously on shifts than in daywork departments, it was very much greater where change *in either direction* was recent.

EFFECT OF SELF-SELECTION

This bring us to another point. In addition to the effects of habit and change of attitudes through time, some process of self-selection is also involved. Labour turnover is most likely to occur immediately before, during and immediately after change. There is an initial self-selection through acceptance or rejection of shiftwork at this point. There is also a more gradual process of self-selection through time, because those who like shiftwork and can adapt to it stay on this type of rota, while those who are unable to adapt tend to drop out. Initial self-selection, as well as self-selection through time, assumes that men are free to choose their work in the first place and to leave it subsequently at will. Where a shiftwork system has been in use for any length of time it is likely to be manned substantially by a "survivor population" (Reid, 1957). There is a sense, as Shimmin has pointed out, in which every job is a selection procedure, and "in time of full employment, it is unlikely that men will stay on shiftwork if they find it unendurable. As a shiftworker said in an interview: 'It's no good asking *us* how we like shiftwork, because we wouldn't be here if we didn't' " (Shimmin, 1962).

WHERE SHIFTWORK IS PREFERRED

The attitudes of shiftworkers in general have been said to be characterised by "resignation rather than adaptation" (Banks, 1956) and by "acceptance rather than acclaim" (Downie, 1963). But attitudes to shifts are often more positive than this.

The literature provides many examples from a variety of countries of an active liking for shifts expressed by substantial proportions of workers. In Finland, 26 per cent of three-shift workers in an electricity plant stated a firm liking for their rota against 39 per cent who claimed a strong dislike (Hakkinen, 1966). In an investigation in a French petrol refinery there was no desire for a radical change in the pattern of the working day among continuous shiftworkers (Vieux, Carré and de Monès, 1962).

In this country a majority in favour of shifts was found among 169 men on a rapidly-rotating shift system in a steel works: 53 per cent "liked" against 15 per cent "disliked" (Wedderburn, 1967). Very similar proportions (57 against 12 per cent) were found among workers in an oil refinery in Canada (Blakelock, 1960). Suggested reasons for liking shiftwork in the latter case were that the group was located in an area in which most of the working population were employed on "unusual" hours; that their pay compared favourably with that for daywork; and that indoor and outdoor recreational facilities were exceptionally good.

It is of interest to note that the examples so far quoted are all of three-shift workers on continuous rotas. Taylor, with continuous three-shift workers in a British oil refinery in mind, comments that in spite of the problems to which shiftwork can give rise, it is often associated with greater satisfaction in the work role than is the case with daywork (Taylor, 1967). This author found a higher degree of job satisfaction and identification with their work among shiftworkers than dayworkers, and considered that this might be the cause of their lower absence in the refinery in question.

But liking for shiftwork is by no means restricted to this type of system. An investigation of attitudes to double-day shifts, for example, showed that "for more than half of those interviewed the benefits outweighed the inconveniences" (Brown, 1959). Women were almost unanimously in favour of double-days in comparison with normal daywork, such shifts making it easier for them to combine employment with housework. Even the 1966 Ministry of Labour (1967*a*) survey, which reported a widespread dislike of shifts, excepts the case of married women "who had been able to select the particular non-rotating shift which suited their domestic circumstance." Part-time shifts, too, of course, have often been quoted as giving widespread satisfaction. Again the advantages here are that hours of work can be chosen to suit individual domestic circumstances.

SITUATIONS PERMITTING CHOICE OF SYSTEM

We are coming here to situations of deliberate choice. Even in the examples quoted above, where majorities of workers expressed a liking for shifts, they cannot always be said to have deliberately "chosen" their hours of work, except insofar as they had chosen their industry and job, and so accepted the conditions of work associated with these.

Examples of active choice between alternative patterns of working hours are on record, however. De la Mare and Walker (1968) have described how men in a service industry were permitted, on achieving a certain seniority, to state an order of preference for three different types of duty: permanent days, permanent nights or rotating shifts. While the majority chose daywork, substantial minorities, 27 per cent in the case of permanent nights and 12 per cent in the case of rotating shifts, opted for shift hours. The authors consider at some length the reasons for this preference (which they investigated both by unprompted questioning and subsequently by ranking of factors). It is of interest to note that the reasons for choice given by the permanent day men were mainly negative, while the permanent night men were more articulate in stating the advantages of their preferred duty. These advantages were mostly associated with pattern and amount of free time; ease of travel to work; and the more easy-going tempo of work at night.

A rather different approach was used in a study of attitudes of nightworkers in a Midlands chocolate factory where McDonald (1958) put the question: "If the money were the same, and job and conditions of work and employment remained unchanged, would you prefer to work on nights, on days, or would you be equally happy on either?" Of this sample 14 per cent said that they would still prefer nightwork. But subsequent questioning led McDonald to doubt whether such statements really did represent these men's "true" preference, and whether in fact they would have been night shift volunteers in a free choice situation.

Among those who are on shiftwork at their own request a preference for regular night work is not uncommon. A number of firms visited by the writer in London and the South-East reported little difficulty in the recruitment of a permanent night force. One even claimed that job applicants were lost because no work on this basis could be offered. In another it was said that payment of a night shift differential resulted in a queue to get into shiftwork from daywork. Of interest in this respect is the experience of two firms in the Medway area in which both alternate day and night and permanent nightwork had previously been practised. Following a redistribution of night shift hours over four instead of five nights a week, and an increase in the night shift rate (plus in one case an additional night shift meal allowance), the numbers of those on a permanent day or permanent night arrangement began to increase at the expense of those who worked on a basis of change. In one case, alternating shifts almost completely died out.

Operators in these factories were free, through informal arrangements with each other and with the shop foremen, to arrange their own systems of shift. As a result of the additional nightwork incentive of extra cash and free time, permanent night volunteers came forward in sufficient numbers to enable those who disliked shiftwork to return to permanent daywork. Money is obviously a factor here, but preference for the shift system itself is also clearly involved.

ADVANTAGES FOR THE SHIFTWORKER

It is no part of the purpose of this chapter to underplay the dislike which many people have for shiftwork or the fierce opposition to which proposals for its introduction can give rise. Some workers will not tolerate *any* disturbance of a regular daytime routine, and will go to almost any lengths to avoid it. A firm in Wales reported: "The people here just don't want to work shifts. When approached they are quite frank about it and say that if this method of working is introduced they will look for employment elsewhere, even if it means accepting lower wages."

Similar reluctance on the part of some employees to abandon daywork conditions is found even where the economic need for shiftworking has been recognised and has been put across by the relevant trade unions in a capital intensive industry.

An interesting comment on the determined pursuit of daywork in a possibly expanding situation of shift-employment came from a Birmingham firm. The company commented that it was having to engage in lengthy discussion and negotiation in an attempt to persuade its employees that the future pattern of employment would be in the direction of ever-increasing amounts of shiftworking, and that, in the end, leaving one company to join another might not ensure the maintenance of a daywork job. "The reaction of employees," this firm concludes, "is that such is not at present the case and, as far as they can see, day shift employment will be available in the Midlands area for very many years to come."

Nor is it intended here to underplay the extent to which shiftwork may be grudgingly conceded as a necessary evil accompanying a particular way of earning a living. To the man who is "born into" a shiftworking industry (such as coal or steel) or whose particular skills may be tied to shift hours of work, very little choice may be available. Such a man may be in the position of having to accept certain hours of work whether he likes them or not. The aim here is simply to illustrate, in the face of much that has been written about the unpopularity of shiftwork, that for many it is a perfectly acceptable way of life, that many others actually like it and that what many employers have described as a "recognisable proportion" and a "substantial core" of their workers go out of their way to seek it out.

What also emerges from this discussion, and what often tends to be overlooked, is that liking or choice of shiftwork is in reality liking for particular forms of shiftwork. People do not choose to go on to shiftwork: they choose to work part-time evening shifts or discontinuous three-shifts or permanent nights. An expression of liking for double-days tells us nothing about a person's likely re-action to alternate day and night work. The refinery process workers mentioned above who were highly satisfied with a seven-day rota would most likely have responded less favourably to the Medway engineers' system of regular nightwork. Equally, the permanent night men on the Medway (Monday to Thursday) would hardly have welcomed a continuous system which deprived them of their long weekends.

The advantages of different types of system are many and varied. They arise partly out of the hours of work themselves. "Early birds" prefer early morning shifts, and late turns suit those who find it more difficult to get out of bed in the morning and the "night owls" who prefer to stay up late. The suitability of different types of shift varies, too, according to family and social commitments and interests outside the place of work. Married women will prefer shifts which best fit in with their family and household responsibilities. If both husband and wife are working, they will normally want their hours of work to coincide, if there are no children. But with a young family they may find it more convenient to have different working hours so that at least one parent is always at home. Some types of shift provide daylight hours which give an opportunity to follow a particular hobby or interest such as gardening or fishing. Others provide an element of variety, with changing duties, and for some this is an attraction in itself. Some rotas permit travel to work in more leisurely and less crowded conditions.

Apart from such considerations connected with the arrangement and distribution of the hours themselves, other advantages arise from the conditions of the job itself which are associated with these routines. Mention has already been made of the higher degree of job satisfaction and identification with their work that Taylor (1967) found among continuous three-shift workers when compared with dayworkers. Shift men at this refinery worked in small groups of two to six, with four such groups successively responsible for a particular unit or task. A high sense of responsibility and mutual trust had been built up within these shift teams, in contrast with the larger and less closely-knit groups of dayworkers.

In the very thorough examination which de la Mare and Walker (1968) made of the factors influencing the choice of shift pattern, an important group of reasons governing preference for permanent nights centred round the "orderliness" of work at night. This sense of order applied to the way in which the work itself was organised, as well as to the regularity of hours. Less "hurry and scurry" and "rush and chaos" was reported at night than with daytime work. The atmosphere was said to be pleasanter, with a greater sense of companionship. There were fewer interruptions from clerical, technical and supervisory staff.

Confirmation of this type of reaction was found in our own factory visits. Nightwork conditions were described as offering "greater freedom in a more easy-going atmosphere in which men can set their own pace." Or, again, "The pressures are off; there are fewer bosses; a man can get on with his work undisturbed by production changes, progress chasers, and the like." The fact that in many night shift situations the degree of supervision is less than with normal daywork means that a greater responsibility is given to the shiftworker with consequent opportunity for increased job interest and satisfaction.

Part of this greater sense of freedom and greater *esprit de corps* at night consists of what can only be described as a kind of mild excitement. This may seem a fanciful word to apply to the apparently humdrum nature of many industrial activities. Nevertheless, comments do suggest that for some workers there is a quality about, say, a Staffordshire pot-bank or a Lancashire mill at night that is quite lacking by day. It is easy enough for the casual visitor to capture this feeling, but in some cases it appears to persist with workers who have spent years on shift.

A suggestion of a similar kind occurs in a wartime report by Mass Observation (1943). This includes a note by the labour manager of a machine shop in which morale had fallen to a low ebb among women operators. The medical officer here suggested the need for some emotional stimulus to improve morale, and one proposition was to switch from a purely daytime shift to a system of alternating days and nights. Morale immediately improved and output rose. "... it was found that working on a night shift provided to those so engaged just that stimulus and *sense of romance* necessary to take a real interest in the job" (my italics).

This admittedly was a special situation in which women were carrying out unaccustomed work in adverse conditions. No information is available about the period over which the improved level of morale was maintained. Nevertheless "romance" may not be too strong a word to use if shiftwork is thought of as providing relief from the tedious character of many daytime occupations.

At the other end of the scale the financial inducement must obviously be included among the job conditions which attract workers to shift routines. For many workers it may be the only, or at least the main, attraction. There is a tendency for employers and management to overemphasise the importance of the financial incentive, just as there has been a tendency for social scientists to undervalue it. "These men are the type who are prepared to put up with the inconvenience of nightwork in return for high earnings." "If they could earn a penny an hour more elsewhere, they'd be out of here like a shot tomorrow." These are typical management accounts of the motives of those who do not mind working unusual hours.

In the de la Mare and Walker (1968) study the financial advantages of night shiftwork received only limited mention from those working this shift, and the authors suggest that this may have been due to "a reluctance to admit to the financial motive so frequently attributed to them by others." Those who did give money as a reason for choosing shift rotas were usually men who had some particular financial need such as hire purchase or mortgage commitments.

Money matters. Many men work shifts for this reason alone. But the generalisation that "they're only in it for the money" is very much of a half truth. Reasons for working shifts are as varied as those for working in a particular job or firm or occupation. Reasons for working shifts are as varied as the particular combinations of needs of the individuals concerned.

Shifts may be worked because no daytime work is available, or because no daytime work with comparable earnings and conditions is available. They may be worked because of certain advantages which attach, or are thought to attach, to them; because such advantages outweigh, or are thought to outweigh, their disadvantages. Finally, shifts may be worked because they are genuinely preferred.

TEN

Personal and Social Factors
Affecting Attitudes to Shiftwork

In the last chapter it was stressed that workers' attitudes relate not to shiftwork in general, but to particular types of shift system. Like/dislike are associated with the advantages/disadvantages which these different types of shiftwork have for the individually different men and women concerned. Generalisations about those who work on shifts are as out of place as are generalisations about shiftwork, and in the present chapter some of the many personal and social factors which can influence individual attitudes will be considered.

AGE

As might be expected there is a certain amount of comment from employers and management about the lower tolerance to shiftwork of "young people nowadays." For example, in a firm in which alternate day and night working had been practised for 40 years, the works director declared: "Young people coming into the company will not put up with night shift work to the same extent as did their fathers and grandfathers." Another informant agreed that youngsters prefer jobs which do not tie them to their work during normal social hours, and so "either do not start with us at all, or leave as soon as they are old enough to go on to shifts at 18, or as soon as they start courting."

There is some confirmation of these unfavourable attitudes to shiftwork on the part of the young in the literature. Brown (1959) found that young men objected more strongly to the loss of social life in the evening than did the older man. Extra hours at home at other times of the day were not adequate compensation for loss of social life in the evening. Taylor (1969) mentions that young bachelors complained that irregular hours hampered regular contacts with girl friends, most of whom were employed on daywork. (Although where couples are employed in the same factory it may be possible to arrange that both work the same shift.) Downie (1963), discussing the labour turnover consequent upon change from day- to shiftwork suggests that this can be minimised by an adequate shift premium combined with adequate advance information about the change: but he specifically excepts the young unmarried group. "Here the turnover is fairly high since many of them will not accept the restrictions on their evening leisure and the interference with their courting."

As an exception to experience of this kind may be quoted the example of the computer software industry where it is not unusual to find young people in the 18–23 year age group who are prepared to work shifts for a year or two as a necessary condition of promotion to more senior jobs in the industry, even though this may involve "burning the candle at both ends."

Attitudes appear more favourable higher up the age scale. A study in France (Dervillée and Bannel, 1969) found that "people seem best adapted to nightwork between the ages of 28 and 54." And in a steel plant in Wales (Wedderburn, 1967) satisfaction with shifts was found to be highest in the 31–40 age group (as well as among married men and those with three financial dependants). Mott (1965) calls the age of the worker "one of the key factors in understanding his attitude towards shiftwork." He sees the higher satisfaction with shifts that comes with age as being due to the fact that older age groups are selected populations—the dissatisfied having left; to greater familiarity with and adaptation to shiftwork routines; and to the fact that the older man is probably earning more money and therefore able to afford more highly compensating features outside the place of work.

Complementary to management's comments about the attitudes of the young is the commonly heard assertion that shift populations tend to feature a high percentage of older men, although such age bias has not been consistently found in firms in which this point has been examined. De la Mare and Walker (1968), for service workers who had chosen to work permanent days, rotating shifts or permanent night routines, quote mean ages of 37.0, 35.1 and 39.6 years respectively. Dayworkers did not differ significantly from the norm of the group as a whole, "but rotating shiftworkers included more short service men and men under 35 years old, while the nightworkers included a large number of long service men and men over 45 years." But de la Mare and the present writer (1968) in an engineering situation where men were also free to choose their rota, found no difference in the age distribution of permanent day and permanent nightworkers, with means for both groups of 41 years.

The general observation that satisfaction tends to be higher with age may have to be qualified at the upper end of the scale. In a New Zealand survey (Griew and Philipp, 1969) it was found that acceptability of shiftwork decreased sharply with advancing age, and the authors recommend that the oldest workers would in most cases be more suitably employed on normal non-shiftwork.

There is some physiological and medical evidence to support this view. For example, recovery after nightwork among Czech railway dispatchers was found to be slower and less complete in workers over the age of 50 (World Health Organisation, 1969). And Japanese work (Anon, 1969) has shown that rate of recovery of body weight lost during a week on nights, in the following week on daywork, is slower for men in their forties and fifties than for those in their twenties and thirties. For this reason 45 has been suggested as an upper age limit for men on rotas involving work at nights. In Scandinavia a series of investigations into shiftwork and health (Thiis-Evensen, 1958) concluded that those over 50 years of age, without previous experience on shifts, ought not to be recruited for work on continuous rotas.

There are two aspects to the problem of shifts and the older worker. One concerns situations where shifts are of long standing. A number of firms in this country are constructively facing up to the problem of their older shift employees, and considering such questions as: "What are the prospects for shiftworkers who are now growing old with the company?" And: "Are they to go on working shifts for the rest of their lives?" In some companies personnel over the age of 50 are not required to work on the night shift, but this will involve financial hardship unless the company is prepared to continue to pay its long-service employees at shift rates.

The other aspect of this problem concerns the older worker in firms going over to shiftwork for the first time. The over fifties are likely to find it difficult to adjust physically and socially to the demands of new rotas. "Technical managers are inclined to forget this problem," one manager is reported as saying (CBI, 1968). "They are more concerned with production and plant utilisation and less with the human problem." For his factory the solution was to allow dayworking for long service employees, while paying them at the new shift rates. This is admitted to be a costly compromise but "it will resolve itself in about 15 years and is worthwhile if only to keep local goodwill for the company."

MARITAL STATUS AND DOMESTIC RESPONSIBILITIES

Associated with the age factor are those of marriage and family responsibilities. The extra money that is paid for shiftwork is of advantage to the man who is buying or setting up a home, or for the additional financial commitments which come with children. [In a study of the psychological effects of night shiftwork (van Loon, 1958) attitudes of married workers tended to be influenced to a greater extent by the shift premium than was the case for single men. And in a comparison of permanent day and permanent night-workers (Walker and de la Mare, 1971) fewer single men and married men without children were found on the night shift, but a greater number of men with four or more dependants.] But shifts may interfere with the time which a man can spend at home with his wife and family. A man may be unwilling to leave his wife at home at night and may be under pressure from her not to do so. Such pressures may be particularly severe on younger married people and many management comments display considerable sympathy for those who must face these problems. One personnel manager comments:

> Men who marry, having worked happily on shifts for some time, are soon anxious to work days.... The man finds himself being torn between appeasing his wife and the extra cash that shiftwork provides. Married men join-ing us to work shifts do not exhibit the same anxieties—at least, not to the same degree. It is not suggested that the subject of shiftworking is ignored by young couples contemplating marriage, but that the impact is greater than anticipated

And in the words of another:

> By the very nature of this shift (a long permanent night shift) men are exposed to physical and nervous strains which they would not be subjected to during normal day shift working. These strains can be accentuated by the lack of understanding of a man's wife. We have found that the men who we are most successful in keeping in our employ after training are those over the age of thirty. Those under this age have probably recently been married, or are married to young wives with small children, and it has been our experience that such men do come under pressure from their wives to return to normal day shift. One resultant factor is that wives of night shift men at the younger end of the age scale seem to be very susceptible to becoming involved in financial troubles, particularly mail order and hire purchase transactions —a problem which causes us concern from time to time

De la Mare and Walker (1968) in their careful study of shift preferences stress the importance of the opinion of wives. This was frequently mentioned as a main reason by those who had elected to work on days. The influence of the wife's opinion on a worker's choice was supported by the fact that a higher proportion of married men, and of married men without children, were found in the day-work group than in any other. The authors consider that there was "...a real relation between a wife's dislike of being left alone at night and a husband's tendency to prefer daywork."

At the same time, although these authors found that men who had elected to work permanent nights ranked "able to see more of family" highly among their reasons for choosing this rota, they could find no supporting evidence for this claim in a greater concentration of home and family-centred leisure activities among this group.

In the case of double-day work Brown (1959) found that married men attached more importance to the advantages of having more time at home than did single men, and more than half her sample preferred double-day shiftwork for this reason.

Marriage and the domestic situation may thus be reasons for either working or not working shifts, depending upon individual family circumstances and upon the work/leisure pattern of the shift system involved.

Opinion concerning the effect of children in the family on a man's attitudes to working shifts is often conflicting. Much depends here on the age of the children and the ability of the wife to cope with a family on her own. For men on systems involving nightwork the presence of young children may present problems of sleep in the daytime. Wives may expect some degree of help with the bringing up of a family, and feel the need of the father's disciplinary influence in the case of teenage children. But again, the presence of children may provide reasons both for and against working shifts, depending upon the people involved and details of the rota in question.

Another factor to be considered here is whether the wife herself is working. Shifts may be disliked by men whose wives are employed on regular daytime jobs (Blakelock, 1960). Young, newly-married computer operators said they hated the 16 00 – midnight evening shift because they had to leave for duty just as their wives were due to come home. A man on permanent nights, with a wife working days, may see her virtually only at weekends. A report on such "shiftwork marriages" in the *Daily Mail* (4 April 1970) quoted the case of a mother of twelve children on a car factory night shift and her day shift husband. They are able to have an evening meal together before she goes to work and sometimes, early in the morning, they pass each other in the street. One of this woman's few regrets —"I'm just sorry that my husband had to bring the baby up."

There is a vast interplay of factors here. Marriage as such is not "the great deterrent" to working shifts that it was called by one informant. A man's attitudes and his willingness to work a particular shift system will depend not only on whether he is married or not, and has children or not, but on whether he is newly-married, on the "success" of the relationship with his wife, on her attitude, whether she is working, the number and ages of his children, his financial commitments and so on.

So far as the employment on shifts of married women themselves is concerned, the arrangement of the double-day system on which so many of them are employed can make the tasks of shopping and looking after a house easier to cope with, and many working women prefer this system to an ordinary daywork shift for this reason. Brown (1959) reported that for housewives "extra time at home during the day was more valuable than leisure time during the evening." Part-time shifts, including evening shifts, are popular among women because they can be fitted in with domestic responsibilities, and also, quite apart from the extra cash involved, because they provide company and a relief from housework. When there are younger children in the family, shiftworking is more difficult to arrange unless provision can be made for them to be looked after while the woman is at work. This depends in large measure on the husband and his ability and willingness to cope on his own.

"I feel sure," one personnel manager said, "that it is the co-operation a man gets at home which is the determining factor in whether or not he will work shifts." But the same can be said of the married woman worker with regard to the husband's cooperation.

TEMPERAMENT AND PERSONALITY

Do shiftworking populations differ temperamentally from those engaged on daywork? Are those who deliberately elect to work shifts, or who can adapt to them, a different "kind" of people?

Management generalisations on this topic are particularly common in the case of permanent night shiftworkers. One works manager was opposed to this type of shift because, he claimed, it attracted "a careless type of worker with personal difficulties." Another thought that a preference for such work indicated an underlying insecurity and quoted "a divorcee, a widower living by himself and a man with marital problems" to support his point. Yet another manager described the permanent night worker as "a lonely man, a non-mixer, one who doesn't want to be bothered."

At one employers' association it was suggested that the permanent night worker was "a special kind of bird," the type that sprang to mind being "the widower, usually with very little social life, devoted to his garden." The dayworker, on the other hand, was "a much more normal type of person." There is some confusion here between statistical and temperamental normality. If day shift is regarded as the "normal" pattern of work, nightwork is "abnormal," and nightworkers, by a process of association, become "abnormal," too —"a race apart," inhabiting "a lost world"—both descriptions from personnel departments.

Sometimes the nightworker is seen as merely temperamentally different, rather than temperamentally "odd." For instance, "He is the man who prefers lack of interruption and the less hectic tempo of nightwork," or, "An independent sort of person who doesn't like interference from the day shift." One machine room foreman even suggested that night men were distinguishable by the "slow and deliberate" way in which they walked on to the shop floor.

Few efforts at personality assessment of different groups of shift-workers, or of shiftworkers against dayworkers, have been made. De la Mare and Walker (1968), for groups which had chosen permanent day, permanent night and rotating systems of shift, used the Maudsley Personality Inventory which provides a measure of introversion–extraversion and neuroticism. They found a striking agreement between the scores for their total sample and the norms for an English population. "Shiftworkers," these authors observe, "are often said to be a selected population, but this group of shift-workers was certainly not selected in relation to either of these personality dimensions." Nor were significant differences found in this study in personality measurements between any of the groups choosing different shift arrangements, although it is suggested that the inventory used may not have been appropriate to identify the aspects of personality involved.

There is certainly scope for research in this field. For the present it is better to regard with scepticism suggestions that shift teams are characterised by "a special kind of bird." If forced to generalise about the temperament and personality of shiftworkers one could well argue that, far from being an odd-man-out, the permanent night man who has deliberately opted for his hours of work shows better adjustment than the day worker who is less likely to have exercised a deliberate choice.

Permanent night volunteers, in the view of one production manager, "never give any trouble because they are doing what they want to do and have asked to do." But the particular combination of reasons behind each volunteer's choice will be different.

THE EFFECT OF TRADITION

The effect of local, industrial and company traditions exert a strong influence upon a worker's attitudes towards shiftwork. Visits to firms in a variety of locations and industries yielded many examples of differences in attitudes in traditional and non-traditional situations. Problems of introducing shiftwork for the first time or changing an existing form of shift vary from factory to factory and from region to region. The importance of local custom and practice is familiar to any company having a number of factories in different parts of the country. Such companies may have difficulty in introducing shifts or a particular system of shifts in one location whereas it may be perfectly acceptable elsewhere. One company commented on a marked difference in attitude that existed in its Home Counties factory and in the North of England. In the latter area, "where there is a tradition of shifts, systems of all types seem to be acceptable to both males and females."

In the North-East a personnel officer in a firm where three-shift working was an established pattern claimed that most of his operatives would find it strange *not* to work shifts, and in the Sheffield area, in what is a traditionally shiftworking community, the three-shift system is said to be still generally regarded as normal, there being "no social stigma attached to being a shiftworker."

Even in areas not traditionally regarded as shiftworking it is possible for a single company to establish its own tradition for this method of work. Traditions may also be built up within sections of the same establishment, as in the case of the firm which commented that: "... three-shift working operates well enough in departments where it is customary—boiler house, security office, etc—but we have always encountered strong objections to any extension of this pattern." Tradition can thus be highly circumscribed in its effects.

LOCAL OPPORTUNITIES AND AMENITIES

Local traditions are closely related to local employment conditions. One firm, operating in a traditional shiftworking district of Yorkshire and experiencing as yet no undue difficulty in recruiting shiftworkers, foresaw the day when the spread of dayworking practices would bring firms face to face with greater reluctance to work shifts. Where alternative opportunities are plentiful the recruitment of shiftworkers is likely to be correspondingly difficult even at shift rates of pay—for example, the difficulty of recruiting women to work shifts in a high female employment area such as Nottingham. Lack of comparable employment opportunity would seem to be a major factor in the success story of a largish and still expanding Midlands firm which a few years ago introduced continuous shiftworking into a dominantly agricultural area where there was previously no record of shifts.

The existence or the lack of social amenities of various kinds for shiftworkers has also to be considered, along with local traditions and the state of the local labour market, as a determinant of attitudes to shifts. Considerable emphasis is given to this point by management informants. "All amenities, public and private," writes a Bristol employer, "are linked to the daywork system. Even TV and radio, where one would think it simple to run recorded programmes in the morning and very late evening, are geared to dayworkers, and the popular programmes are all at peak listening periods." Another, from east London, refers to the "social penalties incurred by being a shiftworker in a daywork community"; sporting, social and recreational events all being timed to cater for majority attendances. The need for improved nursery, shopping and transport facilities are also mentioned in this connection.

In an earlier section dealing with domestic responsibility reference was made to the pressures brought to bear on the shiftworker by his wife and family. Implicit in these last paragraphs is the influence also exerted by a man's friends, workmates and neighbours and by the whole community in which he lives. Little encouragement is likely to be given to the potential shiftworker if his hours of work are considered to downgrade the status of his job. "People here tend to look askance at a night worker," a manager from an agricultural area in Berkshire reported. And from north Staffordshire comes an account of landladies refusing accommodation to men working shift hours. The manager supplying this last piece of information admits that men working shifts may make inconvenient lodgers, but considers that discrimination of this kind is based more on the unfavourable social significance attached to shiftworking. Little progress is likely to be made, he concludes, "until society in general moves away from the concept that shiftworking is abnormal." Other writers support this view and consider the extension of shiftworking to any significant degree to be very much a community matter.

EDUCATION AND SKILL LEVEL

In general it is more difficult to get skilled men and higher grades of worker to accept shiftwork. The higher a man's education or skill level, the lower is likely to be his level of satisfaction with shifts. For a group of power plant operators in the United States (Mott, 1965) liking for shiftwork was negatively related to both education and skill. This was attributed to different levels of aspiration and of expectations from the job among members of the sample. Among Dutch workers (van Loon, 1958) there was greater objection to nightwork among those of higher intelligence and those from the upper educational and social groups. Interference with social and educational activities was the main cause of dissatisfaction here.

In this country Marris (1964) has suggested that to the middle-class person shiftwork may seem not only inconvenient but un-dignified. "One of the most valued middle-class privileges," he writes, "is that of getting out of bed an hour later than the rest of the population, and since few professional workers are under economic pressure to work shifts, an industrial manager working unusual hours will find himself in a much smaller minority among his friends than would a manual worker."

The financial factor is clearly involved here. The greater a man's earnings the less need will there be to earn more through additional shift allowances. Thus the "same" shift premium of, say, 20 per cent for all grades is likely to have less incentive value to a man earning £30 a week than to a man earning £15 a week. In this way willingness to work shifts is probably broadly related to rates of pay in much the same way as differences in amounts of overtime working are so related (Shepherd and Walker, 1958).

NATIONALITY

Certain groups of workers labelled by their place, or supposed place, of origin, were specifically mentioned by management in interview as being more willing to work shifts (see Appendix 6). These included coloured immigrant groups (African, Indian, Pakistani, West Indian), Maltese, Irish and Welsh, constituting what in one factory was called "a cosmopolitan workforce attracted by good wages." A Leicester firm named Indian, Polish and Czech workers as being "more prepared to put up with the inconvenience of working nights." A textile firm in South-West England had Italian women working a double-day shift when "it is virtually impossible to recruit women locally." ("But the trouble with Italians on shift-work," in the opinion of one company (CBI, 1968) "is that they like their wives to be working at the same time. If that proves impossible they would rather work daywork.") In London 80 per cent of one food company's unskilled permanent night shift was made up of African and West Indian workers, many of whom were said to take up shiftwork "simply to tide themselves over until they find a suitable daywork job."

It is unlikely that there is anything about such national, or supposedly national, groups which makes them basically different in their attitudes to shiftwork or more adaptable to it. It is much more likely that the financial advantages of shiftworking may offer a special inducement to sections of the working community whose job opportunities are restricted.

THE TIME FACTOR

Acceptance of shiftwork for a limited period only is also a feature which may be briefly considered at this point. Workers who would not consider shift employment on a permanent basis may find shiftwork tolerable if required to adopt it temporarily during occasions of heavy production demand, or periodically during a firm's busy season.

A worker may also be willing to go on to shifts for a limited period as a stepping stone to another job—for instance, if a period of service on shifts is made a condition of supervisory training.

Very commonly, too, a man may be willing to work shifts in order to earn extra money to pay for a specific object, for example, the deposit on a house, the instalments on a car, even to set up in a small way in business on his own account. McDonald (1958) considered that most men had short term economic goals in mind when embarking on permanent nightwork, and that when these were achieved they were satisfied to transfer to lower paying day jobs. For some, however, earnings gradually became translated into a higher general standard of living, giving rise to fresh economic goals and providing continuing reasons for staying on shifts. [McDonald suggests that shiftwork offers one of the few ways available to the unskilled industrial worker of achieving the material standards of middle-class status. But the pursuit of upward social mobility could lead to a rejection of shiftwork if daywork hours are seen as characteristic of a middle-class way of life.]

But a worker who originally embarked upon shiftworking without reservations about his likely length of service on shifts may find that there are limits to his tolerance of this type of work. One firm reports:

Another problem that is beginning to occur in this six year old factory is that, after a while, people get tired of continuous shiftworking and inquire about the possibility of day work with overtime. It seems that for the first three or four years the worker accepts the inconvenience of shiftworking quite readily, but boredom with this arrangement of hours eventually creates a degree of dissatisfaction

Attitudes change through time for the same worker. Response to shiftwork will vary as he grows older, marries, has children; as his financial responsibilities increase or diminish; as his state of health improves or deteriorates. It must again be stressed that we are not dealing in this book with mutually exclusive categories—shiftwork and non-shiftwork, shiftworkers and non-shiftworkers, those who like shifts and those who do not. A man who willingly accepts a shift arrangement of work at one point in his life may be strongly motivated against it at another.

OTHER FACTORS

Other factors which may influence attitudes to shiftworking include the level of shift payment relative to that for daywork; a man's previous experience on various types of shift; his leisure interests outside the workplace, including whether he runs a second job; and the distance and ease of the journey between home and work. Also important is whether the use of shifts in a company is thought by workers to be governed primarily by technical necessity or economic advantage.

Personal, social and organisational factors interact to an extent which makes generalisations about attitudes to shiftwork dangerous. In certain situations it may be possible to point to one factor or another which appears to dominate. But, as many a research worker has pointed out, wherever there is categorisation there are exceptions. Nowhere is this more true than in the field of shiftwork.

ELEVEN

Effects of Shiftwork
on the Individual Employee

How does shiftwork influence domestic arrangements and family life, leisure and social activities? Does it affect a worker's eating and sleeping habits? What are the physical demands arising from shift hours; is shiftwork "unhealthy?" What degree of adaptation is necessary when a shiftworker has to change from "normal" day-work? This is the type of question which will be considered in the present chapter.

FAMILY AND SOCIAL EFFECTS

If, after half a lifetime of leaving home each morning at 08 15 and returning from work at 17 30, a man is suddenly transferred to shiftwork, it is hardly likely that his life outside his job will remain unaffected. Nevertheless, one cannot generalise that shiftwork always has a disrupting effect upon family and social life. Shiftwork *can* have this effect, and frequently does: but it does not of necessity do so. The influence upon family life and domestic arrangements, and upon social life and leisure activities, depends first upon the features of the shift system and secondly upon the particular characteristics and circumstances of the individual concerned.

Accordingly, shiftwork can be an advantage to a man or it can be burdensome. It can enable him to see more, or less, of his wife and family. It can enable him more easily to follow his leisure interests, just as it can hinder him from enjoying them.

In Taylor's study of oil refinery workers (Taylor, 1969) 76 per cent of the men stated that shiftwork adversely affected their social life, and 59 per cent their family life. Yet presumably, since overall these workers made up a satisfied group, the advantages of shiftwork outweighed its disadvantages, and a satisfactory adjustment had been made. The conditions of few jobs—even single-shift, daytime jobs—require no adjustment at all.

Adjustment has to be made not only by the worker himself, but by his wife and family. Shiftwork can place an additional strain upon a wife, in her physical relationship with her husband, in the extent to which she may have to be alone in the house, in the special responsibilities it may place upon her in the upbringing of children, in the disruption it may cause to domestic routine. On this last point difficulties in providing meals at unusual hours, and in getting on with household chores when the husband is at home and trying to sleep, can create particular problems. With an alternating day and night system in mind, Brown (1959) commented that "the interference with her work was more a serious annoyance to the housewife than restrictions on her own social life."

Certain shift systems can present particular difficulties. In a letter to the London police force newspaper, *The Job*, (27 February 1970) a police constable's wife criticises the nine-week shift rota (three weeks of which are spent on nights) worked by her husband as "barbaric." This writer sees the curtailment of social life as "an accepted drawback and not ruinous," but feels that the stress of spending three weeks with virtually no contact between husband and wife can be damaging to a marriage. She argues in favour of a five-week rota with only one week of night duty at a time, which already operates in some police divisions.

The spread of shiftworking appears to be providing fresh scope for comic stories on the sexual theme. For example, the *Daily Sketch* (1 August 1970) under the headline, "Pints of 'love potion' at a 6 a.m. pub," describes how Lincolnshire steelworkers, coming off night shift, are now able to drink at a pub with an early morning licence, and lightheartedly reports wives' reactions to husbands who come home "too sexy for so early in the day." Entertaining as such stories are, it would be a pity if they in any way masked the very real difficulties in the marriage relationship to which unusual hours of work can lead.

With regard to the general level of success in marriage and cohesiveness in a family, it is doubtful whether shiftwork as such ever "undermined" a marriage. Husband and wife relationships can flourish in the most unfavourable circumstances, just as they can break down when externally everything appears to be in their favour. On this point Mott (1965) concludes that "marital happiness is less sensitive to environmental influences, such as those produced by shiftwork, and is more tied to personality factors." A Norwegian source (Bruusgaard, 1969) reports that no increased divorce rate among shiftworkers has been found.

The extent to which a shiftwork rota interferes with leisure and social activities outside the family depends upon the nature of these interests and whether they are tied to time of day in a way which is determined by a dominantly single-shift, daytime economy. Television viewing, drinking in pubs and clubs, and Saturday afternoon sport are activities most frequently quoted as causing "deprivation" among shiftworkers. And the so-called solitary activities, such as fishing, gardening and making money in a second job are those most often cited as best fitting in with shiftworking schedules.

There is a danger here of seeing different "types" of worker, for example, the isolated introvert and the social extrovert, as being more or less suited to shiftwork routines. But this, as so much else in discussion of shiftworking, is an oversimplification. Supping a pint or cheering on the City can be lonely activities; just as belonging to a fishing club or running an allotment can be among the most companionable and matey forms of behaviour.

Shiftwork routines affect not only hours spent on the job, but the duration and distribution of free time away from work. And the extent to which shift arrangements contribute to a man's satisfaction / dissatisfaction at home and at leisure has repercussions on his performance on the job and on his relationships at work. This highlights the importance of those shiftwork studies which have not restricted their inquiries to the workplace.

Investigating the social problems which arose from the introduction of multiple shifts, Hilda Brown (1959) interviewed her informants at home. And Olive Banks (1956), looking at the effects of a change in shift arrangements from discontinuous to continuous work, talked to the wives of shiftworkers, again in their own homes. Such types of investigation pose their own special problems, not the least of which is the much greater time involved in running informants to earth, compared with the more straightforward interviewing of a "captive" factory population. But such investigations can be extremely valuable in the kind of material which they yield.

THE PHYSIOLOGY OF SHIFTWORKING:
24-HOUR RHYTHMS

The physiological aspects of shiftwork are concerned with bodily functions which show a rhythmical pattern of activity within each period of roughly 24 hours. "Circadian" (equals circa diem) is a term applied to this rhythmical 24-hour functioning. [For a short and readable account of this subject the reader should look at "Circadian rhythms and shift workers," J N Mills: *Transactions of the Society of Occupational Medicine* (1967), *17*, 5–7. For a longer and detailed account, with 253 references, by the same author, "Human circadian rhythms," *Physiol Review* (1966), *46*, 128 is recommended. See also "Diurnal rhythms in human physiological processes," *Report of the Medical Research Council*, October 1963 to March 1965, Cmnd. 2787, HMSO, London.]

Among these physiological and biological variables which show a 24-hours' cycle are body temperature, blood pressure, heart and respiration rates, digestion, bloodsugar level, the excretion of urine and the mineral content of the urine. All these functions are at their highest level during the hours of daylight when a person is normally up and about, and at their lowest after dark when he is normally asleep.

Body temperature is the cycle most often quoted, the first systematically observed and perhaps the most readily measurable. From its lowest point early in the morning about dawn, body temperature rises sharply until it reaches a plateau about midday. This is followed by a further slight rise to a peak in the late afternoon or early evening, when it again falls. (Figure 4.)

Interest in body temperature fluctuations has a long history. This phenomenon was investigated in Austrian bakers in 1913, and in men in the same occupational group in Germany as early as 1881. The topic also features in the First World War studies of the Health of Munition Workers' Committee, and in the investigation of industrial fatigue by physiological methods initiated by the Home Office at the same date.

There is a relationship between body temperature, time of day and the activity/rest cycle and performance. In general, performance is at its best when the body is most active and body temperature at its highest.

In the laboratory various aspects of performance have been

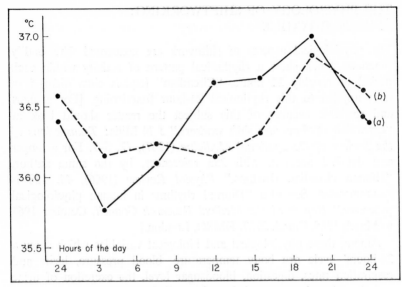

FIGURE 4   BODY TEMPERATURE CURVES
(a) Normal curve and (b) flattened curve achieved
by the same subject during night shift
(*Adapted from J H van Loon, 1963*)

studied during the normal waking period. Kleitman and his associates
(1963 showed a relationship between simple tasks involving
muscular activity—for instance, dealing cards—and time of day.
Over the period 07 00 – 23 00 both speed and accuracy showed a
marked rhythm, with lowest efficiency early in the morning and
late at night, and highest efficiency in the middle of the day. Reaction
time was also found to be related to time of day and body temperature. The ability to respond promptly was best in the middle
of the day, when body temperature was highest, and worst in the
morning and late evening, when body temperature was lower.

Blake (1967b), using naval personnel as subjects, measured performance on a variety of tasks between the hours of 08 00 – 21 00,
and found a variation in performance, with efficiency improving
throughout the day. This trend was closely associated with the movement of the body temperature curve. This author observed: "The
fact that the results were based on relatively large samples of subjects, and that the effect is observable in a number of tasks ranging
from novel laboratory tests to a familiar, highly practised operation,

suggests that the the time of day effect has wide generality."

Time of day effects upon performance have also been investigated in the laboratory over the complete period of 24 hours. Kleitman and Jackson (1950), for example, tested US navy recruits during various routines around the clock on "blind flying" in a Link trainer, colour naming and reaction time. They found in general that the higher the body temperature, the better the performance.

More recently, in this country, Colquhoun, Blake and Edwards (1968a; 1968b; 1969) have carried out a series of experimental studies of "shiftwork" routines over the 24 hours, and have shown that certain aspects of performance on various "mental" tasks (simple calculation, detection of auditory signals, for example) follow the fluctuations of body temperature whether or not this is strictly in phase with the sequence of day and night. Body temperature, as these workers point out, is thus a predictor of performance efficiency. [The first of the papers by these authors (1968a) includes a short and useful review of the literature in this field.]

In the "real life" situation an example of performance following the temperature curve is provided by Browne's (1949) study of the day and night performance of WAAF teleprinter switchboard operators. Response time to a flashing call light was measured over a period of three months for three-shift teams around the clock. Performance improved through the day from 09 00 to midday and remained fairly constant until 17 00: it then fell until 04 00, and after a transient improvement reached its lowest value at 08 00.

In a study of three-shift operatives in a Swedish gasworks (Bjernor, Holm and Swensson, 1955) whose job it was to read figures from meters, make simple calculations and enter the results in ledgers, the greatest number of mistakes was made during the night shift. These authors conclude: "The fact that the same type of variation is shown year after year by different persons and is seen in different series shows that the degree of wakefulness fluctuates in a highly consistent fashion during the 24 hours of the day and night."

The body temperature curve is not constant for everyone. Marked individual variations occur in its rise and fall and this may be paralleled by individual variations in efficiency at different times of day. Kleitman (1963) refers to "morning" and "evening" types who reach their peak somewhat earlier or later in the waking period.

There may also be an association between body temperature and personality. Blake (1967a) found that body temperature of the more introverted rose more rapidly in the early morning, and started to fall sooner in the late evening. He concluded that the performance differences between introverts and extraverts which have been found in various studies may be explained by an association between personality types, body temperature and time of day.

Because body temperature and performance are related it does not follow that nighttime performance will automatically be worse than that on days. In the factory situation the picture may be confounded by the intervention of environmental and motivational factors. Another factor to be taken into account, of course, is the capacity of the worker to adapt, physiologically, to new working schedules. If a man who normally works by day and sleeps by night reverses this pattern, habitual physiological rhythms will at first persist. But, in theory at least, these patterns may undergo changes through time which will bring them into line with the reversed order of activity and rest. Thus, again in theory, a man might become so adapted to work at night and daytime sleep that body temperature and efficiency would reach their peak early in the morning, the time at which they are normally at their lowest point.

In practice, however, such inversion is not a simple matter. While there may be a tendency towards inversion of the temperature curve, there is considerable individual variation. Murrell (1965) quotes a Dutch study in which most men were said to have achieved inversion in 1–3 days. For most factory workers it took place within a week, according to Teleky (1943), although this period might be longer in the case of less physical work.

But for many a week seems inadequate. In the Swedish gasworkers' study previously quoted (Bjerner, Holm and Swensson, 1955), no improvement in performance was noted at the end of a period of seven successive night shifts, as compared with the beginning, as might have been expected had adaptation taken place.

In a more recent study (Pawlowska-Skyba et al, 1968) of women workers on a three-shift system in a Polish textiles factory, in which pulse rate and blood pressure were measured, in addition to body temperature, the authors report that during a weekly shift period "no changes that could be interpreted as the adaptation of workers to the night shift were observed."

It now seems doubtful whether complete inversion of the body temperature curve is ever achieved outside of artificial or unusual surroundings. Under laboratory conditions where it is possible to control the whole environment, and in certain isolated working environments such as those of submarine crews, it has been shown that body temperature rhythm can be synchronised with different time schedules. Occasionally in the normal workaday world one meets cases of nightworkers who have been on shift for so long that they do appear completely to reverse their social habits and stick to an inverted routine even during their free time, sleeping by day and being up and about by night. Under the caption, "Night owl Ernie can't get used to day life," the *Daily Mail* (20 April 1970) reported the case of a retired mineworker who, after 49 years of night shifts, was having to occupy himself with odd jobs about the house at night because "I keep nodding off if I try to stay awake during the day." Nightwork can, indeed, become so much of a habit that one nightworker admitted to "a fear of day work" (de la Mare and Walker, 1968). In such cases, presumably, some permanent shift of the body temperature rhythm may have occurred. Ordinarily, however, industrial shiftworkers continue to live in an environment geared to a daywork routine and in part at least to pattern their behaviour on this.

Observations on three Dutch workers (van Loon, 1963) showed no inversion of the temperature curve during a night shift period of several weeks in succession, but only a modification or flattening of the curve. (Figure 4.) This report suggests that complete inversion of the body temperature curve cannot be expected if there is not a complete inversion of usual day- and night-time behaviour. Most men on nightwork continue to participate to some extent in the normal daytime life going on about them.

In the opinion of a German observer (Rutenfranz, 1967) recent evidence suggests that no inversions of periodical physiological functions take place in man as a result of nightwork, even if continued for a number of months. Such inversions, in this view, should consequently not be sought, but be avoided as far as possible.

What are the practical implications of these findings for the planning of shift rotas? On the assumption that adaptation, in the sense of inversion or adaptation of the body temperature and other rhythms takes some time to achieve, and since this period of adaptation may be one of special physiological strain for the night shiftworker (Teleky, 1943; Lobban, 1965), a number of authors have recommended longer periods at a stretch on the night shift, with less frequent changes.

An early Home Office report (Kent, 1916) was "in favour of lengthening the period over which the day or night shift is worked by individual men, in order that the advantages derived from the adjustment might be enjoyed for a longer time." The Final Report of the Health of Munition Workers' Committee (1918) recommends infrequent change "on physiological grounds." Teleky (1943) suggests four-weekly change for factory workers.

Weekly change, according to this type of argument, is unsuitable because no sooner has a man achieved some degree of adaptation to the night shift than it is time for him to switch back to days.

Long periods on nightwork, however, defeat their own purpose if they are broken up by days off at the weekend or in midweek. A further characteristic of the body temperature rhythm is that in contrast to the difficulties that may be experienced in achieving inversion, reversion occurs as soon as there is a return to the normal pattern of daytime activity and nighttime sleep. From the point of view of adaptation, therefore, long periods on nights would only be effective if they were worked without a break, or if nightworkers retained their pattern of daytime sleep and nighttime activity during their time off.

As a possible solution to this problem much attention has been given in the last few years to the possible advantages of rapidly rotating shifts such as the $2 \times 2 \times 2$ or the $3 \times 2 \times 2$, thus "discarding the ideal of complete inversion of the temperature curve" (Wedderburn, 1967). The theory of this is to work such short periods on nights as to allow no time for the disturbance of physiological rhythms which tend to occur in periods of three nights or more, and to follow each spell on nights with a rest period of at least two days for recovery. Evidence is limited about what happens to the body temperature curve in practice under such rotas, but it has been suggested (Permanent Commission and International Association on Occupational Health, 1969) that circadian rhythms may still be significantly disturbed in such a system.

Another possibility, described by Murrell (1965), is that of a continuously rotating nine-hour system in which four night shifts are worked at a time. The first of these begins at 18 00, and starting time gets progressively three hours later over the four shifts, so that the fourth in the series begins at 03 00. "Obviously," this writer observes, "there can be no question of inversion taking place under this system."

Whatever the physiological merits of such a system—and evidence about what happens in practice is lacking—its social acceptance is likely to be limited. In planning shiftwork there are social as well as biological factors to be taken into account, as the Health of Munition Workers' Committee emphasised over 50 years ago. In the light of physiological evidence, or theory, rotas can be devised which aim at minimising disturbance and facilitating adaptation. But what is physiologically desirable may not be practically feasible or socially acceptable.

Such considerations also apply to various other suggestions which have been put forward regarding the timing of shifts throughout the 24 hours. One proposal, for example, to avoid abrupt change which may be damaging to wellbeing and efficiency, is to calculate the working day as 25 hours, divided into 3 shifts of 8 hours 20 minutes each. A man would work, say, 08 00 – 16 20 on the first day, 09 00 – 17 20 on the second day and so on. Daywork would thus gradually change into nightwork and nightwork into daywork, a full cycle being completed in 25 days (Eranko, 1957).

Other proposals to avoid the type of night shift which is concentrated during that part of the 24-hour rhythm when temperature is normally lowest, and sleepiness greatest, are to time shifts 04 00– noon, noon–20 00 and 20 00 – 04 00, (Kleitman, 1963) or 10 00 – 18 00, 18 00 – 02 00 and 02 00 – 10 00 (Andlaver, 1960).

Such arrangements of hours may involve a "more physiological timing," but would be difficult to implement except in an artificial or isolated community. In the practical, workaday situation some kind of compromise has to be achieved. As de la Mare and Walker (1967) point out: "Factories must avoid the rota which is perfect for physiological adaptation, but ignores the social factors, or the one which permits maximum social satisfaction, but ignores the probable effect on the shiftworker's health."

In this discussion of the physiology of shiftworking we have talked about only one rhythm, that of body temperature. Even if achieved, modification of the body temperature curve may not be accompanied by modification, or modification at the same rate, of other functions. To take only one example, the excretion of water, sodium and chloride in the urine may adjust fairly quickly, but the excretion of potassium take very much longer (Simpson and Lobban, 1967).

"This whole subject of human circadian rhythms," writes one

177

authority on the subject (Mills, 1967), "is more satisfying to the academic than to the practical man, since we know few of the answers; we do not know if these rhythms are of any importance, and there is still plenty to discover."

Such words may bring cold comfort to practising managers. But at least it is important that they should know the present state of play.

PROBLEMS OF SLEEP

A shiftworker on a rota involving nights is unlikely to know very much about variations in his deep body temperature or in the mineral content of his urine. He may be only too well aware, however, of a failure to adapt his habits of sleep to a new work/rest routine.

Complaints about quantity and quality of sleep

Complaints about sleep from shiftworkers are reported in many studies. Such complaints concern the *amount* of sleep obtained during the day, which is generally thought to be less; the *quality* of sleep which is thought to be inferior and affected by noise and distractions of various kinds; and the *effects* thought to be consequent upon sleep difficulties—feelings of fatigue, of general malaise, of being below par.

In the Norwegian paper industry more complaints regarding sleep were found among shift- than dayworkers. (Bruusgaard, 1949). In another industry in the same country sleeping difficulty was a primary factor in the case of 84 per cent of shiftworkers who had been transferred to daywork for medical reasons (Aanonsen, 1964). In Rumania disturbance of sleep after the night shift was reported by 58 per cent of 110 control board operators on a $2 \times 2 \times 2$ system in power stations (Gavrilescu *et al*, 1966).

In this country, 37 per cent of Wyatt and Marriott's (1953) sample of alternate day- and nightworkers claimed that they had less than six hours' sleep. And many of those who reported themselves as satisfied with the amount of sleep they were getting qualified their approval by saying that it was less refreshing than night time sleep. In Japan, on the basis of a survey carried out in 1700 factories (Morioka, 1969), it was concluded that daytime sleep during the night shift period was generally shorter, and thought by shiftworkers themselves to be inadequate to allow recovery from fatigue.

Reasons for sleeping difficulties most often quoted concern, first, "dislocation of the ordinary habits of life," (Health of Munition Workers Committee, 1916) and the repercussions arising from this: " 'nerves,' restlessness, fatigue and bodily discomfort caused by reversal of normal habits" (Wyatt and Marriott, 1953).

Noise is frequently mentioned: ". . . street noises, such as people talking, children playing and traffic. Quite a number said they were disturbed by the wireless next door or in the room above" (Wyatt, 1945b). Scandinavian investigations in particular have stressed the noise factor: ". . . street traffic, trains, factory noises, children at play, etc., and noises in the house, from the kitchen, children, water pipes, radio, etc." (Thiis-Evensen, 1958).

The location and quality of housing is clearly a factor here. Aanonsen (1964) found that whereas only 18 per cent of day men with inadequate housing conditions reported sleeping difficulties, this figure rose to 73 per cent in the case of shiftworkers similarly housed.

In a Dutch study (van Loon, 1958) although daytime noises did not interfere to any appreciable extent with the sleep of night shiftworkers, there were still complaints about sleeping difficulties from 30 per cent of those involved.

Individual differences again occur here. Some workers report themselves unaffected or only moderately so: "A few men were able to sleep 'like a log' whatever the conditions" (Wyatt and Marriott, 1953). And in Wyatt's study of women on war work (Wyatt, 1945b), while 42 per cent gave "can't sleep well in daytime" as a reason for disliking shifts—far more than for any other reason for dislike—10 per cent of the sample actually included "can sleep well in daytime" among their reasons for liking nightwork.

Duration of sleep on different shift systems may vary

A recent Japanese study (Anon, 1969) has looked at this question. The median figure quoted for Japanese male workers as a whole is just under eight hours. Less than seven and half hours were recorded, however, by workers under an alternate day and night system, by those operating a seven-day continuous system with three crews only, and by men who worked an excessively long shift every other day. Equal, or greater-than-average, amounts of sleep were found among discontinuous three-shift workers and those operating continuous systems with four crews. It is of interest to note also, though it is not commented upon by the Japanese authors, that the order of rotation night–afternoon–morning in three-shift work appears to give a higher average amount of sleep than the order morning–afternoon–night.

Different turns of duty within a shift system may also provide varying opportunities for sleep. Among three-shift workers in a Polish hot strip rolling mill (Oginski, 1966) the greatest amount of sleep was obtained by those on the afternoon turn. There was little to choose between morning and night shift in this respect.

Compensation for lack of sleep

In a French study (Lille, 1967) it was found that although a weekly sleep deficit was regularly noted on nightwork, this was made up during the weekly periods of nocturnal sleep on daywork. Similar compensation has been shown on various types of shift rota.

Smith and Vernon (1928) used a sleep questionnaire on 200 women in four factories and found that on the morning shift it was the practice to rest in the afternoon, and on the late shift to stay in bed longer in the morning. And thus "...a deficiency of sleep during the week of morning shifts was usually compensated for during the week of afternoon shifts." Evidence of HM Medical Inspector of Factories before a Departmental Committee in 1935 suggested that compensation on the later shift for loss of sleep on the early shift gave double-day workers more time in bed on average than dayworkers. Hilda Brown (1959) found that men on double-days had about six hours in bed while working the morning shift, and nine hours while on the afternoon shift, although some men mentioned having an additional hour or two's sleep in the afternoon after working in the morning. This study was characterised by a lack of complaints about insufficient sleep.

More recently, Tune (1969) has compared the sleep of a group of 52 three-shift workers and a group of dayworkers, matched for age and occupation, over a period of 10 weeks. He found that shift-workers took a higher average duration of sleep per 24 hours than dayworkers, about 16 minutes. This was achieved by their sleeping about an hour longer during their off-duty periods than during their working periods—an increase due to their taking longer naps during off-duty. Sleep was also significantly less disturbed at this time.

How disadvantageous it may be to a man to have to "catch up" on his sleep in this way, and to do so by a series of short naps outside the main sleep period, is not yet certain. A normal main period of sleep taken at night consists of various stages, and if this main period is shortened and compensated for by briefer spells, shift-workers may be deprived of specific types of sleep, for example, the Rapid Eye Movement (REM) dreaming state. As Tune points out: "The total duration of sleep achieved may well be of less importance than the amount of time spent on various levels of sleep."

In some shift situations there may even be no "catching up," accumulated "sleep debts" apparently remaining unpaid. In a Swedish study (Bjerner, Holm and Swensson, 1948) of a three-shift system, average sleep per 24 hours over the whole cycle was 6.5 hours for shiftworkers, against 7.5 hours for day men during the same period. Again, de la Mare and Walker (1968) found that average "time spent in bed"—that is, not taking account of additional naps—for men on permanent night duty was half an hour less (7.2 hours) than for permanent day men and those on a rotating shift cycle (7.7 hours).

Individual differences in recovery rate
Not only are there individual differences in the amount of sleep required, and in the capacity to sleep at unusual times, but also in the ability to recover from any sleep loss that may occur at night.

An investigation in Czechoslovakia (World Health Organisation, 1969) examined such recovery time after nightwork among a group of railway workers. In 80 per cent of cases a free period of 24 hours after night shift was an adequate interval in which to compensate for sleep loss. But the remaining 20 per cent needed an additional 24 hours to make up the deficit.

Difficulties of measuring duration of sleep
While there is evidence of differing amounts of sleep under different arrangements of working hours, care has to be exercised in inter-preting this, and certainly in comparing the evidence from one study with that from another. Information about sleep is difficult to collect because outside the laboratory one is largely dependent on the accuracy of self-recording techniques. [One recent exception to this is a French investigation (Foret and Lantin, 1970) of long distance train drivers whose irregular sleeping hours were measured by electro-encephalograph.]

Methods of collecting information have ranged from simple

questions during interview about "how many hours sleep you usually get," to carefully designed diaries and sleep charts in which, over a period of weeks, the subject makes a daily note of his hours of sleep. Here again, is he to record time "asleep," "in bed," "resting"? Are short naps in front of the television, on the bus, after lunch, to be included or not? Finally, recording itself, even for the most conscientious subject, is not an easy matter. How is he to assess a main sleeping period in which he may have slept soundly for several hours, lain awake for half an hour, dozed fitfully for perhaps another hour? Underestimation is another problem. "Few admit to being able to have as much sleep as they like, and many attribute its lack to external pressures" (Masterton, 1965b). Overconscientiousness in recording, on the other hand, may even affect sleep! Most self-recording must be accepted as an approximation. A form of sleep chart is best which is kept at least over one complete shift cycle and which combines a quantitative estimate with some kind of assessment of the quality of sleep. These reservations should be borne in mind when interpreting research results.

Possible effects of sleep loss
It is difficult to be unequivocal about the effects of sleep loss. A Home Office report of 1916 (Kent 1916) suggested the "inadequacy of rest obtained by day" as a possible cause of the greater fatigue developed at night (as measured by various tests of reaction time, acuity of sight and hearing) under an alternating day and night scheme. And among women on war work Wyatt (1945b) noted an association between curtailment of sleep and increased sickness absence. But both these studies were carried out during war years when other factors might reasonably be supposed to have contributed to workers' fatigue.

A considerable amount of work has been carried out in the laboratory into the effect of sleep loss on performance, though this has been much more concerned with periods of total deprivation up to a maximum of about 100 hours, rather than with the partial loss that is characteristic of shiftworkers.

Kleitman (1963) quotes a number of studies which illustrate that the deterioration in performance which follows loss of sleep is far from being general or systematic. As well as differences between individuals, much depends on the exact nature of the task being performed, on whether, for example, it is simple or complex.

But closely interwoven with this element of task difficulty, as Wilkinson (1964, 1965) has shown, is the degree of interest which the task holds for the person concerned. Thus the most vulnerable tasks can be the simple, uninteresting ones, while a complex task may be little affected by loss of sleep "if it is complex in an interesting and rewarding way" (Wilkinson, 1964).

There are parallels in such experimental work to the nature of industrial tasks. In general it may be said that lack of sleep is likely to affect simple and repetitive rather than demanding jobs, primarily because the former are lacking in interest and incentive. But the worker suffering from lack of sleep will respond to stimulation whether in the job itself or in the working environment.

Other practical considerations are that prolonged work is likely to be more affected than that which is carried out intermittently over short periods. Sedentary jobs are also more vulnerable than those involving some degree of physical movement. Sleep deprivation is likely to influence accuracy rather than speed, and to result in errors of omission rather than of overactivity. The impact of sleep loss on performance is also greater at night than during the day (Corcoran, 1961; Wilkinson, 1965).

Although some performance after-effects of sleep deprivation in the laboratory have been reported (Wilkinson, 1965), the subject usually appears to be "back to normal" after a recovery sleep of 9–12 hours. On the basis of a study of overworked hospital medical staff, it was concluded (Masterton, 1965) that: "There is no knowledge allowing us to say that sleep deficits have a deleterious effect on life expectancy or general well-being." In view of the fact that the mean daily ration of sleep fell as low as 4.7 hours over 78 days in the case of one house surgeon in this study, another author (Wedderburn, 1967) is moved to observe somewhat wryly that "it is unlikely that many industrial shiftworkers, simply because of the demands of the job, regularly deprive themselves of sleep to this extent."

Reports that nightwork and sleep deficiency can produce irritability and inter-personal frictions at work are not uncommon, and behaviour of this kind is to some extent mirrored in laboratory studies of sleep deprivation.

Suggestions for dealing with sleep problems

Since sleeping difficulties have been shown to be related to *housing conditions* some Scandinavian companies have built special sound-proofed and air conditioned dormitories for their shiftworkers. These, however, are reported to have met with little favour (Andlauer, 1960). In Japan, too, rest rooms are provided in some factories where night shiftworkers can have the opportunity of undisturbed sleep (Rutenfranz, 1967). Special housing for shiftworkers is not a practical solution to the problem in this country, although better housing and the wider use of sound-proofing techniques would benefit shiftworkers, as they would the population as a whole. There may be certain groups of workers, however, in semi-artificial or isolated situations for whom special sleeping accommodation might usefully be provided.

Modification of starting/stopping times may help. In Sweden it was found (Bjerner, Holm and Swensson, 1948) that for three-shift workers with a 06 00 – 14 00, 14 00 – 22 00, 22 00 – 06 00 arrangement the average duration of sleep per 24 hours for the week in which the night shift was worked was 5.21 hours. When shift starting times were changed to 04 00, noon and 20 00, this average rose to 5.78 hours. A 04 00 changeover, however, is unlikely to meet with much approval.

Of wider application are suggestions to *rearrange shift succession* so as to give more favourable opportunities for sleep. With difficulties of sleep in mind some writers recommend the avoidance of continuous night work altogether (Morioka, 1969). Others suggest rotas which ensure additional rest after the night shift, or a minimum of 24 hours without working to give time for recovery (Vieux, Carré and de Monès, 1962; Rutenfranz, 1967). Forty-eight hours is considered preferable (World Health Organisation, 1969).

Another suggestion is to *use some form of selection*, keeping off night shift those who find most difficulty in adapting to it or whose sleep needs are greatest. Another possibility is to *use the quota system of work* wherever practicable, fixing in advance the amount of work to be done during the night shift and allowing men to sleep or to go home when they have finished. Sleeping on the night shift at present appears to be regarded by many managements as akin to high treason. There are various jobs in which short spells of sleep might well be permitted. (They may already be taken unofficially.) In one refrigeration plant it was official practice to work an hour and rest an hour. During rest periods the men used to "thaw out" in the boiler room, and one of the night shift foreman's main duties was to make periodic sorties upon them to make sure that they stayed awake. Such a policy makes little sense.

Finally, of course, there remains the education of the shiftworker himself in *simple rules of sleep hygiene*. At present one reason for sleep difficulties on shiftwork must surely be the failure to adopt regular and reasonable patterns of rest/sleep/activity in off-duty periods.

EATING HABITS AND PROBLEMS

In addition to sleeping problems, difficulties concerning appetite and digestion are also commonly reported by shiftworkers because of meals taken at unusual hours. At times these seem to override problems of sleep. Such difficulties mainly concern loss of appetite and enjoyment of meals, together with disturbance of the digestion and normal elimination of body wastes.

After changing to nightwork 27 per cent of men in one British investigation (Wyatt and Marriott, 1953) reported that it took from 1–3 days to settle down to new mealtimes: 12 per cent needed 4–6 days to adapt and 24 per cent even longer. But 37 per cent considered themselves to be immune from such effects. The proportion of men who claimed to adjust at once to new mealtimes after changing back from night- to daywork was 61 per cent. Most of the remainder took up to six days, but a few took longer. In a study in two automated electric power plants in the USA (Mann and Hoffman, 1960), adjustment time varied from one to four days, with just under half of the sample claiming that four days were needed.

Again, differences are found with type of shift. Complaints are much fewer on double-days. With schedules which include nightwork, reports of disorders of the appetite and digestion appear more common where there is a change of shift than with stable arrangements. Operators who had volunteered to work permanently on nights were asked by de la Mare and Walker (1968) to record meals and snacks when completing sleep charts. These authors report:

> The pattern of meal times ... gives support to the subjective reports that night workers were more satisfied with the convenience of their meal arrangements and less disturbed in appetite than the other rotas. Their meal

times are the most regular and ... whether the main
meal is taken in the middle of the working night or in the
middle of the day when off duty its timing varies little
from day to day

While there is no doubt that many men do suffer bodily discomfort when working on certain shifts, the method of collecting
information and the type of question asked in some interview/
questionnaire approaches may lead to a high proportion of digestive
"problems" being recorded. Moreover, if shiftwork is disliked this
may in itself lead to a high level of complaints. This applies equally
to complaints about sleep and about health generally.

Digestive troubles, as in the case of sleeping difficulties, may also
be due not so much to the effects of shiftwork itself, as to failure
to adopt regular habits within particular rotas.

A number of investigations have looked at the nutritional aspects
of meals taken on various types of shift system.

In a Czech study of miners on night shift (Ceizel, 1962), food was
found to be monotonous and consumed cold and "neither the
preparation nor biological value of this diet were of the standard
stipulated in literature on this subject."

Also in Czechoslovakia (Cirman and Hejda, 1964) the eating
habits of locomotive crews were studied. These men worked fewer
but longer shifts (12–18 hours) than is normal in industry, with
almost a third of their working time on nights. The calorie content
of their food was found to exceed their requirements, especially
as regards proteins and fats. The incidence of obesity (58 per cent)
and hypertension (32 per cent) was high.

Among French chemical workers (Debry, Girault, Lefort and
Thiebault, 1967) although there was no difference between the mean
calorie level for continuous shiftworkers and dayworkers, the normal
balance of meals and their content was affected on the shift routine.

Some rotas may mean that more meals are taken alone, rather
than with the family, and so may be eaten more hurriedly. The
consumption of tobacco and alcohol may also be affected.

HEALTH EFFECTS

To what extent can shiftwork, or certain forms of shiftwork, be
said to be unhealthy? This question has been asked for over a century
and is still unresolved.

"We do not find any difference in the health of those who work regularly by night and those who work by day," asserted an employer witness in the 1860s before the Children's Employment Commission. [Children's Employment Commission, 4th Report, 1865.] But the Commission itself was in no doubt about the harmful effects of nightwork upon children, mentioning particularly lack of daytime sleep and deprivation of sunlight. Nightwork had in fact been forbidden for those between 9 and 18 in certain trades as early as 1833.

The Final Report of the Health of Munition Workers' Committee (1918) makes no *specific* reference to shift or nightwork as "unhealthy," although for a variety of reasons it comes down heavily against nightwork:

> Even for men nightwork is open to serious objection. It is uneconomical owing to the higher charges for wages, lighting and heating. Lighting is generally inferior and supervision more difficult. Adequate sleep by day is difficult owing to dislocation of ordinary habits or from social causes. Social intercourse and recreation can hardly be obtained except by an undue curtailment of sleep. Continuation of education is generally impracticable. Finally it is unnatural to turn night into day

The Interim Report (Health of Munition Workers' Committee, 1917), however, speaks of "remotely injurious effects of permanent nightwork, effects which are not manifested until after a long latent period" as being worthy of investigation from a long-term point of view.

Wyatt and Marriott (1953) have no doubt on the subject. Concluding their paper on nightwork and shift change, they write:

> There is not the least doubt that nightwork is unpopular and, in the long run, is detrimental to health, efficiency, and the enjoyment of life. In every group of workers, some break down in health after a few weeks, months, or years of nightwork. These are the obvious casualties but it is reasonable to suppose that almost all workers are adversely affected in some degree and brought nearer to the point when the effects can no longer be ignored

The only solution, they suggest, is "the abolition of nightwork except in times of emergency and in certain continuous processes."

Against this, another IHRB investigator, Vernon (1940), states: "Men working permanently on shifts for the whole of their working lives, such as steel workers, do not appear to suffer in health as a result." And more recently, Raffle (1967) adds: "In spite of physiological considerations there is little evidence that shiftwork affects physical health."

In certain countries there is legislation making it clear that nightwork is to be avoided or guarded against. In the Netherlands nightwork on a permanent basis is not permitted, and in Japan twice yearly medical examination is required for night shiftworkers under labour standards law. In the latter country a loss of more than four kilograms of body weight over a short period of time is regarded as grounds for taking a worker off nightwork. Some factories supply milk and additional vitamins to nightworkers.

Our own factory visits yielded little information on the question of shiftwork and health. There were a couple of references to the nervous wear and tear involved in night shiftwork. For example, the physical and nervous strain of a long permanent shift of 13 hours (worked four nights one week and five the next) was mentioned by a northern textiles firm where distance travelled to work could mean a total daily absence from home of between 15 and 16 hours. And in the opinion of a Yorkshire iron and steel company nightwork could produce interpersonal frictions at work: "It would appear that the strain of the early hours magnifies any personal antipathies that may exist."

In the opinion of one industrial medical officer:

> There is no definite evidence in this factory that the disturbance of the diurnal rhythm resulting from shiftwork has any harmful effect on the normally healthy adult. There is little doubt, however, that a proportion of our three-shift workers eventually develop stress and psychosomatic symptoms. Investigation of such cases usually indicates that they have not adopted a realistic sleep-work-eat-relax rhythm. The commonest error is to indulge in excessive periods of recreation at the expense of sleep, but questioning also commonly shows that adequate sleep periods are not possible due to noise

and disturbance inside and outside the house. Married men may also meet latent resentment from their wives which affects their mental welfare

A London organisation, which used to carry out a second medical examination of its permanent nightworkers after a year's service on that shift, discontinued the practice when it found "no inherent risks of any consequence." But medical examinations are now being carried out on its "veterans" (five to six years' service). These have shown that such men have put on an average of half-a-stone in weight during their service on nights and there is "no evidence of their health being affected by their work." Their absence record is said to be satisfactory and their morale high.

There is plenty of evidence of the unhealthiness of shiftwork if one accepts the evidence of interviews, questionnaires and inventories in which shiftworkers themselves are required to report on their own symptoms and ailments.

Wyatt and Marriott (1953) state that feelings of fatigue are more widespread and severe on nightwork. Similarly in a Japanese study (Sakai and Kano, 1965) which assessed shiftworkers' subjective feelings of fatigue, using a standard form of inventory, such symptoms were more marked among nightworkers than dayworkers. Drowsiness and eyestrain, stiffness of the shoulders and tiredness of the body and limbs were particularly pronounced. In an investigation in Denmark (Bonnevie and Andersen, 1953, 1957 and 1960) 64 per cent of shiftworkers complained of nervous and digestive disorders compared with 24 per cent of day men. In the USA (Mott, 1965) a significantly higher level of complaints concerning sleeping, appetite and bowel difficulties were found among workers on night or rotating shifts. And in Finland (Hakkinen, 1966), where three-shift workers in an electricity plant were compared with a control group of dayworkers on the same kind of job, it was found that although the majority of workers in both groups reported themselves to be healthy, 70 per cent of shiftworkers said they experienced stomach pains and nervous troubles compared with only 40 per cent of dayworkers. The Finnish report calls these results "typical of those found in many shiftwork investigations."

To what extent can such subjective reports be relied on? An interesting variant of this type of investigation was carried out on 600 shiftworkers and twice this number of dayworkers in Holland

(Dirken, 1966), using a standardised inventory of 58 yes/no questions about health and general wellbeing. Of particular interest here was the fact that subjects were unaware of the investigator's interest in shiftwork. The declared aim was "the investigation of the subjectively-experienced health" of those concerned. Although a slightly lower level of general wellbeing (as measured by the number of complaints) was found among shiftworkers, no important complaints emerged as typical effects of shiftwork. Only one item—"home from work, falls asleep in chair"—scored consistently higher among those on shift. The main conclusion from this study is that "for subjective well-being in both its somatic and psychological aspects shiftwork can in general hardly be called a problem."

Not all investigations of the health aspects of shiftworking have confined themselves to shiftworkers' subjective reports. Use has also been made of medical examinations, sickness absence records, information from health insurance offices and other sources.

By such means as these Aanonsen (1964) in three Norwegian electrochemical plants compared groups of several hundred dayworkers (including men on double-days), continuous three-shift workers, and men on days who had previously had experience of shifts. He found no increased frequency among shiftworkers in any of three main categories of disorders (nervous, gastro-intestinal, and cardio-vascular). Also, as a whole, continuous shiftworkers had 30 per cent fewer days' absence from work both in a detailed one year's investigation and in a retrospective 13 years' study of the 51–65 age group. The shiftworkers also had fewer medical consultations. This author concludes that the main reasons for these results is that the shiftworkers represented "highly selected material ... with a capacity of adaptation and fitness for this form of industrial work, and—above all—that a continuous transfer had taken place of unsuitable labourers to other forms of work."

This tendency is also seen in another Norwegian study by Thiis-Evensen (1949; 1949, 1953 and 1958) who found, among nearly 2000 workers whose medical records he examined, virtually the same amount of illness between groups of shift- and dayworkers. As length of service increased, however, a relatively higher morbidity occurred among the day group, which again suggests a continuous process of selection at work. Evensen also found that workers who had followed a non-daywork routine for over 10 years had a significantly longer life-span after retirement than dayworkers. This is of particular interest in view of the assumption on the part of some workers that shiftwork is not only unhealthy, but reduces life expectancy.

In a four years' study of the sickness and other absence of workers at an Essex oil refinery, Taylor (1967) found that continuous three-shift men had consistently and significantly lower rates of sickness than did dayworkers in similar occupations. Age-related absence showed similar differences between the two categories. Taylor makes it clear that this difference in absence behaviour was not due to medical selection or to the transfer of unhealthy men to daywork on medical advice, but points out that a large element of self-selection was probably at work both in initial choice of hours and through the course of time.

As regards chronic illness, one point in particular needs comment. There is commonly thought to be an association between working on shifts and peptic ulceration. This is widely found in the literature. Wyatt and Marriott (1953) considered that, for some workers at least, change in meal times "may be an important factor in the aetiology of peptic ulcer." Andlauer (1960) claims that gastro-duodenal ulcers are significantly commoner among shiftworkers, and this he attributes to eating, drinking and smoking habits associated with shiftwork. In a Danish study (Bonnevie and Andersen, 1953, 1957 and 1960) clinical examination revealed 23 per cent of men on shifts with gastric disorders of medical signi-ficance compared with only 9 per cent of men on days, while peptic ulcers were diagnosed in 10 per cent of shiftworkers compared with 4 per cent of day men without shift experience. In the Norwegian paper industry (Bruusgaard, 1949), on a questionnaire basis, a greater tendency to peptic ulceration was found among both shiftworkers and those who had previously been engaged on shift rotas. Among employees working irregular hours on the Netherlands Railways (Ensing, 1969) the incidence of peptic ulcer appeared to be much higher than among those regularly working a daytime shift. In Sweden, Bjerner, Holm and Swensson (1948), using the records of health insurance offices, found a slightly higher, though statistically insignificant, incidence of ulcers among men on shifts. "The general impression in Sweden," according to the conclusions of a recent international symposium on night- and shiftwork (Permanent Com-mission and International Association on Occupational Health, 1969), "is still that the frequency of dyspeptic disorders is rather high among shiftworkers."

In the USA, Mott and his co-workers (1965), using a questionnaire approach, found the prevalence of ulcers to be higher among day and afternoon shiftworkers than among those on nights and rotating shifts. They suggest as a "strong possibility" that those on days and afternoons who claim to have ulcers may have developed these while working on some other shift, but were unable to test the hypothesis. Wesseldijk (1961) refers to evidence that the incidence of peptic ulcer is higher among shiftworkers, but acknowledges that "the extent to which shiftwork causes the symptoms of the disease to appear, or aggravates an existing pathological condition, is difficult to judge." Thiis-Evensen (1953), on the basis of extensive investigation among industrial workers in Scandinavia, found no evidence that shiftwork directly causes ulcers. Although the percentage of gastric ulcers among shiftworkers was twice as great as for day-workers in this investigation, most of the shiftworkers were found to have contracted the disease before embarking on shifts.

In this country a study of occupational factors in the causation of gastric and duodenal ulcers was carried out by Doll and Avery-Jones (1951). The effects of shiftwork were among the many factors considered in this large scale and carefully conducted survey. These investigators could find no evidence of any harmful effect of shift-work in relation to ulcers. "The incidence of peptic ulcer observed was not significantly different from that expected among workers doing any type of shiftwork, while the number of men who had given up shiftwork because of having an ulcer was small." Nor did these authors find, although the investigation was not specifically designed to deal with this question, any direct evidence of the harmful effect of irregular meal habits. Such differences as were observed were in favour of an association between peptic ulcer and irregularity of meals, but this association was not considered to be of major importance.

It is sometimes argued that peptic ulceration (and, indeed, a number of other disabling conditions) should automatically disqualify men from working shifts (Thiis-Evensen, 1958; McGirr, 1966; Rutenfranz, 1967). But it has recently been shown by Taylor and Fairrie (1968) that many middle-aged men with a variety of chronic disabling conditions, including peptic ulceration, are able to live and work perfectly satisfactorily under a rotating shift arrangement. It may be advisable, Taylor suggests elsewhere (1969), for men with such conditions not to take up shiftwork for the first time, or to transfer to daywork if they also dislike shifts. But each case, he argues, should be considered from its social and economic as well as from its medical aspects: "Virtually all shiftworkers in this country are paid more than their daywork equivalents, and ... they may often obtain more satisfaction from their work. To take them off shiftwork for 'medical reasons' ... can impose hardship and emotional stress which could aggravate the chronic disease."

SHIFTWORK AND HEALTH: TENTATIVE CONCLUSIONS

1 *Subjective and objective evidence*

The medical evidence is by no means consistent or clear. This may be due in part to differences in methods of investigation and research design. In the Scandinavian series of investigations, the Danish studies tended to show a greater frequency of illness than did the Norwegian, and one reason suggested for this is that the former were largely based on subjective reports and the latter on medical and health statistics (Thiis-Evensen, 1958). The fact that subjects were unaware of the nature of the investigator's interest in the Dutch study quoted earlier (Dirken, 1966) may well account for the much lower level of complaints about health among shiftworkers that was found in this case. In Taylor's (1969) study of oil refinery workers 48 per cent of three-shift workers reported in interview that their health was affected by this type of rotating schedule, and many of these were convinced that their life expectation was less than that of dayworkers. Yet analysis of absence records showed that the shift men had consistently lower rates of sickness than day men in similar occupations. Such evidence emphasises the need for combining various measures of health and sickness experience when looking at this problem.

2 *Self-selection of shiftworkers*

A further difficulty, as has often been pointed out, in comparing health and sickness experience of shift- and dayworkers, is that of selection. Even where there is no initial medical screening and selection of shiftworkers, and little transfer of shiftworkers to daywork for medical reasons, differing degrees of self-selection may take place in the formation of the shift and day groups. Assuming some degree of choice, one can argue that only those who are not deterred by the prospect of working unusual hours—and so in one sense the fittest—will embark upon them in the first place. Secondly, only the more durable—that is, those who can cope with such demands as particular forms of shift work may make—will survive on shifts through time. (Again, assuming an element of choice.) Just how far the process of self-selection applies in a particular situation is impossible to judge: but to the extent that it does apply one may expect it to show the shiftworker to advantage in health terms.

3 Individual differences in adaptation

Too little is known about the factors involved in one man's capacity to adapt to changed hours of work, and another man's failure to do so. Adaptation, however, is not just a matter of a reaction between a worker with particular physical characteristics on the one hand and the physical demands of a particular shift routine on the other. It is also a matter of his attitudes to work and to his job, to his shift hours, to his own health. It depends on his motivation in a particular context of place and time; on the nature of his work and immediate working environment; on wider environmental factors outside the workplace: distance from work and travel conditions, housing, domestic circumstances, attitudes of his wife and family, leisure habits.

4 Relationship with minor ailments and chronic disease

Even allowing for bias in subjective reporting, and for rationalisation of shiftwork as "unhealthy" on the part of those who dislike it, there does seem to be some positive association between bodily discomfort/minor ailments and certain shiftworking routines. But no such association has been established between shiftwork and any type of chronic disease. In association with other factors shift hours of work may, in some cases, have an aggravating effect upon a chronic condition such as peptic ulceration. But in general the existence of such a chronic condition ought not be be considered automatic grounds for taking a worker off shiftwork.

5 Psychological factors

Many people, including shiftworkers, believe shiftwork to be unhealthy, that it can lead to chronic disease and may even reduce life expectancy. Even though such beliefs and fears may be unjustified, the reality of their existence to those who hold them may serve to reduce well-being and morale.

6 *Lack of evidence and research*

Clearly there is a lack of research evidence in this area. The long term health of shiftworkers has never been systematically investigated, and there is no firm evidence to prove or disprove allegations of "unhealthiness." The increasing use of shiftwork requires factual answers rather than qualified opinions. Research in this country designed to provide such information will be briefly outlined in the final chapter.

Part Four

Part Four

TWELVE

Conclusion

FUTURE NUMBERS ON SHIFTWORK

The Ministry of Labour's 1954 and 1964 analyses of shiftworking showed an increase between these two dates in the numbers of hourly-paid manual workers on non-daywork routines. Evidence concerning this occupational category in the Department of Employment and Productivity's "Survey of Earnings" (1969) indicates that the number of those who are in receipt of some form of shift premium is continuing to rise.

Nevertheless this pattern of growth is by no means the simple and automatic process that many people assume it to be. Corner-cutting generalisations about an "increase in shiftworking" gloss over the kind of industrial, regional and shift-type variations which the Ministry's figures so clearly bring out. They also conceal localised decreases in numbers, and shorter term fluctuations, both of which have considerable behavioural implications within companies concerned.

Shift changes are certainly taking place and more are foreseen in both individual firms and industries as a whole. Sugar, cement, paper, baking—to name but a few—are examples of industries where wholesale changes have occured in the recent past. A strong belief was expressed by many of our own management contacts in the need for, and likelihood of, the spread of shiftwork practices, based in the main on increasing capital costs. This belief was given some support by developments either taking place or under consideration in the companies concerned.

But the amount and rate of growth is extremely difficult to assess.

Precisely what is meant by the phrase "on the increase" as applied to shiftwork is often not made clear. "More shiftwork" can refer to an increase in the total number of men and women involved (on a regular basis or irregularly), in the number of establishments using shifts (regularly or irregularly) or in the nature and variety of systems used. Increase in one of these directions does not necessarily mean increase in the others.

Whatever the factors making for "more shiftwork" in the future, a number of limiting factors will continue to apply.

1 Technical development

The first of these is associated with technical developments. While the introduction of new and costly equipment may encourage day-work firms to introduce multiple shifts in order to use such equipment intensively, the extension of automatic or semi-automatic processes in an existing shift situation may permit a reduction in the numbers of shiftworkers involved.

In a number of firms visited machine developments had resulted in fewer shiftworkers or even in the elimination of shifts altogether in certain sections. In a marine engineering firm, for example, where shifts were said originally to have been introduced in order to meet contract time limits, pressure for delivery is now met through a greater element of automation. In a sugar refinery, where seven or eight operators used to handle individual presses, a new filtration plant is now controlled by one man. In water supply, new plant developments have meant a substantial reduction in manpower in recent years, a process which it is said will continue. In a plastics factory, where 1500 were employed on shifts in 1959, the labour force has been contracted to less than half this number since demand can now be met by improved methods. In a firm producing iron castings, where a two-shift system once operated in the foundry, technical developments have meant that subsequent production departments can now be supplied from a single shift. In the bakery industry, where arrangements of working hours are to a great extent determined by customer buying habits, it was suggested that improved keeping properties and packaging methods may eventually make it possible to operate on a daywork basis only.

2 Effect of take-overs and amalgamations

The effect of take-overs and amalgamations can also be considered as a factor in this situation. Such developments, if they result in a rationalisation of production and personnel policies and practices, may produce some economy in shiftworking numbers.

3 Availability of labour

The availability of labour has also to be taken into account. Firms which would like to introduce or extend shiftworking may find themselves frustrated by an inability to recruit men on to shifts. This was the experience in, for example, a number of engineering concerns in the Birmingham and Midlands area at the time of our own visits. "Because of recruiting difficulties," one employer said, "we try to operate shifts only on essential services. Ideally we should like to see all the activities of the factory, including engineering, stores, canteen, production control and transport, working on shifts. But we recognise that we have to compromise." Attempted "shake-ups" in the labour market such as were seen in the mid-1960s do not necessarily help here. Redundancy and redeployment of labour may leave the situation unaffected if "surplus" workers are not made available where shortages exist.

4 Resistance from shop floor workers

Shop floor resistance to changes in working hours is, of course, another factor which will continue to have a restricting influence on extension of shiftworking patterns. A number of firms, as we have seen, have had to modify or abandon their plans for change in the face of employee opposition, while others have hesitated even to attempt negotiation on the subject. This applies especially to certain forms of shiftworking. Continuous seven-day working is probably the most important example, where worker adherence to the traditional weekend is an obstacle in the way of further continuous operation.

5 Resistance from managers

Nor must it be forgotten that shiftwork is often regarded without enthusiasm by management itself. This is particularly the case in the smaller unit operating a second shift, where multiple shiftwork may be seen as creating more problems for management than it solves. "So far we regard our night shift as a necessary evil," was the comment from a small engineering firm in the Home Counties, forced by limited capacity to go outside normal dayworking.

"In organising work," the standing orders of another firm laid down, "managers shall use every endeavour consistent with efficiency to reduce to a minimum the number of members who are required to work on abnormal shifts." There is some paternalistic regard here for the wellbeing and working efficiency of the employees concerned. But not a few managers would welcome an opportunity to get rid of their night shifts simply because of the administrative headaches involved in running them.

THE FUTURE OF WOMEN ON SHIFTS

Further growth in the number of establishments using multiple shifts is nevertheless to be expected over the next decade, as well as in numbers of shiftworkers involved. But this growth is unlikely to be revolutionary in proportions. One of the most dramatic developments in shiftwork practice may come as a result of changes affecting the working hours of women. At present the hours of employment for women in factories and certain other places of work are regulated by the 1961 Factories Act and related legislation. Women must not work before 07 00 or after 20 00, or for more than a fixed number of hours a day or week, without special dispensation.

But the number of women in respect of whom exemption is granted has risen steadily, month by month, in the last two years. The figures for women on night work (taken from the *DEP Gazette*) are of particular interest:

August 1968	10 953
August 1969	15 650
August 1970	20 754

Relatively small as these numbers still are, they give some indication of the readiness of employers to engage women on hours outside "normal," and of women workers themselves to take advantage of this opportunity. Change in legislation, or a relaxation in the conditions under which exemption is granted, could have profound effects on the organisation of shiftwork in this country. It would also raise a whole set of fresh issues—social and domestic, medical, performance—involving women at work.

VARIETY IN FUTURE WORK PATTERNS

In the meantime what is perhaps of more interest and importance than speculation about increases in the amount of shiftwork or numbers employed thereon, is consideration of the likely increase in variety and complexity of arrangements of hours of work.

Shiftworking, as we have already seen, is no more static than it is simple and uniform. Modification and movement are occurring all the time, involving adjustment on the part of both company and employee. Seasonal fluctuations and other varying production demands entail periodic expansion and reduction in numbers. The spread of shift practices is seen in what have previously been regarded as daywork areas, and some contraction is found in traditional shiftwork localities. Multiple shifts are being introduced into new industries and among new categories of worker. Changes are taking place in the skills involved—for example, "less manhandling: more dial-watching."

Availability of labour is a further variable factor and this can mean alterations in the way in which working hours are organised. One Scottish textiles firm, for example, is extending its night shift because it now finds it possible to recruit ex-miners and is able to train them for work previously handled by women. A metal products firm in the South-West reports that the tendency is all the time to use more and more male labour, and that this will mean the replacement of their present system of double-days (women) and permanent nights (men). The reverse is found in an East Midlands food factory, where continuous three-shift working for men is under review as more women workers become available in the district. And the management of a Yorkshire textiles mill foresees "the deployment of males to other departments and sections of the industry" as it seeks to extend a special arrangement it has in one department of three female shifts to cover the 24 hours.

Diversity and change in the arrangement of working hours are factors which have been emphasised repeatedly in this book. They are characteristics which stem from the varied needs and preferences of working men and women on the one hand, and equally varied organisational requirements on the other. In a rapidly-changing social, economic and technical climate these two sets of needs—and the steps taken to accommodate them—are certain to grow rather than to diminish. Whatever the numbers employed 10 years hence on shift rotas with which we are now familiar, we may confidently predict a far greater variety of arrangements within and outside these rotas for the future.

Considerations of this kind will call for a high degree of adaptability, not only from the individual who has to adjust to new patterns of work and leisure, but also on the part of companies and management, unions and their representatives, whose responsibility it also is to decide and agree on such patterns.

CURRENT RESEARCH

Hours of work and their arrangement clearly comprise an area of industrial activity in which our knowledge is still far from adequate. Too little is known about:

1   The demands which different types of shiftwork impose on the worker; their effects on health and/or efficiency
2   Individual differences in the capacity to adapt in various ways to different shift systems and rotas

Further information on these issues would help in the design of working schedules and in the selection of shiftworkers to man them.

Research is nevertheless developing in a number of directions. For example, a series of investigations with special emphasis on the health of shiftworkers is being carried out by the Institute of Occupational Health at the London School of Hygiene and Tropical Medicine under the direction of Dr P J Taylor. As indicated in an earlier chapter, multiple shiftwork is widely believed to be "unhealthy," but little hard and fast evidence exists to prove or disprove such a belief.

The Institute's investigations are concerned with both the long term and more immediate health of men and women who are consistently employed on unusual hours of work. They are being conducted in three stages:

1   A study of the expectation of life and main causes of death among men who have spent at least 10 years on shiftwork postwar, in comparison with dayworkers and with men who reverted to daywork after some experience on shifts

2   A two years' study of time lost through absence of all kinds by various types of shiftworkers in comparison with dayworkers of the same age and occupation

3   In addition to these two stages, which are large scale statistical exercises based on past employment, medical and personnel records, more detailed investigations are being made with smaller numbers of shop floor volunteers who are currently engaged on different types of shift rota. A variety of methods is being used here: interview, self-ratings, medical examination, psycho-physical tests and measures. The aim is to assess the physical, psychological and social demands of different arrangements of working hours and the degree to which adaptation in its various forms is achieved by the men and women involved

Adaptation to shiftwork is also the theme of a field study being carried out by Dr Wedderburn of Heriot-Watt University, Edinburgh, and supported by the British Steel Corporation. This is concerned first with social adaptation, with subjective reactions to the social deprivations, dislocations and benefits of shiftwork. Secondly, it is using sleep logs, body temperature recordings and performance data to measure different aspects of psycho-physical adjustment. This piece of research is particularly concerned with continuously operating forms of shiftwork, and with the advantages/disadvantages of the more traditional "week about" types of rota in comparison with those which rotate more frequently.

From the point of view of efficiency on the job, much of the recent and continuing experimental work in human performance of the Medical Research Council's Applied Psychology Unit at Cambridge is important. Experimental studies of "shiftwork" routines carried out by workers from this group in the recent past have compared stable and and changing rotas of various kinds, and have measured the effects of time-of-day and sleep deprivation on performance at different types of task.

Much of what goes on in the psycho-physiological laboratory, of course, may appear to have more relevance to life in "artificial" work environments than to that in "real life" situations, where social factors usually intervene to upset the best-laid plans. Nevertheless, there will always be elements in what is applicable to the work/rest schedules of submariners or astronauts which are also capable of extension to the more complex world of the factory floor worker. The answers we need will be provided by a combination of field and laboratory research.

PRACTICAL CONSIDERATIONS

Research may be continuing, but in the meantime practising management has the problem *now* of taking decisions which affect the arrangement of working and leisure hours. To the man in production or personnel who is faced with having to choose one way or the other by the time the three o'clock shift comes on duty, it is small comfort to know that the research worker may come up with the definitive answer in 18 months' time.

The manager knows better than most that he must operate in an imperfect world and in a state of imperfect knowledge. In making up his mind about hours of work he has to try to marry up various sets of information:

> What is technically and economically necessary
> What is administratively convenient or feasible
> What is socially acceptable; what, that is, shiftworkers prefer or will put up with
> What is desirable medically and psycho-physiologically: what is known, that is, about the effects of different shift arrangements on health and performance

He has to try to strike a balance between all these factors, and the result will inevitably be a compromise of some kind.

While it is impossible to lay down simple formulae for success, or to recommend one "best buy," two general considerations should be borne in mind.

The first is that provision must always be made as far as possible for what has been stressed throughout this book, namely the highly individual differences of working men and women. Each working routine places certain physical and social demands upon those who must conform to it. The weight of these demands differs according to the personal make-up and circumstances of the person concerned. Some flexibility in shift arrangements to allow for individual differences in workers' capacity to adapt is essential, even if this entails a degree of administrative inconvenience to the company.

Secondly, it should be remembered that every workplace is in a very real sense unique. Because of this, individual analysis of a situation and individual planning are of more importance than taking too much account of what may or may not have worked in the factory next door. What is called for in each case is a strategy tailored to a particular organisation operating with particular human resources. The solutions at headquarters in Halifax and branch factory in Bideford are unlikely to be the same. Nor are these solutions likely to provide the right answer twelve months or a couple of years from now. Periodic reappraisement of shift arrangements to ensure that they continue to meet current needs is also essential.

Shiftworking Terms

Abnormal hours. Commonly used to refer to any arrangement of hours other than a single, main daytime shift. But the term has an emotive quality. Its literal, statistical sense is often confused with a meaning of freakishness or "something that is bad for you." Abnormal hours are worked outside those generally accepted as a standard: it has yet to be shown that they are thereby unhealthy.

Adaptation. In this context refers to the degree to which a person is able to adjust to a change in the habitual length or arrangement of his or her working hours. Adaptation may be (*a*) physiological: adjustment of bodily rhythms and habits, (*b*) social: rearrangement of family, domestic and leisure activities, (*c*) personal: referring to a person's attitudes to change, and the extent to which he or she accepts or resents new working hours. Adaptation may occur in one of these ways, but not in the others. There may be partial adaptation in the sense that one physiological or social habit is modified, but not others. Or there may be partial adaptation in the sense that adjustment of one function—for instance, body temperature—is incompletely achieved. Adaptation, then, is not an either/or state. Adaptation may also be operationally defined in terms of whatever yardstick is used to measure it.

Afternoon shifts. The later turn in a double-day system, or the turn between "morning" and "night" in a three-shift system. Most commonly timed between 14 00 and 22 00. Sometimes used synonymously with "evening" shift, although this is usually timed later, say, 16 00 – midnight. May also refer to a part-time shift between the hours of, say, midday and 18 00.

Alternate pair sequence. Another name for the rapidly-rotating $2 \times 2 \times 2$ or metropolitan system.

Alternating day and night. A system under which the same workers alternate between day and night shifts, most commonly at weekly intervals, but also fortnightly, monthly, etc.

Alternation. Refers to change by the same worker, or the same shift team, between two differently-timed turns of duty. (For instance, early and late turns in a double-day system; day and night shifts in alternating days and nights.) Alternation may take place at any interval of time, though weekly is commonest. Is sometimes used synonymously, though incorrectly, with "rotation" (which refers to change between three or more turns of duty).

Backshift. Usually refers to the late, afternoon or evening shift in a three-shift system. Also used to refer to the nightshift. (See "fore shift.")

Backward rotation. In a three-shift system refers to change by the same shift-team from one turn of duty to another "against the clock" —that is, in the order morning, night, afternoon. Under "forward rotation" change takes place in the order morning, afternoon, night.

Bastard. Not an epithet applied to shift work of all kinds! But to a system which combines such a variety of different turns of duty that it defies simple description. May occur where the nature of the service required is unpredictable, or where there is undermanning.

Before-and-after. Refers to a type of field investigation in which the performance of the same group of workers is compared before and after a change in working hours. Or one in which the performance of an experimental group, which has changed its working hours, is compared with that of a control group which has continued under the former arrangement of hours.

Between shifts. A type of field investigation in which the performance of a group of shiftworkers on one type of rota is compared with that of a second group on another type of rota. Or in which the performance of a group of shiftworkers is compared with that of a group of dayworkers on similar work. (See "within shift" investigations.)

Circadian. Refers to rhythms which regularly recur roughly every 24 hours, such as light and darkness, sleep and wakefulness, rest and activity, and to such physiological functions as body temperature, digestion, urine flow, heart and respiration rates, etc. These bodily functions may be disturbed by shift rotas which interrupt the customary day/night, activity/rest pattern. The term "circadian" (attributed to Halberg, 1960), is generally preferred to the term "diurnal" which now tends to be used in contrast to "nocturnal."

Continental. Refers to the continuous three-shift system which rotates rapidly in the sequence $3 \times 2 \times 2$. Under this system a man works two or three consecutive shifts of the same kind with a 24-hour break between shift changes. The cycle is completed in four weeks.

Continuous. Although sometimes used to refer to 24-hour working round-the-clock, this term is more properly reserved for continuous seven-day (168-hours) working, as distinct from discontinuous or non-continuous work which covers only part of the week.

Dawn shift. Any early morning shift.

Day shift; daywork. Traditionally these terms referred to the hours between sunrise and sunset. What constitutes "day" and "night" may now be differently defined in the collective agreements of various industries. In this book the term "dayworker" is used in contrast to "shiftworker" to refer to anyone permanently engaged on a single, main turn of duty usually within the hours between 06 00 – 18 00. "Day shift" is also sometimes used instead of "morning shift" to refer to the turn between "night shift" and "afternoon or evening shift" in a three-shift system.

Dead fortnight. The afternoon and night shift periods under a traditional continuous three-shift system (in which the sequence is roughly 7 mornings, 7 afternoons and 7 nights) because of the lack of opportunity for normal social life in the evening during these two weeks.

Direction of rotation. Under three-shift working, rotation may take place "forwards" (that is morning, afternoon, night) or "backwards" (that is morning, night, afternoon). These two directions of rotation give different distributions of free hours.

Discontinuous. Usually refers to three-shift operation over part of the working week (for instance, $4\frac{1}{2}$, 5 or $5\frac{1}{2}$ days), as distinct from continuous operation over the full 168 hours.

Diurnal. Has sometimes been used synonymously with "circadian" to refer to a periodicity of 24 hours. But since it is ambiguous it now tends to be used in contrast to "nocturnal" (Mills, 1966).

Double-days. Normally two shifts of eight hours each, 06 00 – 14 00 and 14 00 – 22 00. The system is usually alternating, but can be fixed. Alternation usually takes place weekly, but can be at longer intervals. Is often used to extend the running time of jobs done by women.

Double-jobbing. Or double-job holding, or second-jobbing. Refers to the practice of working at a second, part-time, paying occupation —for example, in the evening or at weekends. Shift hours of work may permit second-jobbing during the daytime, and this is often seen as a disadvantage by employers of shift workers.

Double turn or "doublers". Refers to a normal eight-hour shift followed immediately by an eight-hour overtime stint.

Early turn. The earlier or morning shift of a double-day system. The turns of a three-shift system are also sometimes designated "*earlies*, lates and nights."

Evening shift. The turn between "morning" and "night" in a three-shift system. Most commonly timed between 16 00 and midnight or 15 00 – 23 00. Sometimes used synonymously with "afternoon" shift, although this usually stops/starts earlier (14 00 – 22 00). May also refer to a part-time shift—for example, 17 00 – 21 00, or 18 00 – 22 00.

Fixed shift. Any shift or shift system where workers do not change, alternate or rotate, but remain permanently on the same turn of duty.

Follow-through. Refers to the field technique by which the performance of the same shiftworkers is observed as they change from one turn of duty to the next within an alternating or rotating shift system.

Foreshift. Usually refers to the early or morning shift in a three-shift system. (See "backshift.")

Forward rotation. In a three-shift system refers to change by the same shift-team from one turn of duty to another in the order mornings, afternoons, nights. Under "backward rotation" change takes place in the order mornings, nights, afternoons.

Four-set. Or four-crew. Refers to the operation of a continuous 3×8-hour system by four shift teams. In any 24-hour period three teams will be on duty and one resting.

Frequency of rotation. Or frequency of alternation. Refers to the intervals at which shiftworkers change from one turn of duty to the next. Traditionally, in this country, rotation has been at roughly weekly intervals or longer. (Although there are exceptions to this—for example, in the glass industry.) In recent years such rapidly-rotating systems as the $2 \times 2 \times 2$ or $3 \times 2 \times 2$ have become more popular.

Granny shift. A part-time evening shift, primarily for older women, and mainly found in the textiles industry.

Graveyard shift. A night shift commencing at approximately midnight.

Housewife shift. A part-time shift primarily intended for married women. Usually of about four hours' duration.

Inconvenience payment. An additional payment (calculated either as a percentage of the basic wage or as a fixed supplement to it) made to shiftworkers to compensate them for the inconvenience of their "abnormal" hours of work.

Indemnité de panier. Shift allowance. Originally to compensate the worker on "abnormal hours" for extra expense involved in providing himself with food and drink during a night shift.

Inversion. Describes the complete reversal of a normal 24-hour pattern or rhythm. For example, an inversion of the normal rest/ activity pattern may take place if a shiftworker works at night. In theory, at least, it is possible for the rhythms of body functions to follow suit. The body temperature curve, normally at its peak in the afternoon, would, if inverted, reach its highest point about dawn. In practice, such complete inversion is seldom achieved, a modification or flattening of the curve being more usual.

Late turn. The later or afternoon shift of a double-day system. The turns of a three-shift system are also sometimes designated "earlies, *lates* and nights."

Link-up shift. Usually a short, part-time shift used to fill a time interval between two main shifts so as to secure continuous working. For example, a part-time evening shift used to link the end of the day shift with the beginning of the night shift.

Lobster shift. A night shift beginning at approximately midnight.

"Manchester" system. A continuously alternating system over seven days, using 12-hour shifts and three crews.

Matching. Matched pairs, matched groups, etc. Often in industry one finds inter-departmental or inter-group comparisons being made on the basis of absence, lateness, accidents, turnover and so on without any account being taken either of the composition of the groups or the work on which they are engaged. These factors must be taken into account before assumptions about "better" or "worse" performance are made. In particular, comparisons between the performance of dayworkers and shiftworkers, or of shiftworkers on different types of rota, can only be valid if samples taken from the groups in question are matched on the basis of such factors as age, length of service, job and total working hours.

Metropolitan. The continuous three-shift system which rotates rapidly in the sequence $2 \times 2 \times 2$. Under this system a man works two consecutive shifts of the same kind with a 24-hour break between shift changes. The cycle is completed in eight weeks.

Moonlighting. Is used in the USA and in this country to refer to double-jobholding. But here it is also used simply to describe employment on twilight or evening part-time shifts.

Morning shift. (*a*) The turn between "night" and "afternoon or evening" in a three-shift system. Most commonly timed between 06 00 – 14 00. Morning shifts of 07 00 – 15 00 and 08 00 – 16 00 also occur, but may be called "day shift." (*b*) May also refer to the early (06 00 – 14 00) turn in a double-day system. (*c*) Or to a part-time morning shift.

Multiple shiftwork. Primarily an organisational term indicating the employment of more than one team of workers over a given period of time in the same working situation. Multiple shiftwork may exist whether those employed always work the same period of duty, or take their turn on successive periods of duty.

Night; night shift; nightwork. Like the terms day shift and daywork, "night" has no generally agreed starting and stopping times. Originally its duration was determined by sunset and sunrise. It now often refers to the hours between 18 00 and 06 00, but some collective agreements place very different limits upon it. Some agreements differentiate between "shiftwork" (meaning an alternating or rotating system of some kind) and "nightwork" (indicating permanent employment at this time). "Night" may refer to permanent nightwork, the night shift of an alternating day and night system, or to the night turn in a three-shift system.

Non-continuous. Synonymous with "discontinuous."

Normal hours. "Normal hours" commonly refers to permanent employment on a single, main daytime shift (for example, nine to five, eight to four). What is "normal" and what is "abnormal," however, are only so in particular contexts of space and time. The practice in certain Mediterranean countries of having a long midday period for siesta would not be regarded as normal by employers in Nuneaton or Newton-le-Willows. What were normal working hours in 1870 are abnormal by today's standards. It may be considered normal to work shifts in coal-mining or computing, and abnormal to do so in the furniture trade or the typing pool.

Overtime. Hours worked outside the basic or standard working day or week. One of the advantages most frequently quoted in favour of the introduction of shiftworking is the elimination of excessive overtime practices: the extent to which overtime working is regularly combined with various shift systems, however, is often overlooked.

Part-time. Any shift of shorter duration than a full standard shift, but usually of about four hours. Evening shifts of this length between 17 00 and 22 00 are almost exclusively worked by women. Part-time shifts during the day, however, are becoming increasingly common, and it is not unusual to find a factory operated almost entirely by a succession of such short production shifts.

Permanent. Permanency refers to the regular employment of the same workers on the same hours of work. Most often applied to regular dayworkers and regular nightworkers, but examples of continuous employment on mornings and afternoons also occur.

Rapidly-rotating. Refers to three-shift systems, either continuous or discontinuous, where the movement of shift-teams from one shift period to the next takes place at less than weekly intervals. Applies in particular to the metropolitan $(2 \times 2 \times 2)$ and continental $(3 \times 2 \times 2)$ systems.

Regular. Synonymous with permanent, as in "regular daywork" or "regular nightwork."

Relay. Defined by the *Oxford English Dictionary* as "A set of persons appointed to relieve others in the performance of certain duties." The word was used throughout the nineteenth century in this sense. Marx (1867) refers to the "relay system" and to "relay work" as we would speak of "shift system" and "shiftwork."

Rotation. Change by the same workers, or the same shift-team, between three or more differently timed turns of duty (for example, mornings to afternoons to nights). Sometimes used synonymously, though incorrectly, with "alternation" (which refers to change between *two* different periods of duty).

Shift. Among the many separate meanings which the *Oxford English Dictionary* attributes to the word "shift" are: (*a*) "A relay or change of workmen or horses." (*b*) "The length of time during which such a set of men work." (*c*) "A quantity (of ore) removed at a time." 1812, 1825 and 1839 are the respective dates for the first known use of the word in these senses.

The word "shift" is still widely used both in the sense of "shift-team or crew" and of "shift period or turn of duty," and this can cause some confusion. In the latter sense, of course, a man permanently engaged on days works a day *shift*.

Marx (1867) uses the terms "shifts" and "shifting system" to refer to a "shuffling of 'the hands' about in endless variety, and shifting the hours of work and of rest for different individuals throughout the day." This, he suggests, was a technique used by unscrupulous employers to confuse the factory inspectorate in order to evade the restrictions imposed by the Factory Acts on the length of working day.

Shift allowance, payment or premium. The additional allowance made for working an "abnormal" arrangement of hours. In theory it represents compensation for the inconvenience or hardship—social, physical, financial—of working on shift hours. In practice the level of shift payments depends more upon relative strengths in particular bargaining situations. Shift payments are calculated as a percentage of the basic rate, as a fixed addition to this, or as $x+$ paid hours for x hours worked. There is an increasing demand, and some tendency for this to be implemented, for the shift allowance to be incorporated into a consolidated rate.

Shiftwork, shiftworker. For the purposes of this book "shiftwork" is regarded as involving any shift or combination of shifts used in place of, or in addition to, a single, main daytime turn of duty. And a shiftworker is any person employed on such a shift or combination of shifts.

Split shifts. A full shift divided into two distinct parts, with a gap of several hours in between. Used in passenger transport, catering and other service industries, where there is a need to meet peak demands at different times of the day.

Stable shift. Synonymous with "fixed shift."

Staggered daywork. Overlapping of working hours by different workers or groups of workers. The periods worked may be full- or part-time shifts. Gives an extended working day without overtime hours being worked by individual employees. Used, for example, in seasonal activities such as fruit and vegetable preserving.

Steady. Synonymous with permanent, as in "steady night shift."

Stint. An allotted portion of work and, by extension, the period of time taken to complete this.

Sunset shift. Any late afternoon or evening shift.

Swiftly-rotating. See "rapidly-rotating."

Swing shift. Afternoon or evening shift from about 16 00 to midnight.

Three-shift work. Division of the 24-hour period into three working turns. For instance: (*a*) three rotating shifts: morning, afternoon and night. (*b*) Three stable or non-rotating shifts. (*c*) A double-day shift (often of women) + a permanent night shift (of men). The term "three-shift system" usually refers to (*a*).

Traditional. (*a*) Used to describe, in this country, a system of rotation at roughly weekly intervals, in contrast to rapidly-rotating systems. (*b*) Also used to describe areas or industries where shift-work has long been practised and where it is generally accepted.

Twelve-hour shifts. In spite of suggestions to the contrary, the use of 12-hour shifts is now very common, and is tending to increase. Apart from their use as an occasional temporary measure, they are regularly and consistently employed under permanent night arrangements, alternate days and nights, and various types of continuous seven-day rotas.

Twilight shifts. Part-time evening shifts. "Twilighting" is also sometimes used, as is "moonlighting," to describe the practice of holding a second, part-time job.

217

Two-shift system. Any shift system involving the use of two shift-teams at different times during a 24-hour period. Examples are: double-days; permanent day and permanent night; alternating day and night; 2 × 12 hours.

Veterans. In this context refers to those in any working group who have worked longest on shifts. In traditional shiftworking industries such as steel, glass or coal, veterans may thus have 30 or 40 years' service on shifts. But in an investigation in chocolate manufacturing, permanent nightworkers qualified as veterans after five to six years (McDonald, 1958).

Volunteers. In this context those who, for whatever reason or combination of reasons, volunteer to work on some "abnormal" arrangement of working hours. To volunteer for shift hours implies more than a mere acceptance of particular hours of work: it implies an active choice between alternatives.

Weekend. To some extent a variable concept. The traditional "weekend off" has been extended from Saturday afternoon and Sunday, to all Saturday and Sunday, to (for many nightworkers) Friday – Saturday – Sunday. For some shiftworkers the weekend stops at midnight on Sunday. For many workers in retail trades Sunday and Monday comprise the weekend.

Unwillingness to give up the traditional weekend is a common reason for workers' refusal to change to continuous shift systems. The advantages/disadvantages of different seven-day rotas are often seen in terms of the number of Saturdays and Sundays off which such rotas include.

"Within-shift." Refers to the type of field investigation in which the performance of the same worker is compared as he moves from one turn of duty to the next within a shift system. For example: is his output greater during the day shift or at night; does he take more time off on the morning, afternoon or night shift? (See "between shift" investigations.)

Appendices

Industrial groups in which greatest numbers on various types of shiftwork are to be found

MEN

CONTINUOUS THREE-SHIFT

Metal manufacture	74 000	33%
Chemicals and allied industries	48 000	21%

NON-CONTINUOUS THREE-SHIFT

Metal manufacture	57 000	30%
Paper, printing and publishing	29 000	15%

ALTERNATE DAY AND NIGHT

Vehicles	97 000	41%
Engineering and electrical goods	45 000	19%

PERMANENT NIGHT

Engineering and electrical goods	32 000	27%
Vehicles	24 000	20%

DOUBLE-DAY

Vehicles	21 000	18%
Textiles	20 000	17%

WOMEN

DOUBLE-DAY

Textiles	21 000	43%
Food, drink and tobacco	9 000	19%

PART-TIME EVENING

Engineering and electrical goods	17 000	25%
Food, drink and tobacco	16 000	24%
Textiles	15 000	22%

Figures in the second column refer to percentages of all men (or women) engaged on a particular kind of shiftwork.

The importance of the various types of shiftwork in different industrial groups

THREE-SHIFT SYSTEMS
(continuous and non-continuous combined)

Gas, electricity and water
83% (31 000) of shiftworkers are on three-shift
Chemicals and allied industries
81% (59 000) of shiftworkers are on three-shift
Metal manufacture
71% (131 000) of shiftworkers are on three-shift

TWO-SHIFT SYSTEMS INVOLVING NIGHTWORK

	ALTERNATING DAY AND NIGHT	PERMANENT NIGHT	COMBINED
Shipbuilding and marine engineering	40% (3 000)	54% (4 000)	94% (7 000)
Vehicles	62% (97 000)	15% (24 000)	77% (121 000)
Engineering and electrical goods	36% (45 000)	26% (32 000)	62% (77 000)

"DAYTIME" SYSTEMS

	DOUBLE-DAY	PART-TIME EVENING	COMBINED
Textiles	35% (41 000)	13% (15 000)	48% (56 000)
Clothing and footwear	21% (500)	26% (500)	47% (1 000)
Food, drink and tobacco	24% (21 000)	19% (17 000)	43% (38 000)

Incidence and importance of shiftworking in the different regions

	NUMBERS	AS A PROPORTION OF ALL SHIFTWORKERS IN COUNTRY (%)	AS A PROPORTION OF ALL WORKERS IN REGION (%)
Midlands	204 000	20.2	17.9
North-West	177 000	17.6	20.4
Yorks & Lincs.	121 000	12.0	19.8
London & SE	119 000	11.9	13.5
East & South	107 000	10.6	17.8
Scotland	92 000	9.1	17.9
North	71 000	7.0	22.8
Wales	66 000	6.6	29.6
South-West	36 000	3.6	13.5
N Ireland	14 000	1.4	11.7

Appendix 4

Comparison of numbers and proportions on different types of shift system, 1954 and 1964

	1954		1964		
	NUMBERS (*thousands*)	PROPORTION (%)	NUMBERS (*thousands*)	PROPORTION (%)	PERCENTAGE INCREASE
Three-shift	316.5	48	420.6	41	32.9
Alternate day and night	155.3	23 ⎱ 32	237.3	23 ⎱ 35	52.8 ⎱ 63.4
Permanent night	62.6	9 ⎰	118.7	12 ⎰	89.6 ⎰
Double-day	103.1	16 ⎱ 20	169.8	17 ⎱ 24	64.7 ⎱ 83.2
Part-time evening	27.7	4 ⎰	69.8	7 ⎰	152.0 ⎰
Other	2.3	—	3.8	—	65.2
	667.5	100	1 020.0	100	52.8

Frequency distribution of shift payments as a % of the minimum hourly rate of pay

1 Permanent nights

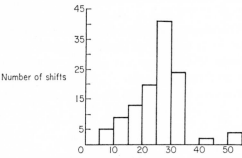

Mean = 24.7 %
Standard deviation = 8.6 %
Range = 7.1 to 50.0%

2 Discontinuous three-shift

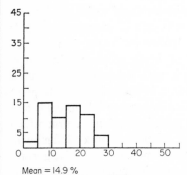

Mean = 14.9 %
Standard deviation = 6.5 %
Range = 2.0 to 29.7 %

3 Double-days

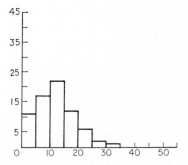

Mean = 12.2 %
Standard deviation = 6.3 %
Range = 2.0 to 33.3 %

Shift premiums as a % of the minimum hourly rate

Shiftworking and "nationality"

In Chapter 10 mention was made of certain "national" immigrant groups found on shiftwork. While it is not possible to estimate the total number of such workers, they appear to constitute a sizeable and distinctive element in at least 15 of the firms visited, sometimes making all the difference between ease and difficulty of recruitment. Particularly in the case of certain smaller shifts they may constitute virtually the whole or a very large part of the labour force. For example:

100% of permanent night shift of 150	(Plastics)
100% of permanent night shift of 58	(Bakery)
99% of three-shift discontinuous team of 153	(Bakery)
80% of permanent night shift of 280	(Biscuits and cakes)
65% of permanent night shift of 130	(Telegraphic apparatus)

In all known cases more are employed on shifts than on ordinary daywork.

Management comment on their satisfactoriness varied as for any other group of workers. There were a couple of comments on their high labour turnover and "nomadic tendencies." One firm thought its night shift had the reputation of being a place where new immigrants could tide themselves over with a temporary job until they found something better. As regards attendance, one informant considered that coloured workers were more susceptible to colds and to longer absences of three to four weeks' duration. A firm which had introduced a supervisory training scheme reported difficulty in finding suitable coloured trainees. There was one surprising complaint about the low level of aspiration of immigrant labour. It was hard, this informant maintained, to instil the firm's standards of performance into such workers. They had "little ambition to raise their wage level" and were "not as interested as a British workman in a larger income." There were finally various comments about difficulties involving human relationships. "It's something of a problem to fit them into teams," one senior foreman said, "because they're touchy and apt to think that any disciplinary action is directed at them because of their colour." A firm employing workers from eight or nine different national groups tried to spread them evenly over each shift in an attempt to avoid friction. The policy of another company was to restrict such workers to 10 per cent of the total.

Against these views must be set a number of highly complimentary comments on the performance of coloured employees. A bakery manager described his three-shift discontinuous workers (99 per cent Indian and Pakistani) as a stable group of which half had 10 years' service or more. Of the Indian and Pakistani permanent night shift workers in a factory making radio and electronic equipment it was said that while their piecework efficiency might be a little lower, they compensated for this by their greater reliability in starting work as soon as they arrived, etc. And in a firm producing moulded plastics, unit production was said to be higher on permanent nights because of "the team spirit of the coloured man." Night shift was also described here as a stable group, with lower turnover and an absence rate that was certainly no higher than on days.

An article in the *Observer* [*"The night shift from Pakistan,"* by Dilip Hiro, 16 March 1969] considered two groups of such workers, Pakistanis in the textiles industry in the West Riding of Yorkshire and a West Indian group in a variety of manufacturing industries in the High Wycombe area. This interesting account emphasises the extent to which industry is dependent on such groups, their high financial motivation and their general satisfactoriness to the employer from the viewpoint of attendance and production.

Who works longest?

As a little light relief, consider the following examples of long work hours, randomly culled from press and television. The reader may care to build up his own collection.

WORKING STINTS OF "LONGER DURATION"

12 hours. "They didn't have a lunch break, and now they've been hard at it for 12 hours." BBC programme "Twenty-four Hours," 21 November 1968, reporting on meeting of "Group of Ten" finance ministers and central bankers in Bonn on the international monetary crisis.

12 hours. "He works coalman's hours—often getting up at four in the morning, sometimes working a 12-hour day, six days a week—and after a day's filming he's so tired all he wants to do is go to bed." Mr Richard Burton's secretary describing the actor's working hours: *Daily Mail,* (26 October 1970).

14 hours. Mr Bryan Forbes, in television interview, refers to Dame Edith Evans working 14 hours a day over an eight weeks' period while making the film "The Whisperers."

14 hours. Report in London *Evening News* (1 May 1968) on the presidential campaigning of Senator Robert Kennedy: "... in high spirits. After a 14 hour day that left most of the Press Corps exhausted he was in a mood to relax and chat."

Up to 15 hours. Book review (*The Times,* 4 March 1968) of A J Merrett's *Executive Remuneration in the UK* (Longmans, 1968) refers to Merrett's sample of salaried directors who were asked how many hours they worked "yesterday." Over half worked 10 or more, with a maximum of 15.

16 hours. Mr Tommy Docherty, interviewed for television about his new appointment as manager of Rotherham United Football Club, said that he was at the ground for 16 hours a day.

16 hours. Under the title, "Double-shift talks all night," *The Times* (24 May 1968) reports that the parliamentary Finance Bill committee "concluded their second all-night session at 07 52 on Tuesday morning after nearly 16 hours of complex discussion on life policies, life annuity contracts and capital redemption policies."

18 hours. From a *Times* report (26 August 1968) on a Midlands murder hunt: "These two tired men, who have worked 18 hours a day for a year, with no summer holidays and only a couple of days off for Christmas. . . ."

20 hours. Lord George-Brown (then Mr), after his resignation from the government, talking to Anthony Barber of the London *Evening News* (4 April 1968): ". . . I have left an overfull life—working from six or seven in the morning until often after two the next morning." And so on, up to such one-off performance feats as:

72 hours. "Trevor plays his way to chess record" London *Evening News* (23 February 1968) headline over a story of a schoolboy who played chess non-stop for three days and nights in aid of charity.

LONGER-THAN-AVERAGE WORKING WEEKS

66 hours. Letter to the *Daily Sketch* (14 June 1968) from the wife of a shop assistant in a chain store whose official weekly hours were 42, but whose actual working time reached "the staggering total of 66 hours with not one penny overtime pay." "I call it slave labour," writes M of Chelmsford.

100 hours. Feature on the small shopkeeper in London *Evening Standard* (28 October 1968). Two sisters running a sweet shop are quoted as saying: "We never knew it was such hard work. We start at six in the morning, cleaning up the shop, which we open at eight. We work through the day, right until nine at night. . . . This business means working more than 100 hours a week, every day of the week—but we love it. We would never give it up."

108 hours. Report in the *Daily Telegraph* (14 January 1970) of an Old Bailey case in which two directors of a haulage company were charged with causing goods vehicles to be driven excessive hours. Although under the Road Traffic Act the maximum number of hours a driver could drive in a day was 11, with 10 hours' rest in each 24, "One man had driven 108 in one week."

Up to 110 hours. Under the heading, "Scandal of a 110 hour week," the *Daily Sketch* (4 September 1968) reports the "professional blackmail" of junior hospital doctors as being attacked by the General Secretary of the Medical Practitioners' Union. He appealed to TUC delegates to support the junior doctors' fight for recognition of proper standards of pay and duty times, and referred to a "scandalous situation" in which doctors were working between 80 and 110 hours a week.

Unspecified. A report in the London *Evening News* (4 March 1968) spotlights the problem of undermanning in the prison service: "They have to work shifts, bank holidays, and every other weekend and overtime when they're told to—there's no pleasing oneself in a disciplined service."

Bibliography

AANONSEN, A (1964) *Shiftwork and Health*, Scandinavian University Books, Oslo

ALDEN, J D (1968) "Double jobholding—an economic phenomenon: a regional analysis of Scotland," Unpublished report, Department of Economics, Heriot-Watt University, Edinburgh

ANDLAUER, F (1960) "The effect of shift working on the worker's health," European Productivity Agency, *T U Information Bulletin*, 29

ANON (1969) "Occupational Health in Japan," Organising Committee of the XVIth International Congress on Occupational Health, Tokyo

BANKS, OLIVE (1956) "Continuous shiftwork: the attitudes of wives," *Occupational Psychology* volume 30 pp69–84

BELBIN, E, and SERGEAN, R (1963) *Training in the Clothing Industry*, Twentieth Century Press Limited, London

BJERNER, B, HOLM, A, and SWENSSON, A (1948) "Studies on night and shiftwork," reported in Aanonsen (1964)

BJERNER, B, HOLM, A, and SWENSSON, A (1955) "Diurnal variation in mental performance—a study of three-shift workers," *British Journal of Industrial Medicine* volume 12 pp103–10

BLAKE, M J F (1967a) "Relationship between circadian rhythm of body temperature and introversion-extraversion," *Nature* volume 215 pp896–7

BLAKE, M J F (1967b) "Time of day effects on performance in a range of tasks," *Psychonomic Science* volume 9 pp349–50

BLAKELOCK, E A (1960) "A new look at the new leisure," *Administrative Science Quarterly* volume 4 pp446–67

BOHR, R H, and SWERTLOFF, A B (1969) "Work shift, occupational status and the perception of job prestige," *Journal of Applied Psychology* volume 53 part 3 pp227–9

BONNEVIE, P, and ANDERSEN, J E (1953, 1957 and 1960) Reported in Aanonsen (1964)

BRADDICK, W A G (1966) "Shiftworking: a survey of the literature," Papers in Management Studies: Ashridge Management College

BRANDT, A (1969) "The influence of various shiftwork systems on the health of workmen," XVIth International Congress on Occupational Health, Tokyo, (Abstracts)

BROOKES, R P (1968) *GKN Report and Accounts, 1967*, Guest, Keen and Nettlefolds Limited, Warley, Worcestershire

BROWN, Hilda G (1959) "Some effects of shiftwork on social and domestic life," *Yorkshire Bulletin of Economic and Social Research*, Occasional paper number 2, Department of Economics of the Universities of Hull, Leeds and Sheffield

BROWN, I D (1967) "Measurements of control skills, vigilance and performance on a subsidiary task during 12 hours of car driving," *Ergonomics* volume 10 number 6 pp665–73

BROWN, I D, TICKNER, A H, and SIMMONDS, D C V (1970) "Effect of prolonged driving on overtaking criteria," *Ergonomics* volume 13 number 2 pp239–42

BROWNE, R C (1949) "The day and night performance of teleprinter switchboard operators," *Occupational Psychology* volume 23 pp121–6

BRUUSGAARD, A (1949) "Shiftworkers," *Recommendations on the Shortening of Working Hours in Certain Occupations*, Ministry of Local Government and Labour, Oslo, Reported in Aanonsen (1964)

BRUUSGAARD, A (1969) "Shiftwork as an occupational health problem," *On Night and Shiftwork*, National Institute of Occupational Health, Stockholm

BUZZARD, R B (1958) *Coalminers' Attendance at Work*, National Coal Board, Medical Research Memorandum 3

CEIZEL, P (1962) "The diet of miners on night shift," *Ceskoslovenska Hygiena* (Prague) volume 7 number 4 pp240–3

CIRMAN, V, and HEJDA, S (1964) "Work, rest and nutrition regimen of locomotive crews on long-distance runs," *Pracovni Lekarstvi* (Prague) volume 16 number 9 pp404–7

COLQUHOUN, W P, BLAKE, M J F, and EDWARDS, R S (1968*a*) "Experimental studies of shiftwork I: A comparison of 'rotating' and 'stabilized' 4-hour shift systems," *Ergonomics* volume 11 number 5 pp437–53

COLQUHOUN, W P, BLAKE, M J F, and EDWARDS, R S (1968*b*) "Experimental studies of shiftwork II: Stabilized 8-hour shift systems," *Ergonomics* volume 11 number 6 pp527–46

COLQUHOUN, W P, BLAKE, M J F, and EDWARDS, R S (1969) "Experimental studies of shiftwork III Stabilized 12-hour shift systems," *Ergonomics* volume 12 number 6 pp865–82

CONFEDERATION OF BRITISH INDUSTRY (1968) *Shiftwork*, CBI, London

COOK, F P (1954) *Shiftwork*, Institute of Personnel Management, London

CORCORAN, D W J (1961) "Sleep: alertness during the night shift," *The Manager* volume 29 number 11 pp866–8

DEBRY, G, GIRAULT, P, LEFORT, J, and THIEBAULT, J (1967) "Enquête sur les habitudes alimentaires des travailleurs à feux continus," *Bulletin de l'INSERM* (Paris) volume 22 number 6 pp1169–1202

De la MARE, Gwynneth (1967) Unpublished report

De La MARE, Gwynneth, and SERGEAN, R (1968) "Who are the night workers?," *Personnel* volume 1 number 3 pp20–23

De la MARE, Gwynneth, and SHIMMIN, Sylvia (1964) "Preferred patterns of duty in a flexible shiftworking situation," *Occupational Psychology* volume 38 pp203–14

De la MARE, Gwynneth, and WALKER, J (1967) "Stress on the shifts," *Management Today*, January 1967

De la MARE, Gwynneth, and WALKER, J (1968) "Factors influencing the choice of shift rotation," *Occupational Psychology* volume 42 pp1–21

DEPARTMENT OF EMPLOYMENT AND PRODUCTIVITY (1969*a*) "Results of a new survey of earnings in September 1968 Part 4—Make up of earnings and joint distribution of earnings and hours," *Employment and Productivity Gazette* volume LXXVII number 8 pp725–36

DEPARTMENT OF EMPLOYMENT AND PRODUCTIVITY (1969b) *Time Rates of Wages and Hours of Work,* HMSO, London

DERVILLEE, E, and BANNEL, F (1969) "Technical and medical aspects of night-work," Symposium on Occupational Health Aspects of Shiftworkers; XVIth International Congress on Occupational Health, Tokyo, (Abstracts)

DIRKEN, J M (1966) "Industrial Shiftwork: decrease in well-being and specific effects," *Ergonomics* volume 9 number 2 pp115–24

DOLL, R, and AVERY-JONES, F (1951) "Occupational Factors in the Aetiology of Gastric and Duodenal Ulcers," MRC Special Report Series 276, HMSO, London

DOWNIE, J H (1963) *Some Social and Industrial Implications of Shiftwork,* Summary of an investigation by the study groups based on HRH the Duke of Edinburgh's Study Conference, 1956, Industrial Welfare Society, London

DUNLOP COMPANY LIMITED (1969) *Shiftwork in Dunlop,* Personnel Policies Report number 1, Central Personnel Division

ENSING, H (1969) "Occupational aspects of peptic ulcer," *T. Soc. Geneesk,* (Assen, Holland) volume 47 number 6 pp178–86, (Abstract in *Excerpta Medica,* November 1969)

ERANKO, O (1957) "25-hour day: one solution to the shiftwork problem," XIIth International Congress on Occupational Health, Helsinki

EVANS, A A (1969) "Work and leisure, 1919–69," *International Labour Review* volume 99 number 1 pp35–59

FARMER, E (1924) "A comparison of different shift systems in the glass trade," IFRB Report number 24, HMSO, London

FORET, J, and LANTIN, G (1970) "Le sommeil des conducteurs de trains," Proceedings of NATO Symposium on the effects of diurnal rhythm and loss of sleep on human performance, Strasbourg

GAVRILESCU, N, et al (1966) "Control board shiftwork turning every two days," Proceedings of XVth International Congress on Occupational Health, Vienna

GEORGE, M Dorothy (1966) *London Life in the Eighteenth Century,* Peregrine Books, Harmondsworth, England

GRIEW, S, and PHILIPP, E (1969) "Workers' attitudes and the acceptability of shiftwork in New Zealand manufacturing industry," Research paper of the New Zealand Institute of Economic Research

HAKKINEN, S (1966) "Psychological and physiological reactions to shiftwork," XVth International Congress on Occupational Health, Vienna, 1966

HALBERG, F (1960) "The 24-hour scale: a time dimension of adaptive functional organisation," *Perspectives in Biology and Medicine* volume 3 pp491–527

HEALTH OF MUNITION WORKERS' COMMITTEE (1916) Memorandum number 5 "Hours of Work," Cd. 8186, HMSO, London

HEALTH OF MUNITION WORKERS' COMMITTEE (1917) Interim Report, "Industrial Efficiency and Fatigue," Cd. 8511, HMSO, London

HEALTH OF MUNITION WORKERS' COMMITTEE (1918) Final Report, "Industrial Health and Efficiency," Cd. 9065, HMSO, London

HIGGIN, G W, *et al* (1957) "Comparative study of mining systems: composite cutting longwalls: development of task-shift rotation systems," Tavistock Institute of Human Relations, Document number 470

HOLLAND-MARTIN, Admiral Sir D (1969) Final Report of the Committee of Inquiry into Trawler Safety, Cd 4114, HMSO, London

HOME OFFICE (1935) "Departmental Committee on the Employment of Women and Young Persons on the Two-Shift System," Cd 4914, HMSO, London

HUTTON, G (1953) *We Too Can Prosper: The Promise of Productivity*, Geo Allen & Unwin, London

INDUSTRIAL FATIGUE RESEARCH BOARD (1924) "Results of Investigations in Certain Industries," Report number 27, HMSO, London

INDUSTRIAL HEALTH RESEARCH BOARD (1940) "Industrial Health in War," Emergency Report number 1, HMSO, London

INDUSTRIAL SOCIETY (1963) "Double-jobbing," Information Survey and Report Series, number 107

INDUSTRIAL SOCIETY (1966) "Shiftwork—current practice in Great Britain," Information Survey and Report Series number 140

INTERNATIONAL CONFEDERATION OF FREE TRADE UNIONS (1964) *Trade Union Handbook*, Brussels

JARDILLIER, P (1962) "Etude de 14 facteurs influant sur l'absentéisme industriel," *Le Travail Humain* volume 35 pp107–16

JINDRICHOVA, J (1960) "The possibility of rotating shifts in a three-shift system with reduced working hours," *Pracovni Lekarstvi*, (Prague) volume 12 number 10 pp500–504

KENT, A F S (1916) "Second interim report on an investigation of industrial fatigue by physiological methods," Cd 8335, HMSO, London

KLEITMAN, N (1963) *Sleep and Wakefulness*, University of Chicago Press, Chicago

KLEITMAN, N, and JACKSON, D J (1950) "Body temperature and performance under different routines," *Journal of Applied Physiology* volume 3 number 6 pp309–28

LILLE, F (1967) "Diurnal sleep in a group of night workers," *Le Travail Humain* volume 30 numbers 1 and 2 pp85–97

LOBBAN, Mary C (1965) "Time, light and diurnal rhythms," in *The Physiology of Human Survival*, ed Edholm, G, and Bacharach, A L, Academic Press, London

LOSKANT, H (1957) "Experiences of the influence on health of various types of shifts," XIIth International Congress on Occupational Health, Helsinki

MCDONALD, J C (1958) "Social and psychological aspects of night shiftwork," University of Birmingham Ph D thesis

MCGIRR, O (1966) "Health considerations," *The Benefits and Problems of Shiftworking*, Production Engineering Research Association of Great Britain

MAKOWIEC-DABROWSKA, T, *et al* (1967) "Night work and alternate shiftworking," *Medycyna pracy*, (Warsaw) volume 18 number 4 pp340–9

MANN, F C, and HOFFMAN, L R (1960) *Automation and the Worker*, Henry Holt & Co, New York

MARKS, D (1970) "Flexible working day successful in Germany," *Science Journal* volume 6 number 4 pp9–11

MARRIOTT, R and DENERLEY, R A (1955) "A method of interviewing used in studies of workers' attitudes," *Occupational Psychology* volume 29 pp69–81

MARRIS, R L (1964) *The Economics of Capital Utilisation—A Report on Multiple Shiftwork,* Cambridge University Press

MARRIS, R L (1966) "The economics of shift working," *The Benefits and Problems of Shift Working,* Production Engineering Research Association of Great Britain

MARX, Karl (1867) *Capital,* Translation from 4th German edition by E and C Pane, J M Dent & Sons Ltd, Everyman's Library, 1930

MASS-OBSERVATION (1943) *War Factory,* Victor Gollancz, London

MASTERSON, J P (1965a) "Patterns of sleep," *The Physiology of Human Survival,* ed Edholm, G, and Bacharach A L, Academic Press, London

MASTERTON, J P (1965b) "Sleep of hospital medical staff," *The Lancet number* 7375 pp41–42

MAYEDA, K, *et al* (1969) "Analysis of industrial sickness absence in relation to the assessment of health," Proceedings of the XVIth International Congress on Occupational Health, Tokyo

MENZEL, W (1950) "Physiology and Pathology of Shiftwork," *Arbeitsphysiologie* volume 14 pp304–18

MILLS, J N (1966) "Human Circadian Rhythms," *Physiological Reviews* volume 46 pp128–71

MILLS, J N (1967) "Circadian rhythms and shiftworkers," *Transactions of Society of Occupational Medicine* volume 17 pp5–7

MINISTRY OF LABOUR (1947) *Ministry of Labour Gazette* volume LV number 7 pp218–19

MINISTRY OF LABOUR (1953) *Ministry of Labour Gazette* volume LXI number 8 pp266–7

MINISTRY OF LABOUR (1954) "Shift Working," *Ministry of Labour Gazette* volume LXII number 10

MINISTRY OF LABOUR (1965a) "Shift Working," *Ministry of Labour Gazette* volume LXXIII number 4

MINISTRY OF LABOUR (1965b) "Shift Working: Regional analysis," *Ministry of Labour Gazette* volume LXXIII number 6

MINISTRY OF LABOUR (1967a) "Shift working practices," Personnel Management Information Series number 3, 1S(3)67, p4

MINISTRY OF LABOUR (1967b) *Introduction of Shift Working,* HMSO, London

MORIOKA, M (1969) "Physiological burden to shiftworkers: a study of their sleeping hours," XVIth International Congress on Occupational Health, Tokyo (Abstracts)

MOTT, P E, MANN, F C, MCLOUGHLIN, Q, and WARWICK D P (1965) *Shiftwork—The Social, Psychological and Physical Consequences,* University of Michigan Press, Ann Arbor

MURRELL, K F H (1965) *Ergonomics: Man in His Working Environment,* Chapman and Hall, London

NATIONAL INSTITUTE OF INDUSTRIAL PSYCHOLOGY (1969) *Personal Communication*

BIBLIOGRAPHY

NATIONAL UNION OF GENERAL AND MUNICIPAL WORKERS (1969) *Handbook of Wages and Conditions*

NEWBOLD, E M (1926) "A contribution to the study of the human factor in the causation of accidents," IFRB Report number 34, HMSO, London

NOACK, W (1967) "On the problem of a 12-hour shift," *Arbeit und Leistung* volume 21 pp63–5

OGINSKI, A (1966) "Comparative research on three-shift work: morning, afternoon and night," Proceedings of XVth International Congress on Occupational Health, Vienna

OSBORNE, Ethel E (1919) "The output of women workers in relation to hours of work in shell-making," IFRB Report number 2, HMSO, London

PAFNOTE, M, et al (1967) "Some aspects of human adaptation to weekly turning of working shifts," IIIrd Congress on Ergonomics, Birmingham

PAWLOWSKA-SKYBA, K *et al* (1968) "Night work and shiftwork III Effect of three-shifts work system on the body physiological activity," *Medycyna Pracy* (Warsaw) volume 19 number 4 pp321–32 (Abstract in *Excerpta Medica* volume 15 number 8 pp605–6)

PERMANENT COMMISSION AND INTERNATIONAL ASSOCIATION ON OCCUPATIONAL HEALTH (1969) Sub-committee on shiftwork, Proceedings of an international symposium *On Night and Shiftwork* Oslo, 1969, Published by the National Institute of Occupational Health, Stockholm

PIERACH, A (1955) "Night work and shiftwork among healthy and unhealthy workers," *Acta Medica Scandinavica* Supplement 307 pp159–66

PIGORS, P F (1944) *Human Aspects of Multiple Shift Operations*, MIT, Cambridge, Massachusetts

PIKE, E Royston (1966) *Human Documents of the Industrial Revolution*, Allen and Unwin, London

PRADHAN, S M (1969) "Reaction of workers on night shift," Society for the Study of Industrial Medicine, Bombay

RAFFLE, P A B (1967) "Automation—another change in working environment," *Abstracts of World Medicine* volume 41 number 9 pp657–70

REID, D D (1957) "Records and research in occupational medicine," *Royal Society of Health Journal* volume 77 p675

REID, P C (1961) "The human problems of shift operation," *The Manager* volume 29 number 4

RUTENFRANZ, J (1967) "Psychological aspects of night and shiftwork," *Arbeitsmedizin-Sozialmedizin-Arbeitshygiene* (Stuttgart) volume 2 number 1 pp17–23

RZEPECKI, H, and WOJTCZAK, J J (1969) "Night work and shiftwork IV Changes in the performance of psychological tests during work in various hours of the day," *Medycyna Pracy* (Warsaw) volume 20 number 1 pp40–9

SAKAI, Y, and KANO, H (1965) "The Manifest Fatigue Scale," *Journal of Science of Labour* (Tokyo) volume 41 pp390–7 (English Summary)

SERGEAN, R, and BRIERLEY, Jean (1968) "Absence and attendance under non-continuous three-shift systems of work," *Nature* volume 219 number 5153 p536

SERGEAN, R, HOWELL, D, TAYLOR, P J, and POCOCK, S J (1969) "Compensation for inconvenience: an analysis of shift payments in collective agreements in the UK," *Occupational Psychology* volume 43 pp183–192

SHEPHERD, R D, and WALKER, J (1956) "Three-shift working and the distribution of absence," *Occupational Psychology* volume 30 pp105–111

SHEPHERD, R D, and WALKER, J (1958) "Absence from work in relation to wage level and family responsibility," *British Journal of Industrial Medicine* volume 15 pp52–61

SHIMMIN, Sylvia (1962) "Extra-mural factors influencing behaviour at work," *Occupational Psychology* volume 36 pp124–31

SIMPSON, H W, and LOBBAN, M C (1967) "Effect of a 21-hour day on the human circadian rhythms of 17-hydroxycorticosteroids and electrolytes," *Aerospace Medicine* volume 38 number 12 pp1205–13

SMITH, May and VERNON, M D (1928) "A study of the two shift system in certain factories," IFRB Report number 47, HMSO, London

ST DAVID'S DIOCESAN EVANGELISTIC COMMITTEE (Undated) Report, "The 3-shift system and church attendance."

TAYLOR, P J (1967) "Shift and day work: a comparison of sickness absence, lateness and other absence behaviour at an oil refinery from 1962 to 1965," *British Journal of Industrial Medicine*, volume 24 pp93–102

TAYLOR, P J (1968) "Pilot survey of attitudes to present shift arrangements," unpublished memorandum

TAYLOR, P J (1969) "The problems of shiftwork," *Journal of the Royal College of Physicians, London* volume 3 number 4 pp370–84

TAYLOR, P J, and FAIRRIE, A J (1968) "Chronic disability in men of middle age," *British Journal of Preventive and Social Medicine* volume 22 number 4 pp183–92

TELEKY, L (1943) "Problems of night work—influences on health and efficiency," *Industrial Medicine* volume 12 pp758–79

THIIS-EVENSEN, E (1949) "Shiftwork and health," (English summary to Norwegian text) Eidanger Salpeterfabriker, Norsk Hydro, Porsgrund, Norway

THIIS-EVENSEN, E (1949, 1953, 1958) Reported in Aanonsen (1964)

THIIS-EVENSEN, E (1953) "Shiftwork and gastric ulcer," *Sartryck ur Nordisk Hygienisk Tidskrift* volumes 3–4 pp69–77

THIIS-EVENSEN, E (1958) "Shiftwork and health," *Industrial Medicine and Surgery* volume 27 pp493–7

TRANSPORT AND GENERAL WORKERS' UNION (1966) *Handbook of General Minimum Time Rates and Conditions of Service*

TUNE, G S (1969) "Sleep and wakefulness in a group of shift workers," *British Journal of Industrial Medicine* volume 26 pp54–8

van LOON, J H (1958) "Psychological aspects of shift working," *Mens en Ondern* (Haarlem) volume 12 pp357–65 (Abstract in *Psychological Abstracts*, April 1960) volume 34 pp341–2

van LOON, J H (1963) "Diurnal body temperature curves in shift workers," *Ergonomics* volume 6 pp267–73

VERNON, H M (1918) "An investigation of the factors concerned in the causation of industrial accidents," Health of Munition Workers' Committee, Memorandum number 21, Cd 1046 HMSO, London

VERNON, H M (1919) "The influence of hours of work and of ventilation on output in tinplate manufacture," IFRB Report number 1, HMSO, London

VERNON, H M (1920) "The speed and adaptation of output to altered hours of work," IFRB Report number 6, HMSO, London

VERNON, H M (1940) *The Health and Efficiency of Munition Workers*, Oxford University Press, London

VIEUX, N, CARRE, D, and de MONES, P (1962) "Continuous shiftwork in a petroleum refinery," Shell Berre, Petit-Couronne, Seine-Maritime, France

WALKER, J (1961) "Shift changes and hours of work," *Occupational Psychology* volume 35 pp1–9

WALKER, J (1966) "Frequent alternation of shifts on continuous work," *Occupational Psychology* volume 40 pp215–25

WALKER, J, and de la MARE, Gwynneth (1971) "Absence from work in relation to the length and distribution of shift hours," *British Journal of Industrial Medicine* (in press)

WANAT, J (1962) "Accident incidence in various periods in pits," *Prace Glow. Inst. Gorn.*, Ser A, Kom 285 (Poland)

WEDDERBURN, A A I (1967) "Social factors in satisfaction with swiftly-rotating shifts," *Occupational Psychology* volume 41 pp85–107

WESSELDIJK, A T G (1961) "The influence of shiftwork on health," *Ergonomics* volume 4 pp281-2

WHYBREW, E G (1967) *Overtime Working in Britain*, Royal Commission on Trade Unions and Employers' Associations, Research Papers number 9, HMSO, London

WILD, H W, and THEIS, H (1967) "Effect of beginning of shift on accident rate," *Gluckauf* (Essen) volume 103 number 17 pp833–8

WILKINSON, R T (1964) "Effects of up to 60 hours' sleep deprivation on different types of work," *Ergonomics* volume 7 pp175–86

WILKINSON, R T (1965) "Sleep deprivation," in *The Physiology of Human Survival*, ed Edholm, G, and Bacharach, A L, Academic Press, London

WILKINSON, R T, and EDWARDS, R S (1968) "Stable hours and varied work as aids to efficiency,' *Psychonomic Science* volume 13 number 4 pp205–6

WORLD HEALTH ORGANIZATION (1969) Note on work at the Institute of Industrial Hygiene and Occupational Diseases, Prague, *WHO Chronicle* volume 23 number 1 pp40–2

WYATT, S (1927) "Rest pauses in industry," IFRB Report number 25, HMSO, London

WYATT, S (1944) "A study of variations in output," Industrial Health Research Board, Emergency Report number 5, HMSO, London

WYATT, S (1945a) "A study of certified sickness absence among women in industry," Industrial Health Research Board, Report number 86, HMSO, London

WYATT, S (1945b) "A study of women on war work in four factories," Industrial Health Research Board Report number 88, HMSO, London

WYATT, S, and FRASER, J A (1928) "The comparative effects of variety and uniformity in work," IFRB Report number 52, HMSO, London

WYATT, S, and MARRIOTT, R (1953) "Night work and shift changes," *British Journal of Industrial Medicine* volume 10 pp164–72

WYATT, A, MARRIOTT, R, and HUGHES, D E (1943) "A study of absenteeism among women," Industrial Health Research Board, Emergency Report number 4, HMSO, London

ADDENDA

Since this book went to press three useful additions to the literature of shiftworking have appeared:

CONROY, R T W L and MILLS, J N (1970) *Human Circadian Rhythms,* J & A Churchill, London

MARRIS, R L (1970) "Multiple Shiftwork: a problem for decision by management and labour," NEDO Monograph 1, HMSO, London

NATIONAL BOARD FOR PRICES AND INCOMES (1970) "Hours of work, overtime and shiftworking," Report number 161, HMSO, London

Index